Donald Francis Tovey

SIR DONALD TOVEY AT HEDENHAM, AUGUST 1935

(*a snapshot taken by the writer*)

Donald Francis Tovey

A BIOGRAPHY BASED ON LETTERS

MARY GRIERSON

GREENWOOD PRESS, PUBLISHERS
WESTPORT, CONNECTICUT

Originally published in 1952
by Oxford University Press

Reprinted with the permission
of Oxford University Press

First Greenwood Reprinting 1970

Library of Congress Catalogue Card Number 70-104237

SBN 8371-3935-X

Printed in the United States of America

This book, to the memory of a great man,
is dedicated to the musicians
for whom he worked so devotedly—
the men and women who were members
of the Reid Symphony Orchestra

PREFACE

I WISH to thank all those who have been so kind as to allow me to use their letters in the making of this book, and to make grateful acknowledgement to Sir Denys Bray and others for their own accounts of certain events; also to Messrs. William Heinemann for their permission to quote an extract from *A Number of People* by Sir Edward Marsh; to Miss Betty Dickson (Mrs. Sidney Newman), and to Messrs. Drummond Young of Edinburgh, for allowing illustrative material to be reproduced.

I wish, in addition, to thank Mr. Hubert Foss for generously making available to me all the material which he had collected.

My deepest debt of gratitude, however, is due to Mr. and Mrs. R. C. Trevelyan for their continued help and encouragement. Despite failing health, the late Mr. Trevelyan read every word of my manuscript and I am encouraged to think that nothing which he approved would have occasioned any distress to those about whom I have written.

Though every effort has been made to trace the copyright owners of letters and other matter from which I have drawn, it has not always proved possible to do so, and I apologize in advance for any lapses in this respect which may have occurred.

This is not a comprehensive biography, and much interesting material has inevitably been crowded out. I hope that it may be used on a future occasion by someone, more skilled in the task than I, who will be able to assess the place of Sir Donald Tovey among the great musicians of this century.

M. G.

April 1951

CONTENTS

ix

CONTENTS

LIST OF ILLUSTRATIONS

I

THERE was a sound of clapping in the next room, and Miss Weisse went to the door to look in. A small boy of 10 was applauding vigorously, and the score of a Haydn Quartet which he had just finished reading was lying on the table in front of him. He looked up in confusion and said 'Oh, I beg your pardon, I thought I *heard* it'. Miss Weisse, at that time a young and gifted teacher of about 30, kept a 'Dames' School' for the children of some of the masters at Eton, and the young Donald Tovey was living with her in term time.

Donald Francis Tovey, born on 17 July 1875, was the younger son of the Rev. Duncan Crookes Tovey, whose other children, two daughters, had died in infancy. The Rev. Duncan Tovey was a scholar of Trinity College, Cambridge. Graduating in 1865, he first became assistant master at Haileybury, then returned to Cambridge as Chaplain to his old college. Thence he went to Eton in 1874, where he was assistant classics master for twelve years. Finally, he became Rector of Worplesdon, combining his duties there with a considerable amount of literary work. He published an edition of Thomson's Poems and, in 1897, a volume of *Reviews and Essays*. He was a recognized authority on the poet Gray, and his most important literary works were *Gray and His Friends*, and *Letters of Thomas Gray, including correspondence between Gray and Mason*. As he said in his preface to this work, his two sons Duncan Tovey and Donald Francis Tovey gave him substantial help, the first by investigating for him in the British Museum, and the second in the notes bearing upon music.

In the beautiful little church at Worplesdon a portrait of the Rev. Duncan Tovey is enshrined in a small stained-glass window of which he is the central figure—a fine-looking old man with a flowing white beard. He was a great favourite with children, and his general disposition was genial and rather easy-going, despite the fact that he had a formidable temper, which was liable to sudden but brief explosions. He possessed a beautiful speaking-voice which both his sons inherited; and in holiday times, especially at Christmas, when there were always family gatherings at Worplesdon, the boys used to read the lessons in Church. The explorer Stanley was for a time a parishioner at Worplesdon. 'I could not resist asking him on one occasion', said Mr. Tovey, 'whether he really *had* said the famous words to Livingstone. "Yes", was the reply, "I couldn't think what else to say." ' Worplesdon is one of the Eton livings, and the Toveys maintained close connexions with former friends, in particular with the family of the Vice-Provost of Eton, Dr. Warre Cornish. When the Rector retired, the masters at Eton presented his younger son with a beautiful Broadwood Grand to take the place of the little upright piano on which he had played during his school days.

Mr. Tovey married a Miss Mary Fison, one of six sisters, a delicate and charming woman with a very ready wit—'One of the most original women I have ever met, and with a turn of humour all her own', is how Sir Denys Bray described her. She was also a considerable scholar, who was reputed to know Dante by heart and to be interested in astronomy. There was, however, nothing academic in her manner, though she could apparently be exceedingly disconcerting at times in her conversation and in her behaviour. One day at tea she remarked that there was no tea-cosy and that she needed a new one; picking up a pair of scissors, she reached out to the velvet window-curtains hanging at her side, and cut a large square from them, remarking that this would do very nicely! All the Fison sisters were married to dons, and one, who was the wife of a canon of Bangor, 'became so Welsh that they made her a bard!' Mrs. Tovey herself was a lively story-teller and used also to amuse her children with clever drawings and rhymes. She had a tendency to be absent-minded, and life in the big untidy rectory was not without its cares: 'Mother was delighted with "The Trials of a Country

Parson",' wrote her younger son, 'and thinks it a little like
Worplesdon.' She could, however, make fun of her trials, and
when part of the rectory was burned down, her letters the
following week were headed 'The Wrecktory'. A High Church
friend who sent her a letter dated 'St. Jude's Day', received a
reply simply headed 'Washing Day'.

Her sons were both devoted to her. From an early age the
little Donald used to play the piano at tea parties in the rectory.
He protested at the clatter of teacups, however, and said that
there should be a part written for them in the score. On one
occasion he had started to play before tea was announced; the
piece was a long one and was succeeded by another. The guests
thought of cold and stewed tea; another piece followed, and at
length his mother absent-mindedly took leave of her visitors,
forgetting that she had offered them no tea at all that day. Mrs.
Tovey suffered latterly from iritis, and spent the last years of her
life in a perpetually darkened room lit by candles. During this
period her mind was much occupied by thoughts of an unseen
world, and it is possible that she resigned herself too readily to an
invalid's existence; but the flash of her wit remained undimmed.

Neither Mr. nor Mrs. Tovey was musical, but their elder as
well as their younger son had in some degree a gift for music.
Duncan, who made the stage his profession for some time after
leaving Cambridge, had a 'flair' for writing attractive popular
songs, composing both the words and the music, although he
had no musical training whatever. His brother was quite proud
of these songs and wrote accompaniments for several of them.
A press-cutting of 1901 records—' "Brown of B Company" is
written and composed by Mr Duncan Tovey, brother of Mr
Donald Tovey, whose concerts in London last season were such
a success. "Brown" is a capital little piece, with plenty of fun in
it and half a dozen very catchy songs. Mr Tovey took the part
of the Colonel and brought the house down with a great gag on
the War Office. His song "The Big Drum Major" was encored
vociferously. Mr Tovey possesses a happy knack for writing
tuneful and humorous music.'

The education of young Donald was in Miss Weisse's hands from an early age, and this came about in a curious way. He had heard from his brother that there were singing classes at the little school which the latter attended, and demanded to be taken along. 'I remember the first day', Miss Weisse wrote; 'he was not yet five years old, and I took him on my knee as I sat at the piano during a singing class. To my astonishment, I found presently that he was singing the *second* part from the music that was on the desk. When the other children had gone I put Schubert's *Haidenröslein* in front of him, and slowly, like the fluting of a bird, the whole tune—the modulation in the second phrase and all—came out absolutely correctly. It was an incredible experience for me, . . . and thenceforth my life was devoted to the care of what was a very delicate child, in whom I recognized an unusual mental endowment and an almost incredible musical talent.'

That such a gifted child should from an early age come under the care and influence of so remarkable a woman was one of the happier accidents of Fate. Miss Weisse belonged to a family distinguished by unusual teaching ability, and she herself was probably the most exceptional character in that family. Here, written fifty years later, is her pupil's revealing account of the way in which she guided the all-important early years of his training. 'Both my parents were, and remained, completely unmusical, though my father intoned in Church in very good tune. Miss Weisse developed my musical capacity in the face of consistent opposition. I remember my first pianoforte lessons, comprising some "This—little—pig—went—to—market" finger exercises, which eventually turned out to be fundamental compositions in Deppe's Pianoforte Method,—which in its turn was the foundation (by coincidence or influence) of Tobias Matthay's method, now the Athanasian Creed of British Pianistics. . . . Until I was about twelve Miss Weisse had to deal with some scepticism as to whether I was really musical, some doubt as to whether I was otherwise "all there", and strenuous opposition to every step she took in my education. My father was for a long time convinced that no musician but a Church organist could have any social status at all. He was enlightened by a visit to Eton of Joachim, whose ambassadorial presence, perfect command of English and obviously profound general culture completely changed his ideas of what a musician might be. He never forgot how when Joachim was told of my progress in Latin and Euclid he asked, "And does he know it *gründlich*"?

'Miss Weisse consistently secured my training being in what she called the right hands. Thus at nine I became the pupil of Parratt at Windsor, instead of going to Barnby who was Precentor of Eton. Although I was born at Eton where my father was a master for twelve years, Miss Weisse succeeded in preventing me from going to a Public School at all. When my father took a country living at Worplesdon, I kept terms at Eton with Miss Weisse and got from one source and another the substance of a proper school education, plus a terrific pianoforte training which included almost literally the shaping of a naturally inefficient pair of hands into quite serviceable instruments.'

The hands were *very* small and weak and necessitated, besides extraordinarily careful training, many hours of patient massage. An accident in which he was pitched out of a dogcart and received minor injuries to his back in the summer of 1892 further endangered the boy's career as a pianist, and probably left as a legacy the slight lack of co-ordination in larger movements which was sometimes noticeable.

It was necessary for his musical education not only to develop his hands, and to train his natural instinct for the pianoforte: 'I found when he was about eight', Miss Weisse records, 'that he was writing quite large compositions in full sonata form, and after some little difficulty I got Dr. Parratt to begin his instruction in counterpoint.' Many years after, however, Parratt's pupil wrote,[1] 'The one great lost opportunity of my early years was that, under the mistaken idea that organ playing would be bad for my pianoforte touch, I never learnt the organ from Parratt; but I *did* form all my notions of that instrument from hearing

[1] In *The Training of the Musical Imagination.*

and watching him every Sunday in the Organ Loft of St. George's Chapel at Windsor, and I grew up in the happy and stimulating delusion that the organ was a rhythmic instrument, and that the use of its stops was analogous to good orchestration. In Parratt's hands both these propositions were true.'

The child began to acquire a library of music very soon. Haydn's Pianoforte Sonatas are inscribed 'An Easter Gift 1885' (he was not yet 10); Bach's *Wohltemperirtes Klavier*, January 1886; Mozart's *Three Symphonies*, July 1886 (his eleventh birthday), are inscribed 'My First Full Score D. F. T.' Writing to Miss Weisse in 1893 he remarked, 'These Three Symphonies are the first score I ever had. The Ninth Symphony was the first score I ever *saw*. You showed it me I remember'. All his sixpences were now spent on miniature scores and his small jackets were padded with them 'for reading in the train', as he once said.

When he was 12 he paid one of his first visits alone to his cousins in Wales. He started at an early hour from Surrey and in the course of the journey lost successively his luggage, his hat, and his return ticket. But he arrived with twenty-four small scores tucked under his arms; he lost none of them!

The training of a child so precocious, so delicate, and so gifted was fraught with many difficulties. He could not fail to realize at an early age that he was different from other children, but his essentially sweet nature, and, possibly, the unwillingness of his family to recognize that his musical gifts were of serious importance, seem to have saved him from self-conceit and from the various tragedies which befall musical prodigies. That he was regarded as such there can be no doubt. Even his father could not fail to recognize that he was abnormally sensitive to music, for when the organist played one chant and the choir by some accident began to sing another, the little boy rushed out of the church and was sick in the churchyard! Lady Pollock writes to Miss Weisse in March 1887: 'I must thank you for letting Don come to us. He behaved charmingly and played delightfully, his exquisite touch particularly striking the musical ones. . . .

Dear little boy, it is a shame to treat him as a wonder, but I hope and think he felt at home with us.'

Mary Beasley, later Principal of the Northampton School of Music, was a pupil at Miss Weisse's school, and made the following entries in her school-girl diary of 1887:

'*Eton, May 18th*. Donald is poorly tonight; Miss Weisse seems in a great way. I truly hope that it is nothing much; the Doctor came and thought him far from well. If Don was very ill I believe dear Miss Weisse would nearly go out of her mind, for she has greater hopes of him than of anyone she has ever dealt with. He is a most marvellously intelligent boy, only eleven, and reads quantities; and added to that we hope he will be one of the greatest musicians that has ever been; and besides he is such a dear sweet boy.'

'*June 25th*. I went up to London with Donald to see "*Der Freischütz*"; he had never been to any Opera before. . . . His compositions seem to me so wonderful and he is always full of new themes. . . . He told me he was going to write a Concerto in the holidays as a surprise for Miss Weisse. He loves surprises.'

'*July 19th*. We had an astronomy examination on the lessons given to us by Mr Porter; in the evening we heard Donald had got the prize.'

'*July 20th*. A day long looked forward to. The Ensemble Practice was great fun; it was in the Cornishes' house, as our schoolroom has been kept for the Whooping-Cough children. I played my E Flat trio of Beethoven; Donald his own sonata for piano and violin with Blagrove; Donald played Mozart's Quartet; Dorothy the Quartet arranged from the Quintet of Beethoven. We were about four hours and thoroughly enjoyed it. Donald read at sight the last movement of the Quintet as Dorothy had not finished it. Wonderful, wonderful, as Mr Parratt always says of dear Donald.'

7

In spite of being the centre of a great deal of interest and conscious to some extent of his own powers, he grew up oblivious of the fact that many of his remarkable musical gifts were anything extraordinary. It is doubtful, for instance, whether to the end of his life he ever realized that the faculty which he already possessed at the age of 12 for reading a musical score as easily as the average person reads a book (and generally with a much more accurate memory of its contents) is a faculty which, if acquired at all, costs most musicians years of practice. The alert eye, the vivid sense of sounds, both heard and imagined, the retentive memory and the quick mental grasp of all that was music, were to him part of a normal equipment.

Early letters bear witness to a happy relationship between teacher and pupil. Here is an exuberant letter from the twelve-year-old Donald, headed 'Christmas Day 1887':

'Dear Miss Weisse,

You're beyond thankability! The scores arrived yesterday safe and sound, *and* the PASTORAL SYMPHONY arrived today! It's a most bbbbeeeeaaaauuuuttttiiiiffffuuuullll Christmas present, —it is, it is, it is, *it is*! When I ordered the Mozart Divertimento for Strings and 22 Horns (Oh dear, I didn't mean 22 I meant 2), I expected about eight pages but instead there arrived forty eight! They're all exceedingly beautiful and I quite admire my own choice. There is a Serenade for Wind Instruments in B Major[1] by Mozart in the Payne's miniature scores, which I guess I shall get some time or other, as I am growing windy (I don't mean brassy). It looks vast for it is two shillings; the number is 100, and I shall probably get another to throw at somebody. Nearly all the Haydns are only eightpence.

'I'll also tell you something else. In the list on the back of the Schumann Quintet *all* the Haydns have opus numbers, up to Op. 76! I've got five shillings for a Christmas present! Very nice isn't it? I shall soon have to ask them to publish more! At present I want No. 100 (2/-) and No. 3 (6*d.*) and No. 10 (6*d.*).

[1] He must have meant B flat—mistranslating the German *B dur*.

Your discount will reduce it to about 2/4, because last time I got 5/9*d.* worth for 4/5*d.*! 1/4*d.* off.

> I am,
>> Yours affectionately,
>> DONALD F. TOVEY.'

A year later he was writing: 'Hallé and his wife played in Guildford yesterday. Father and Aunt Janet said I might go. Father scooted to London; sent a telegram to say he must stay another night, and then Aunt Janet changed her mind, so they recompensed me with mangy. So now I've got all the Beethoven published that I want, all published of Haydn, all ditto of Mozart and all Schumann that I want. . . . There is a Quintet of Boccherini that looks tempting and two Quartets which are the smallest in that edition, and they're actually by Schubert! The two are in one book and together cost 9*d.*, as they are shorter than any Haydn and the themes are really exquisite! I think I shall get them for they *can't possibly* be long.' [An eight-bar quotation follows.] 'The last two bars are my guess, but *isn't* that a beautiful theme! I'm sure it must be worth getting.'

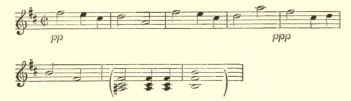

Beethoven's Symphony No. 7 was an Easter present in 1888, and of it Miss Weisse told the following story: 'Never having heard a note of it, he learned it by heart during the course of a journey to Germany. I really couldn't believe it and said to Joachim, "You know, the child says he thinks he knows that Symphony I gave him by heart!" "We shall soon see," said Joachim, "though it does scarcely seem possible." After dinner he said to Donald, "You are very fond of the Seventh Symphony I hear, could you play me a little of it on the piano?" And there and then Donald sat down and played.'

When he was just 13, in October of the same year, the boy wrote, 'I've now got the C Major Symphony and the D Major, the *Eroica* and the C Minor and the *Pastoral* and the A Major and the F Major. May I quote some of the finest passages in the world, which I have found in them?' A musical quotation (bars 260–8, first movement) follows with the remark, 'Isn't this a splendid passage, and wasn't Beethoven artful in using the E Flat and the B Flat of the Drum as D Sharp and A Sharp, and so bringing the Drums out in E Minor? It is startling to hear the Drum harmonizing in such a far off key.' Another quotation (bars 192–6, last movement) is accompanied by the comment, 'That birr-fizz is a Flute! Rather remarkable at $\downarrow = 76$. It's from the finale of the Eroica Symphony. That Symphony takes an hour to peruse senza replica! I hope your [*sic*] enjoying yourself very much.' Beethoven's *Missa Solennis* was also a Christmas present this year.

Dr. Parratt said that his pupil ought to work at advanced counterpoint with Mr. James Higgs, the Counterpoint Master at the Royal College. So he went up to London every week and 'came back radiant after his lessons'. Presently Miss Weisse records, 'I was swallowing tons of criticism and good advice by this time, and I did seriously debate with myself whether to yield and send him either to the Royal College, or to Frau Schumann at Frankfurt. But when Mr Higgs told me that Donald was by far the finest contrapuntist he had ever had, I resolved he should never measure himself against fellow-students *whom he could easily beat*. And I think I was right.'

He was encouraged to take part in some of the more usual boyish occupations. He played football regularly for a time with the boys of an Eton House, but he was 'obviously not an athlete by temper or conviction!' Tennis was not his strong suit either; on 22 May 1889 he wrote: 'The day before yesterday I was invited to a Tennis Party by Miss Sackville West who lives at Bangor. Of course I expected to be a looker-on, but imagine my surprise at being suddenly supplied with a pair of tennis shoes and a racquet and asked to play! I said I was only a very so-so player etc. but someone said, "Oh yes; but everybody says that" (If he had seen me play before, that remark *might* have had another meaning).' Very many years later during a leisurely and unorthodox game at Hedenham, he remarked that he was quite ready to 'take on' Mlle Lenglen provided only that she should use a soup ladle for a racquet!

He learned to row, and struggled unsuccessfully to dance: 'I skated through a waltz, managed two polkas, tried the lancers three times, and might have succeeded the third time, only I had to do a lady; managed a Galop the second time, and capered through a Highland Schottische. I enjoyed it very much and nobody swore at me, not even in the lancers.' But the only exercise out of which he got real pleasure as a young man was walking, and if any composition on which he was engaged came to a standstill, he got into the habit of 'taking it for a walk'. He had a long erratic stride, deceptively swift; and years after, in the summer of 1915, the police, on the look-out for German spies, made inquiries about 'the gentleman who is so often seen running through Windsor Forest'.

When he was quite a child Miss Weisse took him to see two old ladies at Slough, the Misses Herschel, grand-daughters of the famous astronomer, to whom Haydn paid a visit in 1797. The great telescopes on their moveable platforms were still there, and the small boy was allowed to look through them to his heart's content. The interest in astronomy which this thrilling visit awakened remained very real throughout his life, one of his most cherished possessions being a beautiful telescope chosen for him by Professor Newall of Cambridge and given to him by Miss Weisse.

From his earliest studies with Dr. Parratt and Mr. Higgs it was obvious that young Tovey was a born contrapuntist, and these two excellent teachers were the predominating influences in the formation of his musical style. He came to think naturally in terms of counterpoint. A birthday card to Joachim, dated 28 June 1888, takes the form of a neat three-part round to the words 'Herzlichen Glückwunsch zu Ihrem Geburtstag' repeated six times.[1]

The young Donald Tovey was deeply attached to Dr. Parratt, in whose organ loft at Windsor he spent so many happy Sundays. He had a lifelong affection and admiration also for his two later masters, Mr. Higgs and Dr. Parry, with whom he started to study composition at the age of 14. The profoundest musical influence in his life, however, was that of Joachim. The great violinist 'was, very wisely,' says Miss Weisse, 'slow to believe in the child,—he was so quiet and timid. But I remember when Donald was seven, Uncle Jo strummed out the themes of Fugues from the *Wohltemperirtes Klavier* on the table of my sitting-room at Eton and made the little boy tell him which they were. And when Donald was twelve he played a violin sonata of his own with Joachim, and I remember how carefully and tenderly dear Jo played it.' The close association and friendship flourished for twenty years until Joachim's death.

In the autumn of 1889 the young Donald paid a visit to Professor and Mrs. Newall at Cambridge, and went with them to the Leeds Festival. He wrote to *Mrs.* Weisse: 'I used to ride on Polly every day bare-backed (except for a rug to modify the malignity of the animal's backbone), at first with a leading rein, because she was not so peacefully disposed as dear little Hänschen at Pyrmont,[2] but afterwards the leading rein was not necessary because I became able to manage her. Indoors I practised one hour a day, and sometimes Mrs Newall would ask me to show her things about Herr Deppe's Method, and Mr Jenkinson came sometimes and Mr Sedley Taylor came twice. He told me a lovely story about Hallé when he heard an Opera by Wagner. Hallé just listened for a long time and then suddenly said that "Ach! *Ein* Takt *piano*". He also played me Weber's *Last Waltz* in boarding school style and I was in roars of laughter.'

[1] A six-part birthday canon of a later date bears the following explanation: 'The six voices represent ten years each of your English career. The canon is, in any case, infinite and will have many more parts as time goes on—and why fix a limit?'
[2] He paid several visits to Pyrmont with Miss Weisse to play to Deppe.

A long and amazing letter to Miss Weisse gives an account of the Leeds Festival of 1889:

'It began with Mr Parry's *Ode on St. Cecilia's Day* which I thought exceedingly fine. It was so moderate, and artistic, and refined, in fact it was *classical*. The only "extra" instruments were the Harp and the Organ, but the words required them. When this was over there came an interval of half an hour, occupied by jam sandwiches. Then followed Mendelssohn's Violin Concerto played by Sarasate. I was very much struck by his playing, how it suited the piece, and the wonderful sort of thrill in every note. In the cadenza he began the arpeggios quite slowly and instead of getting gradually quicker, he *suddenly* whirled you off your feet. Then came the Ninth Symphony. I needn't say how I enjoyed it, but between you and me and the gate-post, I didn't think Sir Arthur Sullivan at all a good conductor. There was *no piano* (unless you count mf.) and he conducted sitting down. I wished Mr Parry had conducted. He would have at least stood up, and would have raised his left hand in the *pianos*.

'In the evening we heard Stanford's *Voyage of Maeldune*, which I liked very much. Then came the third *Leonora* Overture, which was well done, but for the absence of *piano*. Madam Albani sang a scena out of *Freischutz*—so imagine! After this came the *Midsummer Night's Dream*, and it was delightful. How funny it is, when the fairies tell the long-legged spiders and black-beetles to go, the flute accompaniment changing to the lowest region of the Clarinet.

It is so *very* long-legged and beetlish.

'Next morning after breakfast we just went and did another concert. Programme, Brahms' *Requiem* and Mendelssohn's *Lobgesang*. The Brahms was not so well done as it might have been, one thing in particular being, that in the score the Harps are marked "wenigstens doppelt besetzt"—which of course means that there must be at least two *if the orchestra is only a middle sized one.* The orchestra here was very large though, and it had double wind, so of course it ought to have had *four* Harps. The result was that some of the most beautiful passages were entirely lost. That Requiem is really very beautiful. . . . The performance had no *pianos,* and the oboes drowned the flutes, but the solo singers were very good. . . . It seems to me that it is the most beautiful thing ever written since Beethoven.

'After this came an interval, followed by Mendelssohn's *Lobgesang.* It didn't seem very fine after the Requiem, there was such a lot of blaring Trombone in the fortissimos. . . . All the same much of the *Lobgesang* is very beautiful, for instance the Adagio of the Sinfonia, and everywhere in the first movement where the Trombones don't blare that everlasting theme:

(N.B. I don't mind that phrase when it isn't done by the Trombones.) All the *piano* arias are lovely, and if Brahms had written the choruses it would be most beautiful. Perhaps if I heard it by itself without such a beautiful thing as the Brahms coming directly before it, I should think it more beautiful. It was much better done than the Brahms.' Such criticism from a lad barely fifteen reveals not only astonishing musicianship but a mind of the first quality. 'After the Concert', he concludes, 'there was just time to fly into a kibsir and miss the train.'

Another lively letter of criticism is dated January 1891:

'Dear Miss Weisse,

I got your Postal Order all right, and I thank you for it. I have spent more than a pound, but father had given me 3/6. I enjoyed my stay at the Alderson's very much, and the *Messiah* was splendid, except Barnbyish and too much left out. I can't help thinking there must be a focus in the Albert Hall; it looks an exact ellipse. I wonder if a focus distracts very much from the sound in the rest of the building. . . . On Saturday Mr Middleton most kindly met me at St. James's Hall, and he and Miss Pratt and me enjoyed the most delicious string quartet Spohr ever wrote, and Mrs Henschel sang some nice songs by Mr Henschel, accompanied by Mr Henschel, and then Stavenhagan whacked Chopin with no juice in the tone, and played the C Minor Trio of Beethoven as one would play Boulanger, while Madame Neruda and Signor Piatti played it as one would play Beethoven. I have been to Breitkopf and Härtel's place in Oxford Street, and bought

Mozart—2 Divertimenti for 2 Flutes, 5 Trumpets, 4 Drums (!!!)
   ,, —Concerto for Flute and Harp!!
   ,, —Adagio for Violin and Orchestra (*Loverly*)
   ,, —Concerto for Horn!!! (And possible to play! there are four of 'em)

all as delightful as if for a sane combination of instruments.

Ever your affectionate,

DONALD FRANCIS TOVEY.'

Extract from a letter from Cambridge:

'April

[In later life this musical method was his way of remembering telephone numbers.]

'Could you send me some music paper; if not from the very bottom of my box, from the Stores. It is just *ddubble* the price here! And I cannot afford more than three sheets.'

A letter from Moffat in June discloses part of the use to which the music paper was put. 'The Symphony is quite well. This is the latest [quotation of theme of Adagio]. It is still raining, but only *non legato pp*.'

The following short account by Mrs. Desmond MacCarthy (Miss Mary Warre Cornish) gives a delightful picture of Tovey at this time:

'Donald is first recalled to me in my father's Eton garden standing by a little quince tree on the lawn. His age was 16, mine 9. He was a friend of my two elder brothers near him in age: and he constantly passed from his own home at Eton into our garden to come and find these friends. The following picture has remained in my mind. I should say it was early November, the quinces picked, the leaves of the quince tree not all shed, and I can remember the mossy lawn was damp, the afternoon misty; I had my hoop; it was cold; and Donald was clad in a rather overwhelmingly big homespun ulster, a rational garment, not in the least picturesque; a tall boy, clumsy, talking, dreaming and wandering round about the quince tree. "Would one get to Australia on the other side of the world, supposing one could dig right through the garden earth?" I had asked him. There! I cannot remember a single word more of the talk beyond that babyish question. But I remember that Donald answered in a long, long, monologue during which I noted to myself that one could not possibly talk, oneself, with Donald. He was far, far too clever for a child. I was his sole audience, quite attentive, standing still with my hoop and stick as he philosophised on and on, aloud, but follow I could not. But this did not seem to me funny. Oh, no, quite rightly I regarded his mind with the greatest respect. If he had been a conceited boy or a boring one I am sure I should have just run off, bowling my hoop away. Donald's mind was higher altogether than most people's. I felt a sense of something "going on" when he talked; higher, taller, more distinguished; "higher up", while I listened below. But when others were there, I silently enjoyed the amusing talk he had with my brothers or the grown-ups. I remember a joke he made when a visitor placed a letter for the post out in the hall, and asked whether the letter was safe. "Oh, yes, perfectly safe—it won't go." Little things like that I still remember, and most amusing jokes at the piano.'

2

MISS WEISSE'S mother was a concert pianist, but she herself was not a player. She had, however, studied Deppe's pianoforte method carefully, and her great insight and wonderful gift of imparting knowledge made her a remarkable teacher for a remarkable pupil. The pianoforte training which he received was, as he said himself, 'terrific'. Two of the notable features of the method consist in the cultivation of a high degree of sensation in the finger-tip, and a slightly 'crab-wise' position of the hand—a position which an eminent surgeon once declared to be the only anatomically correct position for pianoforte playing.

The first recorded concert in Miss Weisse's diary is at Eton on 13 April 1886, but a programme of May 1885 contains the name Donald Tovey as playing two 'Instrumental solos', a Haydn sonata and a Dussek sonata. 'When he was twelve I took him to Deppe to show him his work, and Donald did quaint things there—such as one day mistaking an order which Deppe gave and *inverting* a whole long study of Czerny bodily by heart!' But Deppe refused to deprive Miss Weisse of her pupil; 'I will teach you,' he said, 'and then you can bring him up yourself.' 'What Deppe did do,' continues Miss Weisse's record, 'was to conduct for him—and admirably. I used to take him to Pyrmont with say half-a-dozen concertos and we hired the orchestra, and Deppe made him practise with them.'

In June 1890 at Windsor the boy played Schumann's Introduction and Allegro for pianoforte and orchestra at the request of Princess Beatrice, who was studying the piece herself and sent to ask if Master Tovey would play it for her. He did not know the piece at all, and Miss Weisse, who insisted on never pressing the boy, was a little anxious as to whether he could get it up to concert pitch in a few weeks. 'But it proved not very difficult', she records, 'and Donald was not at all tired.' All his life this remained one of his favourite works.

The list of pianoforte music which he was studying at the age of 15 is a formidable one. It includes many Beethoven sonatas, the B flat Concerto, the *Prometheus* and C minor Variations, and the Choral Fantasia; along with Bach Preludes and Fugues, Mozart D minor Concerto, works by Chopin, Schubert, Haydn, and many others, and a considerable amount of chamber-music including the Mozart Wind Quintet, Beethoven trios, Brahms D minor Violin Sonata, and so on. In February 1891 he played the Fantasia for Pianoforte, Choir, and Orchestra by Beethoven at a concert of the Choral Society in Windsor, Mr. Parratt conducting. Miss Weisse writes, 'My dear Don played this very beautifully and everyone was very enthusiastic; "just a little boy with a round collar" they kept saying.'

There is no doubt that, with her genius for imparting knowledge to the young, Miss Weisse succeeded in teaching the boy at a very early age the rare art of practising. He practised regularly but not for long periods, and he was not allowed to overtire himself. His holiday letters frequently contain some such remark as 'I practise for an hour every morning, and spend most of the rest of the day in the open air'—(unless he were able to escape to a quiet corner to read a score or to get on with his composition). The key-note of Miss Weisse's teaching, and presumably of Deppe's method, was mental control and the avoidance of physical strain, and such teaching was admirably suited to the development of the young Donald. 'You ought *never*,' she wrote some years later to another young man,[1] 'to have had pain from practising,—never, however long or fast you may play even in public, feel *any* strain but the mental and artistic one of recreating a musical work. Do let me beg you to be careful; you know that I not only value but really know the possibilities of your playing.'

A jotting in a diary records: 'Don played on January 19th 1892 at Broadwoods, to Mr Hipkins and me, the *Goldberg*

[1] F. W. Kelly.

variations of Bach, by heart. Perhaps the best he has yet done.'
An entry dated 1893 is headed 'Pianoforte Playing—(faults to
be got rid of)

'Sitting not quite upright.

'Swinging the right side away from the piano.

'Looseness of the thumb joint, consequently sticking out of
the middle finger knuckle, and no "weitergehen" in the wrist
at all. *And* consequently, you carry your elbow where'er you
roam, instead of your hand.' There follows a list of 'A few things
for Repertoire for the Northlands Concerts' (which were started
that autumn). The 'few things' include, the *Diabelli* and the
Prometheus Variations, the *Waldstein* Sonata, op. 101 and op. 109,
Schubert G major Sonata, Schumann C major Fantasia,
Brahms-Handel Variations, and a host of smaller works.

Thus at the age of 17 Donald Francis Tovey was a very
accomplished player with an immense repertoire. The tireless
devotion of his teacher never ceased, however, until she had
developed to its fullest perfection his great gift for pianoforte
playing. At last she was able to write 'And so his playing
was "*free*", as I meant it to be, from all physical shackles,—
and it became, as his own mind was, more eloquent than any
speech.'

When he was 14½, Miss Weisse made great efforts to arrange
for young Donald to have lessons in composition from the best
master she could find, and Mr. Jenkinson (of Cambridge) wrote
regarding an introduction to Dr. Parry:[1] 'I shall be glad and
proud to form even the tiniest link in the chain of progress. He
is such a dear boy, apart from his music.' Dr. Parratt, however,
was the real intermediary: 'I took Donald's packet up to Hubert
Parry this morning, and I was very much impressed when I saw
him later by the obviously cordial approval of what he had
seen.'

On 1 April 1890 a letter arrived from Dr. Parry: 'Dear Miss
Weisse, You honour me very much by your proposal to bring
your pupil Donald Tovey to see me. I have heard a great deal

---

[1] Afterwards Sir Hubert Parry.

about him, and should be very glad and interested to hear him myself.' The lessons in composition began in May on the basis of a fortnightly lesson of two hours' duration; but these were far from regular, as Dr. Parry was a very busy man, and his pupil was too shy to press his claims.

The boy's head was continually full of musical ideas. Later that year he writes: 'Father has a bad cold and Mother mayn't put her foot to the ground. Duncan was a week in camp at Dorking and has now gone to Yorkshire. I've got themes of 3 string quartets [quotations follow]. No. 3's the sweetest, No. 2's sombre and tragic and No. 1's pastoral and stirringly melodious. I'm pleased with 'em all. . . . P.S. My pen sputters. I've got *all* the movements of all the quartets. Let me write them down' [quotations follow].

The symphony which was begun at Moffat in the summer of 1891 came up for criticism by Parry in December:

'Worplesdon. Excuse writing,—hard frost, heating apparatus gone mad, impossible to get hands warm. . . . When I got to Dr. Parry he was very jovial as usual. He welcomed me and bolted upstairs for the Boshphony and the Blutundblitzen variations. First he said "Now play this straight through," so I did. At the 4th bar he said that it wanted a few more harmonies, such as:

Dr. Parry embellishes a pupil's piece of platitudinous ponderosity by extracting the juices of the pupil's brain, and concentrating them into an essence while he mysteriously *increases* the quantity! Q. E. D. . . . Then we went on waking up a few sleepy places, till we arrove at the development. *Rayther* too long. Spasmodic. . . . Scherzo was all right. Dr. Parry made me a present of a joke on repetition. . . .

'He was encouraging about the Finale, and even said something to the effect that he would not have died of grief if the

theme had been his own. He said it wanted variety of intensity, and a certain amount of piano and delicate orchestration.

'Then I played the variations. It didn't take long to conclude that they hadn't come off. Dr. Parry said, "You see, if you go on altering things like this, till you're black in the face, you lose all your notions, and get utterly wrong." Well, I said I would start those again. . . .

'Then he asked about the part songs, so I played "Jock o' Hazeldean" to which he did not at all object. Nor did he shake his head at the Elizabethan lyrics; so I think they will eventually succeed. Oh! I quite forgot to tell you about our discussion as to a new adagio! . . . He counselled me much to keep things *clear.* . . . Well after two full hours during which we discussed incessantly, I went away in the swift but expensive hansom with more in my head than one could possibly imagine. . . .

'I had a very warm reception from my family, and a very cold one from the house. . . . I couldn't have composed three bars when I got home, if I had squeezed my head in a hydraulic press.'

The lessons, if infrequent, were evidently therefore exhaustive, and exhausting too,—probably on both sides. The above letter continues (a few days later) describing the bitter cold: 'Then I got somehow acclimatised, but I couldn't remember things and couldn't think. I developed seven coughs, three colds and a quarter, most of which have utterly gone. Worst of all, though I did a good many Christmas cards, I'm ashamed to say I utterly forgot to post them, so I had to send them as New Year cards, regardless of consequences. . . .

'I have got an utterly new first movement (to the Symphony):

Rayther mild it looks. But crikey you should hear it ff! It has exactly $53\frac{5}{8}$ as much gunpowder as the old 'un. . . . Happy New

Year!' At the end of this effusion his mother added—'and from us all kind love and best wishes!' Dr. Parry at the same time writes to Miss Weisse: 'He is very scatter-brained and uncon-centrated, and needs firm discipline to correct flightiness from growing into a confirmed habit.'

After the next lesson Donald writes: 'As far as I can make out, those parts of the Symphony which I *altered* from the old work are hopeless, while whatever I created again is successful. . . . The finale causes him to talk about public houses, which is encouraging.'

The account of a lesson at a later date concludes: 'Then I took the underground to the British Museum, where I met an acquaintance of mine, by name the Rev. D. C. Tovey. He re-tired to work at some manuscripts of Gray and I toured around the rest of the museum. I saw some autographs. . . . I couldn't read the Beethoven and Schubert because it was in German handwriting and written in a hurry! And you know Beethoven writes in his diary "I took a letter myself to the post office and was asked where it was meant to go!"'

There was some danger that the boy's absorbing interest in composition and the reading of music should crowd out equally important matters of general education. 'Dear Father, There is a concert on Thursday evening in London, where a thing of Dr. Parry's will be done; and Miss Weisse and I might get a glimpse of him there. The concert is either on Wednesday or Thursday evening so I shall come either on Thursday or Friday. I will let you know which.

'Meanwhile I have finished the 9th book of the Odyssey, and I here enclose that bit of Cicero. I wish the memory *was* weak-ened! I put off doing this, on purpose, till Saturday, then I copied out the English, as amended by you, so that I might not be guided by my own close translation. Yet I find I remember the original far too nearly to get the full benefit of thinking it out for myself. There are, I am sure, places where I have got wrong, which shows that I don't remember *every* word; but the bulk I think you will find is much as if I had learnt the Latin by

heart. For instance, the singular verb "permaneat" at the place "if only zeal and industry remain".'

During a visit (January 1892) to Dr. Archibald Dickson of Hartree, Biggar, in whose fine music library he had earlier made his first acquaintance with the works of Palestrina, he received a letter from Miss Weisse: 'I want you back as soon as can reasonably be for the sake of your work for Cambridge. The time is so very short before the end of March.' And later she adds, 'You must read History and General Literature and get a grasp on life.' But the weather, and illness at home, kept him at Biggar until the end of February and Miss Weisse wrote again: 'I have a letter from Hubert Parry, written out of the midst of the "Frogs."[1] . . . He says he is waiting to receive work from you or words to that effect. I hope staying till Tuesday will clear the editing of the Airs off, but I confess I should like to see the Preface before it goes to print.' This is one of many references to the arranging or editing of some old airs in which Dr. Dickson had interested him, and with which he was temporarily preoccupied.

The time *was* evidently too short to prepare for the Cambridge examination before March, for in July he received a letter from Moffat, where Miss Weisse had a house for many years: 'Tell your respected Papa that if he will leave it to me . . . we will manage the Senior Cambridge somehow. You can do what is absolutely necessary to get you a certificate this year, and add what is necessary for the University next year. The new Schoolmaster coming here will be handy for this.' In September, however, he was staying with friends[2] in Arran, and Miss Weisse was becoming anxious:

'Dearest Don,

It is *most* nice to think of you in that delightful place with such delightful and kind friends, and "racing on" with your Symphony. I should not grudge you an hour of your possible stay . . . except that I am getting uneasy about your playing a little. . . .

---

[1] Incidental music to *The Frogs* of Aristophanes.   [2] The Glen-Coats.

On the other hand, if you really get this batch of writing off your hands now, you will be all the more able to give yourself up to your playing and your other "lessons" with all your mind.' Moreover, in addition to *getting* lessons, he was also *giving* them: 'Miss Beard is waiting to have some lessons in counterpoint from you. And you are also to teach Miss Edgell through the winter.' He was more than qualified to give these. A counterpoint exercise dated 'Moffat May 1892' consists of thirteen bars combining a six-part canon on a *canto fermo* with imitative treatment of three other counterpoints—twenty parts in all. 'This is not really in 20 parts,' says a note at the bottom of the page, 'though it would take 20 persons to sing it and an infinite number of persons to endure it. Some of the parts do not enter till the pedal, so that there are never more than 16 parts moving.' Mr. Higgs acknowledged his pupil's work as follows: 'I received your excellent and interesting counterpoint.

'There are one or two points I should have remarked upon had you not disarmed criticism by yourself calling attention to such matters as consecutive ninths etc. etc.' [There follow comments on technical exercises.]

'With regard to the rest of the work I think it beyond price in giving you mastery over contrapuntal movement and resource . . . on the whole I like the twelve-part example best. The twenty-part is so rich in design and imitation of one kind and another that it rather obscures itself, or at least wants much effort to duly appreciate.'

By giving a few lessons, and by occasional fees paid by hostesses whose consciences would not allow them to exploit the extraordinary young pianist who played at their musical parties, Tovey helped to defray part of the cost of his manuscript paper, and to add to his library of scores.

This library he used continually, and in these years, with his growing and phenomenal memory, he laid the foundation of the vast comprehensive knowledge of classical music for which he became famous. 'I find it most uncomfortable to be without all my scores,' he complained to Miss Weisse when on a visit to his cousins in Wales, during which time he was also writing a quintet. 'I must break it to you that I want another six [scores]. *Please* send them. *I promise you faithfully* that I won't go poring endlessly over them.' He studied them in order to learn from the classics themselves the real technique of composing. When a composition got 'stuck' he writes, 'I find I want all manner of curiously out of the way scores just for about a quarter of an hour, and then I manage to get out of it somehow.' He also found holidays the best time for composition: 'I can't possibly consider before and behind the time when I sit down to compose, and if I wait till our outings, I lose all the connection. *All* the *large* things I have tried in the term have failed for that reason.'

In the autumn of 1892 it was suggested that he should try for the Mendelssohn Scholarship at the Royal College, but Dr. Parry wrote in December, 'There is no Mendelssohn Scholarship awarded next year. The fund has got low, and we must wait a year to let a little money accumulate.' There is no doubt also that there was a certain amount of official 'coolness' on the part of the College authorities towards the brilliant young musician who was withheld from shedding lustre on that great establishment; and the slight but chill shadow cast by the unexpressed official disapproval fell over the rest of his life. Mr. Higgs confirmed his impression of his pupil to Miss Weisse in April 1893: 'You ask me what I think of his contrapuntal powers. My answer is very plain and simple, *most highly*. I do not remember ever to have met with a student of his age who could do anything like what he can do. Indeed, he seems to me to have so much skill and readiness in contrapuntal combination that he may be in some danger of mistaking the means for the end.' It is impossible to imagine what the authorities at College thought they could have made of a boy who would have started at a point far beyond that at which most of their students left off.

Work for the Cambridge 'Schools' continued in 1893, and the pressure of study, combined with that of his musical activities, the after-effects of a carriage accident, and his sudden shooting up into a tall thin youth, made this a year of rather broken health. But his interests were always lively and varied. He wrote to Miss Weisse from home: 'Mrs. Glen-Coats has invited me to dinner at their hotel and to go to *Hypatia* afterwards. The incidental music is by Dr. Parry! Isn't it nice, and doesn't it fit in with all the other things?

'Thank you so much for *King Lear*. Where I saw Irving's acting edition ("deprived of all superfluous horrors") I know not, but I rather think it was at Ferguslie Park. The blinding of Gloucester and that sort of thing is, I suppose, absolutely impossible nowadays, and no wonder! But they don't alter the ending.

'The Beethoven 33 take 36 minutes as I play them. There are 54 repeats, of which I do 30.' (This referred to the *Diabelli Variations*—which took longer as he played them in later life.) A quotation of eight bars from a *Fantasie of three Parts* by Orlando Gibbons:

evokes the remark 'All the accidentals are there that ought to be, so don't mind its being in two keys at a time (Dorian mode transposed) but see how it makes one's tail wag, especially the 5th bar!'

A later letter comes from 'Hartree', Biggar: 'I am just writing preparatory to proceeding with the annotation of Biltoe's[1] *Paradise Lost*. I did three-quarters of an hour between Jeannie's heliolatrous observance and breakfast.' (Jeannie was a little Dandie Dinmont from Moffat.) 'Quensequently I also do some practising,—at Mazeppa. It *is* a fraud. Now look at this.

But it is very good practice, and I *know* it won't sound hard. . . .

[1] i.e. Milton's.

'Jeannie sleeps in my porkmantew! I slump my dressing gown into one side of it, and in she jumps.

'I am afraid I must stop now, for I must take a walk this morning (doctor's orders), and do another three-quarter hour's Biltoe.' Comments on 'Jeannie's' introduction to the family were:

'Mother still regards Jeannie as she regards most animals, but as to Father, well—Jeannie, "by sitting on a table and continuing to smile, has softened the heart of that cow!"'

He played in May at Rugby, at a concert of the School Musical Society, Beethoven's 1st Pianoforte Concerto (with orchestra) and Chopin solos.

In August he was staying with the Arnolds at Lowestoft.[1] 'This place is most delightful. My room looks towards the sea (on the surface of which I have just counted 16 different colours), and there is a palatial writing table. . . . Father's pound goes a long way, for the single fare is only 9/10½. But I fear cabs and refreshments also go *another* long way!' He spent a happy time exploring the old churches of Norfolk and Suffolk with his host, but the legacy of his accident was still with him. Writing about a new pair of boots in September he says, 'The last bill we can find mentions 1 pair Surgical, 1 pair ditto Clumpsoles. Can you make out what "clumpsoles" are and whether we ought to get them? P.S. There is now a *hard mattress* on top of the spring of my bed. It is perfectly flat.'

Letters from Miss Weisse to the boy, who was to all practical purposes her adopted son, make it evident how very anxious— even over-anxious—she was about his health and general well-being at this time. He was, she admitted, perhaps a *little* odd, i.e. preoccupied with his music. 'Dearest boy', she wrote, 'Do, like an angel and an ordinarily orderly human-being, date and locate your letters!'

He was increasingly absent-minded and careless about his

[1] One of the Arnold brothers kept a preparatory school at Wixenford, where Miss Weisse gave occasional lessons in piano-playing. 'Ah, you should hear my Donald playing that,' she said one day to a pupil, who recalled her words twenty years later in a London concert hall.

clothes. 'Best and beloved boy, do pack *everything before* you go
to the dinner-party on Monday. Bring up the Gladstone bag
with you containing dress clothes for Great Orme Street and
sleeping things; but wear your warm brown tweed suit, a clean
shirt and a black tie,—and your overcoat and white muffler and
top-hat and gloves,—and a warm pair of stockings,—put a cap
in your pocket for the journey and your bowler in the hat-box.
Now *do* finish your packing by daylight on Monday so as to get
a good rest and plenty of breakfast on Tuesday, and have the
vehicle in plenty of time for 11.35. You used to be so splendid
when we were abroad in being all ready!' Most boys of eighteen
would have resented being fussed over to such an extent; this boy
just never noticed, and tried biddably to carry out instructions
if he remembered about them in time—which was not always.

Miss Weisse insisted that he should write frequently when he
was away on visits: 'I have been expecting to hear from you by
every post. So do write and give me a full, true and exact
account of yourself and how you do, and what and how your
hosts do. I *hope* you have written home copiously.' There were
frequent injunctions of this sort, and Miss Weisse treasured
every scrap written to her by 'her boy'. The bond of affection
between the two was strong in these years, unclouded as yet by
the difficulties and stresses which warped it in later days.

From Hartree again in September, he writes, 'Thank you
very much for Dannreuther on *Ornamention*. It is perhaps the
best treatise on *any musical subject whatever* that I have ever seen.
. . . Do you remember my lending my Dieupart[1] to Dr. Parry
and its coming back with remarks on the fly-leaf by Dannreuther? Well, I think that gentleman must have found it not
altogether useless.'

In October 1893 there began the 'Northlands Chamber
Music Concerts'. This series continued, with a few breaks, until
July 1914, and the beautiful music-room of Miss Weisse's distinguished and fashionable school at Englefield Green was the
scene of many remarkable concerts.

[1] A treatise by Dieupart on musical ornaments.

A description of Northlands School has been given by Lady Barlow, who was a pupil there. ' "I don't care if you leave here unable to add two and two together so long as *you want to know*", this was Miss Weisse's dictum. Of course there was a timetable; —we started the day with porridge and Gregorian Chants. But if Miss Weisse had an inspiration or there were some interesting contemporary events, did we have to wait upon it? Certainly not! . . .

'No one could possibly have described the education as sound. No girl could have gone from Northlands to College or to earn her living; but when, in my turn, I had to chose a school for my daughter, I found myself looking for one that would teach her the values Miss Weisse taught us. . . . The two things for which the school was famous were the music and the art lectures, but more especially the music. That was about us all the time, every event was celebrated with it, and our birthday present to Miss Weisse was some part singing. . . . Then, and I think it chanced during my last term, we discovered the Bach Mass in B minor, and the place was pandemonium. We parsed that Mass, we analysed that Mass, and we sang that Mass. It crept into every lesson and during playtime each one of us aspired to its B flats. Finally, hoarsely, we grumbled at that Mass. Indeed we did. But Miss Weisse said, "I don't care. Once you have got this thing into your heads you have a treasure nothing can take from you".

'Then came the evening when the Mass was to be sung by the Windsor Choral Society in St. George's Chapel. . . . We clumped cheerfully to our seats. Sir Walter Parratt conducted. We listened. We knew that Mass. Did we? Utter stillness pervaded our rows. "A treasure nothing can take from you". Yes, she was right.'

The programmes of the first four concerts given at Northlands included such works as the Schubert B flat Trio, Brahms and Beethoven sonatas for violin and piano, the *Waldstein* Sonata, Schubert and Brahms songs, &c., &c. The singer was Miss Fillunger (a friend of the Schumanns) and the pianist was

Donald Tovey. The programmes were of course of his making, and he already had very definite views on the subject:

'*La Fileuse* & Co. is nice enough in itself, but it hasn't enough backbone for this programme. And it and the Dutchman[1] are too much alike. You can't do with two cantabiles on buzzing accompaniments. Besides, the Liszt[2] on Nov. 21st is surely enough "concession to the public". Mrs Pitman likes Brahms. Let's have the Hungarian Variations Op 21 No. 2. Send them to me and I'll put them into shape. We have no other Brahms except two songs, and these variations take five minutes and are most "effective".

'And I think two *Spinnerlieds* would make the programme a sort of mutual disturbance society! Certainly have the Beethoven at the beginning if necessary. But don't let's have a chronological programme!'

In this year there was founded the Nettleship Scholarship at Balliol, in memory of the famous philosopher, who lost his life in the Alps in 1892. The examination on which the first award would be made was due in the spring of 1894. 'I think', wrote Dr. Parry, 'that the Balliol Scholarship would be just the very thing for Donald if he could get it. It seems just cut out for him and he for it.' Dr. Parry was much overworked during this winter and the lessons in composition lapsed. He did, however, write a long letter to Miss Weisse during a period of convalescence after influenza, containing much useful criticism of the rewritten 1st symphony, and the first draft of a 2nd symphony which his pupil had hopefully sent him. He adds 'Donald is in the state in which it will be excellent for him to wrestle by himself a lot. . . . He has great abilities, but his success in composition depends mainly upon the development of his personal character. I sincerely hope opportunity will be found for him to go to Oxford. It is of great importance.'

When the question arose later as to whether the 2nd symphony could be submitted among 'unassisted compositions' for

---

[1] The Spinning song from *The Flying Dutchman*.
[2] Second Étude de Concert, *La Ronde des Lutins*.

the scholarship, Parry was quite firm that it should be: 'I can't find that since last year I have given Donald more than the equivalent of two lessons. More 's the pity—for my responsibilities towards him. . . . I don't think I did more than give general advice about the 2nd symphony.' No one was more pleased than he when the award was finally made: 'It will really be the grandest start for Donald. I wish him good luck with all my heart.'

Tovey's first public appearance with Joachim took place this spring at a concert in the Albert Institute at Windsor on 15 March 1894. The programme opened with Brahms' G major Sonata for Piano and Violin and closed with the *Kreutzer* Sonata; Joachim played the Bach *Chaconne* and Tovey the Beethoven Pianoforte Sonata op. 109; Miss Fillunger sang songs by Schubert, Schumann, and Mendelssohn, which Tovey accompanied. This was three months before his nineteenth birthday.

3

IN the autumn of 1894 Donald Tovey went up to Balliol
instead of going to Cambridge like his father and his brother.
His friend and contemporary, Sir Denys Bray, remembers
him as 'a strange youth with flashing eyes and a noble brow and
ways very different from ours, full of enthusiasms and thoughts
which few of us could share, yet with a gift of quick sympathy
that made him eager to share our thoughts and enthusiasms and
a simplicity that won our hearts'. It is easy to imagine how very
different his ways and his thoughts must have been from the
usual freshman; there were no doubt many others who shared
his inaptitude for, and lack of interest in, games and sports; but
there can have been few who came up with the already mature
mind of an artist. There were other differences too: by virtue of
Miss Weisse's upbringing, of many visits to Germany, and of
contact with numerous foreign artists, his outlook was broader
than that of most British boys of his age. On the other hand, his
inexperience of his own contemporaries was incredible.

Sir Denys Bray sheds further light on the early days at Oxford:
'Donald had not been at a public school and the few boy friends
he had (the Cornishes for instance) he had apparently known
from childhood. They were, as it were, as humdrum as brothers.
Then he was suddenly thrown into a completely new world at
Oxford. It was strange to him; he also seemed strange to us who
regarded ourselves as men of the world. So at first he came
in for a little good-natured, mildly bullying, but not unkindly,
chaffing. By a lucky accident I threw my weight about and
stopped it, and he forthwith adopted me as guide, philosopher
and friend, and accredited me with a wealth of attributes that
were not mine. Some wag at once dubbed him the "slithy Tove"
—the epithet being curiously descriptive of his movements as a
youth; but the epithet soon fell off and he was known every-

DONALD TOVEY AND
HIS FATHER
(c. 1892)

DONALD TOVEY AND MISS WEISSE
(c. 1885)

A GROUP TAKEN IN THE MUSIC ROOM AT NORTHLANDS
(*c.* 1911)

Back row: R. C. Trevelyan, D. F. Tovey, Adila d'Aranyi, Pau Casals
Seated: Mrs. Trevelyan, Miss Weisse, Professor Röntgen, Mrs. Röntgen
In front: Jelly d'Aranyi

TOVEY AND THE JOACHIM QUARTET AT NORTHLANDS
(1905)
(J. Joachim, R. Hausmann, Em. Wirth, and C. Halir)

where affectionately as "The Tove", a nickname of which he himself became rather proud.

'As far as I can remember he played no games and I first thought him weakly. But his stamina was extraordinary. He used to walk for miles with a heavy satchel filled with scores and books of all kinds without apparently feeling any exhaustion. He had an extraordinarily changeable face; after a bad night for instance, it seemed shrunken; at the piano it seemed to expand and at once became ennobled. (The only other face I can remember with so many changes was that of Lord Reading, which in some curious way used to remind me now and then of Donald's.)

'Of course his appearance at the first Balliol Sunday concert altered all our views about him, and I myself realized that instead of extending my patronizing protection to a weakling, I had won the devotion of something like a genius. So the tables were turned, and when I shyly produced my manuscript copies of songs of Schubert and Schumann transposed a tone lower than they had ever been transposed before, his delight was unbounded and he forthwith took my musical education in hand. He could not believe that I had not been taught a note of music, and it amuses me to think that I in turn may have had some small musical influence over him in making him realize that hunger and taste for good music is not confined to those who know the grammar and syntax. On the other hand, I fancy I proved a handicap; my voice was unusually low; had it been more normal, his song-writing would probably have flowed more easily.' (Both of the published sets of songs are dedicated to Denys Bray.)

It was quickly apparent that, shy though he was, Donald Tovey took great pleasure in the company of others and he soon acquired a circle of congenial friends. Nevertheless, there was a fundamental lack of *Menschenkentniss* and a generous natural tendency to accept people at their own valuation (unless this were *palpably* false), a tendency which proved to be the cause of many misfortunes which he suffered later in life. The large number of letters which he wrote to Miss Weisse sets forth clearly the story of his undergraduate years; those which he wrote to his family have unhappily vanished, but doubtless they were fewer. The letters quoted in this chapter are all to Miss Weisse, unless otherwise stated.

He got in touch at an early date with John Farmer who was the moving spirit in University musical life, and one of the first letters from Oxford records: 'I have just had ¾ of an hour with Mr Farmer! He has banged away at his own Balliol Student songs (some of which are rather good) and has given me the most sensational thrills and palpitations for my poor piano. . . . He is quite remarkably kind in a rough-and-ready way. . . . He gets together really good musicians, and as he really likes good music and dislikes bad, they don't mind doing anything for him. . . .

'I am only able to practise in the afternoon; it is forbidden in the morning.'

John Farmer, who was organist at Balliol for sixteen years, was one of the most striking personalities in Oxford in Tovey's undergraduate days. He started the Balliol Sunday concerts in 1885, 'in the face [says an account of him by the late Ernest Walker] of violent personal abuse, and with the sole support of Dr. Jowett at his back. He was a single-minded enthusiast of fiery downright temperament, absolutely devoid of self-consciousness or fear of what anybody might think or say of him. Though he had been an intimate friend of Brahms, Joachim, and other great continental musicians, he mixed on the whole but little with the British members of his profession; he did not like them as a body, and they in their turn did not like him. He believed that music is for the many rather than for the few; but though in many respects an artistic democrat to the core, he never for one moment compromised with his ideal. He knew the

differences between good music and bad through and through.'
This was obviously a man who, however much they might differ
in taste, the young Tovey would respect.[1]

A later letter this term remarks: 'At present my interest in
classics is hampered by grubby ignominious little elementary
considerations which effectually prevent me from having any
ideas. . . . If I could acquire "contrapuntal facility" in classics I
should find nothing a bore or a toil. . . . If I could arrive at
a fluent reading in classics, I know we should hear absolutely
the last of Father's slightly remaining view of music as a mere
amusement. Above all, I should not incur my music's being
made an excuse for my deficiencies in other respects.'

A Christmas letter says: 'It is a singular fact that whenever I
have a cold I develop diabolical contrapuntal propensities! You
remember what a stunning big cold I had when I wrote those
three portentous fugues for Mr. Higgs? Well, here is an innocent
little tune I have just sent him on the back of a Christmas card,

A mer - ry X - mas and a hap - py New Year! A
mer - ry X - mas and a hap - py New Year!

[1] Writing more than forty years later to Henry Havergal when he was appointed
music master at Harrow, Tovey said:

'As to your predecessors at Harrow—the one whom I would like to see better
understood is John Farmer. Very few people even now see what he was driving at—
I should perhaps have missed it myself if I hadn't known him at Balliol. . . .

'John Farmer very nearly succeeded in the task, quixotic at the time, of inculcat-
ing an enthusiastic sense of purity in musical style in public schools. Do look carefully at his tunes and see if you can find in them what he would call a "slawmy"
phrase or harmony. He didn't try to impress people as an educated man, and he
looked as if he had been a bandmaster in a circus—as happened to be the case; but
his talk was full of a Schumannite—E. T. A. Hoffman—Jean-Paul mystical whimsi-
cality, and, to the lasting credit of Bowen and Jowett, they understood him.

'But nobody else—neither Stanford nor Parry nor our academic vulgarians—
saw the difference between Farmer and any other writer of merely popular tunes;
and Farmer did nothing to get himself liked by our musical leaders. Sullivan was
to him as Liszt to Joachim, and he didn't spare the feelings of a Parry pupil, telling
me that Parry and Stanford were dead with spiritual pride and dry-rot.'

[Farmer's own opinion of Tovey will be found on p. 77.]

Now this gentle little tune is a canon with a good many solutions [four examples follow]. This sort of thing isn't altogether waste of time when it is made to sound nice. . . . I shall amuse myself considerably finding solutions. Perhaps there are enough to make it worth while wishing you as many happy Christmases. Perhaps there are about three hundred! . . . Oh dear, what a very bad cold I must have!

Dodald Fradcis Tovey.'

A letter written during the second term at Oxford is enthusiastic: 'That ambrosial creature Bray is giving me priceless lessons in how to write for the voice, though he doesn't know it. . . . I really must begin to read something some day. I feel uncommonly silly in the company of Bray, though nothing could be more unlike him than to "come it over me" in any way at all. . . . But when someone of very nearly my own age has read about as much literature as I have music, and I have read so little besides music, it makes me feel a trifle inadequate. . . . Some day I'm going to write a string quartet and a violin sonata, both in G major; and a pfte. quartet in B flat, and to finish the concerto and revise the E minor symphony and write a new one in D minor, and write 14 pfte. lyrics and turn four-fifths of the _Golden Treasury_ into songs, and write a fourth new first movement to that F sharp minor pfte. sonata; and write a 'cello sonata in D major and a sonata in G minor for the organ; and an unaccompanied 8 part psalm, and a _Magnificat_ in D major for chorus and full orchestra, and 20 part songs, and incidental music to _King Lear_, and a violin concerto in A minor. Now when is this going to get done? The trios have vanished into the silly [_sic_] night and perhaps some of this will too; in fact I think the violin sonata is rapidly fading, and dying of my old disease of "thematrophy" or absence of any definite entity in the first theme; but some of the stuff is sure to rear. . . . I was at Paddedroomski's[1] performance in the capacity of steward. I only got five people to stew, and I mismanaged them

---

[1] Paderewski.

entirely. But it was great fun.' A detailed criticism of the concert follows:

'Occasionally, as in the second theme of the first movement of the Brahms A major quartet there was an incomparable majesty to be seen, but on the whole there was twice as much bang as tone. . . . The Chopin G major Nocturne was stark mad. Not one bar in any rhythm one can extract out of the notation, and all the moonshine in the middle either knocked on the head with a sledge-hammer or played with the end of a pocket hand-kerchief. . . . The execrable acoustics of the Sheldonian might explain away the banging, but they won't explain the rhythm and the incessant soft pedal.'

One of the trios which had 'vanished into the silly night' was written during a hectic week in February, and it temporarily exhausted his capacity for other work: 'I have been perfectly well when not working, but if I work I become as stupid as a boiled owl at once. It's quite natural. There was really twice as much work in that trio as in the E minor symphony . . . and it was all planned in 10 days. . . . I believe I must have done 9 hours of mere writing a day from the 20th to the 28th and the stuff was never for a moment out of my head. . . . I shall try and scrape through Collections at the end of this term somehow, and I expect I shall be all right again soon.'

This trio was written to be submitted with other works for the Mendelssohn Scholarship. The decision to enter was made late; on 17 February he wrote: 'I hear that the Mendelssohn Scholarship is open now, and that the scholar may carry on his studies *at home or abroad*—£100 a year. . . . If I got it, it would solve pretty nearly everything for the next three years, and if I didn't get it, I should at least have been urged to write something. I always turn out my best work when I absolutely must.' (How true this was of him at all times!) 'And whereas my object in the Nettleship was to come here and enjoy myself, my object in the Mendelssohn would be to relieve "certain persons of my acquaintance" from much of the weight of providing such en-joyment.' Dr. Parry, who was consulted, advised him to enter;

but time was short, for names and the works submitted were to
be in by 28 February. It is not therefore surprising that a letter
three days later (20 February) was begging: 'Can you send me
a telegram authorizing me to knock off all work except practising, at once? I can *easily* get enough to send in. . . . I shan't
overwork. Only I can't write to Mr Hardie to say I've knocked
off my general work without your authority, and I sincerely
trust that you will see that the strain of putting things on paper
will be *nothing* to the strain of letting things slide.' Next day,
permission having been received, he wrote: 'I have to stop indoors with a common cold, but there's nothing else the matter
with me, and a cold, as you know, sharpens my counterpoint!
Bray has been taking care of me in the most seraphic way.'
Another card of the same date says: 'I am boiling over this trio.
I send you the themes of the first movement; the broadest,
clearest acres of melody that ever entered my head.' The trio,
which is on a large scale and did *not* win the scholarship, was
afterwards published as op. 1 and dedicated to Parry; possibly
the work was revised later, but the themes remain those quoted
on the card. The Mendelssohn Scholar of the year was one
Christopher Wilson, a student at the Royal Academy of Music.

During this frantic week there was also a concert by the
Joachim Quartet, with Beethoven's Op. 130—not to be missed:
'I can't *possibly* come out to lunch. Every instant is *momentous*
(pun not intended). You see it's the day before posting the trio
and things. But I shall go to the concert. . . . I am doing the 3rd
movement "Presto e feroce". It is exciting me half out of my
wits.' This, curiously, is the one movement in the printed version
which seems rather stiff and dry. It is little wonder, however,
that the young composer was unable to do any reading for ten
days after such a concentrated effort.

The Northlands concerts continued during Tovey's first year
at Balliol, there being three in the autumn of 1894 and three in
the spring of 1895. After the concert on 5 February at which he
played—as well as chamber music and song accompaniments—
the great C major Phantasie of Schumann, he writes: 'I very

much want to know how the concert on Tuesday really went. Beyond my having had a certain feeling of ease when I was playing, I really haven't the faintest idea of what it was like, and I am anxious to know for the future whether this feeling of ease is a good sign or not. . . . I knew you would like Bray. It dawns upon me more and more that he is about as good as they make them. His friends are very characteristic of him also. Never very much on the surface, always very quiet, and of really first-rate abilities. . . . I feel very fortunate at being thus half-accidentally drawn into this particular set of men.' There follows news about his brother: 'Duncan's visit was a success I think. Balliol fêted him in a way which greatly pleased me, and I think he had a good time.'

The long letter of 17 February which raised the subject of the Mendelssohn Scholarship, refers to the next Northlands concert: 'I am trying to get op. 57 (the Sonata "Appassionata") into shape for the 5th [March]. . . . I honestly doubt whether it is humanly possible to appreciate the Appassionata or feel it more strongly than I do; . . . but I shall not be able to make an audience which is familiar with the sonata feel it afresh. . . . I can *interpret* self-contained music, of chiefly intellectual interest, which I could *appreciate* seven years ago, but the things that are now well within my appreciation will not be within my interpretation till I don't know when. This doesn't mean that I won't play the things; far from it. The consolation that there are still bigger fools loose about the world, and ruining the public taste, is the poorest and most misleading consolation in existence. But man cannot live by early Beethoven alone.' A college contemporary (Mr. Kenneth R. Swan) records of his playing at this period: 'Tovey's piano playing was to me a liberal education in the sense that from his performance of any particular composition I learnt more of the meaning of the music than from anyone else I ever listened to. . . . No one who had heard him playing Beethoven's "Appassionata" Sonata could fail to realise the depth of feeling with which such music could inspire him. He was a notable character among my contemporaries at Balliol not only on account of his outstanding musical ability, but also by reason of his unconventional habits and odd manners. He wore his clothes, which always seemed too large for him, as though he had dressed in extreme haste, which was probably the fact, for he was a very belated riser.'

There is also much Oxford news in the long letter of 17 February already quoted: 'The Master asked me if I would come for a walk with him last Wednesday. . . . He got onto the subject of Greek music; and he, as a Greek scholar knowing no music, and I as a musician knowing no Greek, tried to supplement each other; the results being distinctly interesting for me, though I wouldn't venture to judge of the Master's feelings.'

'He was', says Sir Denys Bray, 'the only undergraduate I ever saw go for long walks with the Master (Dr. Caird), in whose presence a man like myself was always tongue-tied. Donald's learned conversation was however sometimes too much for the men in Hall and they tried to tone it down by sconcing him; but they only did it once, for instead of beer, which he never touched, he took the sconce in his usual beverage, milk, and floored it—a feat he was proud to remember in talking over old times with me.'

The letter of 17 February then continues:

'On Monday evening I had to dine with the Dean to meet the first Torpid. I was next the Dean on one side, and Belloc, the president of the Union and one of the most brilliant and most talked-of undergraduates in Oxford, on the other. Belloc and the Dean were conversing at the rate of 90 miles an hour on everything from the French Revolution to the conflict between Astronomy and Geology and the Glacial Epoch. I have not often been so interested or anything near it.

'I have to write an essay on the treatment of Homeric subjects by later Greek and Latin poets,—a theme on which my mind is a perfect blank and about which I can't talk phrases;—the only alternative being "The prospects of peace in Europe", a theme on which *everybody's* mind is a perfect blank, and about which everybody talks phrases. Why this visitation should come upon me I cannot think, especially as I shan't get any really searching criticism on my effusions. No, I think the Mendelssohn scholarship is the thing for me to go for.'

The concert at Northlands on 5 March was cancelled owing to Miss Fillunger being ill, but this cancellation came as a relief to her colleague: 'I must confess, sorry as I am, that I should not have played very well; I can't honestly say I am up to *anything* just now.' A fortnight later he wrote: 'You see I am in a vile temper;—but this isn't because of the Mendelssohn, but because I have just come from doing a Collection paper, and am rather tired.'

The question of the Mus.Bac. examination was now raised by Dr. Parry: 'He certainly should go in for Mus.Bac. this year [1895] so as not to interfere with his reading for his University exams.' On 10 May Miss Weisse received a very irritable letter: 'Please don't think me a Beast! I have 8 lectures a week and I lost so much time last term that I am really very behindhand indeed.

'And why, oh why, should Dr. Parry be personally conducting the finest modern oratorio,[1] while I, who have never heard it or read it, have to waste the afternoon over 4 little counterpoint exercises for the preliminary Mus.Bac.????!!!!!

'Last Tuesday I had a six hours examination for the beastly little affair. It didn't take me much more than 4 hours, but I thought I had better copy the things out; so it wasted the whole day. This sort of thing is very tiresome when one has things to do.

'Dr. Parry came into the examination room and talked to Sir John Stainer and tipped me a wink. Most people look austere in a cap and gown. Dr. Parry looks positively rakish! Of course on Tuesday he went to Newbury at 12 (for the concert) and came back next morning. I'd done the harmony paper by 12. *Why* was there a counterpoint paper at two?'

There was no end to music-making at Oxford. 'The Balliol Sunday Concerts', wrote Sir Denys Bray, 'were then, I suppose,

---

[1] This referred to Parry's *Job*.

at their zenith, with John Farmer still there to give them drive, and Ernest Walker and Donald Tovey to perform.' Later in May Miss Weisse got the invitation, 'Can you stay for the Sunday Concert. *Do.* And hear my orchestration of *Die Forelle*!!!! Farmer has been giving me a lesson in instrumentation that has endowed me with a violent stomach-ache which I shan't get rid of for a week. . . . He has also arranged for me to give a pianoforte recital in Hall this term, which is awfully kind of him and very congenial to me.

'I haven't got any time for anything at all, and I get nothing properly done. I think I must be absolutely the worst classical student in Balliol. . . . I have overcome Walker's prejudices and persuaded the Musical Club to consider the desirability of performing Stanford's splendid A minor quartet next term.

'Come on to the Balliol Barge on Saturday with me and Mrs Drew, and see the eights. It's the most scrumptious way of meeting one's friends that there is. . . . Can you bring the Couperin I left? I've got to play it at the Club next Tuesday.'

In the words again of Sir Denys Bray: 'Though [he was] the mainstay of those classical concerts and the chief means of luring Joachim and other great musicians to take part in them, Donald was never more happy perhaps than in the far from classical atmosphere of our informal Song Club, where week by week each gave his favourite turn, ranging from Schubert's "Litanei" to heaven knows whose "High up on the Lighthouse Tower". And who that ever heard the "Tove", as we loved to call him, make his piano miraculously alive with humour and amazing music over his "You are old, Father William", or—perhaps the most famous of his masterpieces in lightest vein—"Harry and the Hornets", has ever forgotten it, or not regretted that Donald could never be persuaded to put it in writing?' Another contemporary, Lord Kilbracken, recalls that 'Donald's skill appealed to rowing men, and he was present at many convivial bump-suppers, and entertained the company with his amusing settings of limericks and parodies of Handel. He liked conviviality but he never really got out of himself. He was quite ludicrously shy; but he would talk night after night on the theories of art. I remember him also on a visit, telling a long and involved story to my mother, and when her attention wandered he was in agonies of embarrassment.'

Despite, or perhaps because of, his shyness, his eager delight in making new friends and acquaintances was characteristic. 'Last Thursday, by a great *tour de force* I got up to date! On the strength of that I accepted Dr. Joachim's[1] invitation and went out for the rest of the day on the river with him and a great and shining light of the name of *Dale.* . . . If I were a novelist I should have plenty of material to work on in Balliol; as it is I trace a good many of my themes to characters. This isn't fanciful; every musical idea is an embodiment of one's state of mind after receiving some impression. I can trace a place in the Rhapsodie of my trio to Dale with absolute certainty' [quotation]. . . . 'Why can't I study classics like music? . . . I *ought* to learn *easily* to read Plato as I read Bach, but there is no prospect of that for a dreary long time yet. And as to the use of words, I am nowhere here. I can think and feel, but I can't communicate. It's not because my thoughts are deep (gracious!) but because I can only put them satisfactorily in musical guise. What a ridiculous condition! I have (this sounds like fantastic nonsense, but it isn't) frequently caught myself positively *solving* some problem (of a more or less philosophical nature), in, say, the key of A minor, where I had utterly failed to reason it out in words. . . . I have a theory that the reason why the character of *Hamlet* is quite inexplicable, and yet quite convincing, is that it is brought out by a series of subtle artistic devices which are vividly significant and yet quite out of the depth of words. Words do not represent ideas, they only represent *particular cases* of ideas; but I think that artistic devices of the vital order really do represent ideas. Oh dear! Pity my doddering condition and excuse this solemn prosing.' Did Oxford possess any tutor capable of meeting this young man on his own ground?

The trio which had failed to win the Mendelssohn Scholarship

---

[1] Harold Joachim—nephew of the great violinist and a tutor at Balliol.

was performed at the end of June at the Musical Club, and the composer was excited to find that the 'colour' of various special effects turned out to be just as he had imagined it. 'I shall have full confidence henceforth in being able to use any combination of strings with any kind of instrumental effect I wish to produce.' [This unerring faculty for imagining the *quality* of sounds produceable by every kind of instrument was one of his unique gifts.] 'As to the more important and serious qualities of the thing of course I can have no opinion. I only know that it was well received . . . and that Gibson and Ould were quite angelic and rehearsed at it for *two hours and a half,* and never lost their tempers once. . . . Oddly enough it is the most fearful thing for ensemble that I've ever seen!

'. . . Well, well. Collections pull me by a single hair, as Bray says; and I had such a bad night yesterday that I could hardly make out what the paper was about this morning. *P.S.* I must tell you at my next opportunity of a very ideal little hour I had in my rooms, before the Club performance, with my father, Bray, Cotterell, Irving, Mathews and Gow. Mother had presented me with a basket of strawberries and we had coffee and strawberries and cream.'

It is not surprising that July found him much in need of a holiday. 'I was very sorry not to go to the Hipkins; . . . but I must confess that the chief reason was that I find myself much more tired than I was even just after finishing the trio, and consequently I find myself talking too much and altogether effervescing in the way you know.' Shortly afterwards he writes from Durness, in Sutherland, where he was on holiday with his brother: 'It is delightful up here. We're out *absolutely* all day, and my quintet[1] is coming out in the most extraordinary fashion; as is also the revision of the E minor symphony. We are going to-day to use the pound you munificently sent by going to Cape Wrath and spending the night in a lighthouse!!!' [Quotation of a theme in 8 real parts from the quintet.]

Later from Hartree: 'I have *never* had such a collection of

---

[1] Published later as op. 6.

things in my head. The Pfte. 4^{tet} and 5^{tet}, B flat trio, string 4^{tet}, C major Symphony, Pfte. concerto, Mass in G and others are *all* postponed till next vacation. Meanwhile Agamemnon, Bray, Oxford in general, Durness, the Firth of Forth, the delightfully quiet and gay and intellectual Cornishes and their absurd live seagulls and cormorants, and the pompous Chester and the sea-fog with the glassy water, and the clear ring of cold gray sky with a perspective of cold gray clouds seven layers deep, have suddenly turned into an extremely gay and jovial 'cello sonata in F major,[1] and a very romantic and melancholy and pre-historic trio in C minor for pfte., clarinet and horn.[2] . . . The romantic and utterly unearthly effect of the mere combination of instruments (pfte., clar. and horn) has gripped me strongly, and I think I can ensure that it does not pall.' [Several quotations.] . . .

'The Mus.Bac. exercise will just go to the Devil. I mean it'll be done in the last fortnight of the vacation.'

This highly 'effervescent' letter must have caused Miss Weisse some anxiety as to the results of the impact of Oxford life, with its excitements and overwork, on the sensitive and delicately balanced mind of the writer.

During this summer Tovey completed his first set of songs. While on a visit to Namur in the latter half of August, a number of letters passed between him and Bray concerning points of 'alterations or repairs' to the manuscripts; a post-script to one of these adds, 'I am immersed in the deadly dulness of a Mus.Bac. Exercise, and shan't have any more songs for the next few days. Wow!' His comment on the place itself is characteristic: 'The scenery is very beautiful, and there is a peculiar vastness of distance all round'—distance always at-tracted him.

The last week of vacation came: 'Time has been flying at a most awful rate, and I've found that the Mus.Bac. exercise is to have an *unaccompanied* vocal quartet in the middle of three

---

[1] Published later as op. 4.
[2] Published later as op. 8 (*Trio in tragischem Stile*).

other accompanied movements! A more impossible and utterly futile request was surely never made by mortal man. I've been cursing and swearing at the thing, till it suddenly occurred to me that it would work as "Holy, Holy, Holy" in a Te Deum. So here goes, and I'm in the thick of it. Divinity Mods. is next Saturday!!!'

In September Bray paid a visit to Worplesdon. 'Father hasn't looked depressed for a moment since Bray arrived. . . . Do you know I have hit upon what I think might do for my first publication' [list of songs follows]. 'They're all for a bass, in fact five of them are for Bray. . . . I'm afraid they wouldn't pay, but they would be a beginning.'

Bray was critical of Miss Weisse, rather to his friend's dismay, but he established a very pleasant relationship with the Tovey family. 'By a happy accident,' writes Sir Denys, 'my mother had just moved to Guildford, three or four miles from his father's rectory at Worplesdon. . . . Somehow, my memories keep moving away from Oxford to the Worplesdon–Guildford days, and our long walks home in the dark to his house or ours—only to be retraced half-way together, and sometimes retraced more than once. I was devoted to his people, and they to me—not so much on my own account, as because I was a link that kept their beloved Don to their side. I like to remember that when his mother died he wrote "You always understood her. Sing *Schlummert ein* when you think of us tonight". He was devoted to her.

'And he was devoted to my mother, and they delighted in teasing each other. She was fond of music and very proud of him. But she used to creep off to bed when it went on too long for her, and to come downstairs again if she thought it went on too long or too loud for her neighbours, and to turn him— which meant me also—out of the house. "Now, Don" I can still hear her say one evening at supper, "I won't have you play those *Goldberg* Variations again tonight!" "Oh, won't you?" he said; promptly laid down his knife and fork, and grinning up impishly in her face, stretched his arms back on to the upright

Schiedmayer behind him, and went on playing the Variations until she could control her laughter enough to make him stop. It all amazed me as a triumph not so much of technique as of brain. It seemed like reading of Aristotle up-side-down in a looking-glass. Or am I wrong? Curiously enough I never remembered to ask him.'

This is probably the most amazing of all the curious musical feats for which he had an uncanny knack; but he did them quite casually and attributed no importance to them. Mr. George Marshall (late director of the B.B.C. in Northern Ireland) says, 'I can well remember on one occasion Tovey playing a very curious piece in our drawing-room at Moffat. On my mother asking him what it was, he said "That was God Save the King played backwards".'

4

THE conflict between music and University work was constant and became intensified each year as both increased their claims on the young man's time and energy. 'I have been thinking', he wrote at the beginning of his second year (1895–6), 'about Mods. and the concert problem'—the concert in question was a proposed appearance with Joachim at Oxford. 'On the whole I think it would almost be wiser to wait another year for the concert. . . . I noticed that many men last term when they were in for Mods. kept very quiet, although they were quite up to the mark in their work. . . . I shall certainly not play more than once at the Club, and I shall see that it is at the beginning of the term.'

Some weeks later he writes, 'Work, I think, doing tolerably; I believe I could have been a considerable scholar if I had begun sooner'. Others thought so too, but this was the only time the student himself expressed any such opinion. When he was Reid Professor at Edinburgh he stoutly declared to the late Sir William McCormick that he ought never to have read for Classics at all, but that he ought certainly to have gone for Science.

After a long account of recent musical doings at Oxford, the above letter continues, 'I think I shall write something of the treatise order next vacation. . . . I am rather seriously thinking of a group of Essays on "Musical Art-problems and how they have been treated". Such as for instance, the Concerto, the Instrumental Fugue, the growth of differentiation between choral and instrumental forms; and, for problems not yet solved, Modern Organ Music.'

In November, however, he wrote, 'I have got very badly bitten with this old pfte. quintet; and I am incessantly distracted by the actual *effects of the instruments* sounding in my head. . . . I am so crammed full of the thing that I should have thought my attention was hopelessly distracted, whereas work really seems to be looking up a bit'. And in the Christmas holidays: 'When I have a thing like this quintet on, I lose count of time in the most singular way. . . . Rather to my delight the monster is stranded at the beginning of the scherzo, and it won't budge for some time to come, so that I shall have peace and quiet' [Pages of quotations]. . . . 'Even now that I've finished the sketch [of the 1st movement], the thing goes round and round in my head, and as the movement takes a quarter of an hour straight through, I get rather a jump sometimes when I find I've gone twice through it since I sat down in a chair to do something. . . . I seriously don't believe that it will always be thus. It's because I haven't enough technique that my work drives me frantic.'

The quintet was evidently still 'stuck' at the beginning of next term, though it was still causing him to neglect other matters. 'The other day Duncan asked me for the music of his play. I began on it at once, as I could see it was really urgent. But I told him I couldn't send it off all at once, and that it wouldn't be any use sending merely the tunes without any accompaniment (as he very thoughtfully suggested). Result, an urgent letter from Father. . . . I hope the play will get taken on and succeed.'

In February he wrote: 'I have been wading through what is to me boundless regions of reading, but which only gives me material for very scrappy work. . . . However the Dean seems pleased, though I myself should have thought that the sort of stuff I enclose was about 9th rate. . . . I am absolutely certain that the Dean's view of it as a first-class paper if only there had been five questions instead of four is quite outside the mark. . . . With philosophy I feel a little better off. . . . The Master said my logic papers were fairly well done.'

During this spring he complained that he knew nothing about modern orchestration, and he tried to make good that defect by studying Dvořák and Tschaikowsky. 'I came across the analytical programme of Dvořák's *Requiem* the other day, and it is a keen regret to me that when I heard it I allowed the false touches in his views of death, and the errors in his structure and vocal writing, and the amazing badness of the performance, to swamp my appreciation of what I can now dimly see, by the light of Dvořák's other music, must be one of the greatest works of these days.' And later he remarks, 'Tschaikowsky seems to me to have died twenty years too soon. He has left us to make him out by a body of work that only represents him as Wagner is represented from *Rienzi* to *Rheingold*.'

The strain of trying to absorb new features of orchestral technique, and at the same time of producing satisfactory work for his tutors at Oxford, became greater during the summer term, as is only too evident from his characteristically ingenious methods of disclaiming it: 'Now I want you to see the "rationale" of the following. I find that what really tires my head all along is the perpetual trying to think things out and collecting materials up and down for essays. But this last week I have got tremendously into the swing of getting up texts and knowing the words thereof; *and as long as I do that I'm quite at ease*. But if I read, say, a chapter of Nettleship, then I find myself spending four hours in a whirlwind of speculation and confusion and am very tired afterwards. *The same holds good if I do nothing*. . . . I bought a sixpenny copy of *Lorna Doone* the other day for leisure moments, but I daren't read it, for I find myself promptly trying to draw up a sort of classification of novels and styles and aesthetic devices and goodness knows what. When I go out for a walk I come back with a new theory about consecutive 5ths (and a very good one too). Now grinding at texts is giving me about the most complete rest I've had for years. . . . So if you will let me continue chewing the cud in this way you will effectively stop my tiring my head, and I shall have a better chance for the exams.'

Yet this over-active brain was presently making plans for more composition on a large scale: 'Would you advise me to begin next vacation with my C major symphony or my G major string quartet or my trio in C minor? I ought to get them all done before October if I'm to keep out of the lunatic asylum! . . . Father has got the Clarke Lectureship ('97–98) and I have been skipping like the 27th power of a flea ever since. It will set such a lot of things right.'

Some of the completed compositions reached Dr. Parry for criticism in the autumn, at the beginning of the third year at Balliol 1896–7. Dr. Parry was immersed in his new duties as Director of the Royal College, and had not much time to give to them; but he had some positive advice to give on his pupil's general course of studies, which must have been very helpful in the crisis which was approaching. 'From what I saw', he wrote to Miss Weisse, 'I gathered that Donald was making distinct and strong progress. I think it absolutely unwise for him to "leave his music entirely aside" unless he means to make something else his life's work. That would altogether alter the complexion of things. If not, the shelving of all music for Greats would be a mistake. It will make him neither better as a man or as an artist. . . . There is such a thing as overworking academic studies and coming out pretty parched from the ordeal.' The strain told badly this term on the young man, who was now making the quality of his mind felt in his Oxford work, and Parry writes again to Miss Weisse in December, 'It seems to me that it would be a very singular waste of remarkable gifts if Donald was to give up the idea of making music his profession. . . . I don't know whether his gifts in respect of classics and philosophy are even more pronounced than his musical gifts, . . . but if not, surely music is marked out for him with exceptional clearness.' His pupil was, however, on the verge of a breakdown, and everyone was concerned for him.

A letter from the Master of Balliol to Dr. Parry dated 24 December 1896 shows plainly how anxious were the University authorities: 'I venture to ask you to give me your counsel about D. F. Tovey, whom you will remember was elected to the Nettleship Musical Scholarship on your recommendation after examination.

'He is a man of real ability and I should say that he might distinguish himself highly if he could be got to give thought and attention to other subjects than music. I have had excellent essays from him, and the tutors tell me that he has a good feeling for language, and might improve rapidly in scholarship as in other subjects if his mind were steadily devoted to them. But he is so possessed and drawn away by his musical interests that he makes little progress. From time to time he becomes filled with some musical conception and absolutely exhausts himself with the effort to produce a piece of composition in which it is expressed. The consequence is that he altogether failed to take honours in Moderations, and that it is probable that, if things go on as they are doing, he will not succeed better in the Final Schools, though he is quite capable of doing so. . . .

'Is it expedient for the eventual good of a man like Tovey who wishes to devote himself to music, that we should insist strictly on the conditions of the scholarship, or should we regard him as an exception to the ordinary rule? . . . Would it really stand in the way of his ultimate success as a musician, if he were to give up all musical composition for the next two years?' Even so great and discerning a man as Sir Edward Caird had not the faintest notion that this was a physical impossibility, like asking a poet not to speak. In the end, however, the authorities were both wise and humane.

Returning to Balliol after the Christmas vacation, Tovey at first is more cheerful in his letters to Miss Weisse: 'I want you to reserve your dark thoughts of the Master's letter till later in the term. I am much more forward with my work now, and, above all, the things that distressed me so last term are all right. . . . I am uproariously well!' Later, 'I think my term is a good one; though I find my essays awfully difficult and often write three pages of elaborate material only to find on reflection that it's off the point.' Soon he was again driving himself too hard and was tormented by the music he could not get on with: 'I have been put behind-hand by several headaches, and I literally can't tell the difference between a fortnight and two days. . . . Abbott seemed rather pleased with an essay I wrote on the political insight of Herodotus, or the square root of $-2\frac{1}{2}$, which comes to about the same thing. Herodotus would have accounted for the Franco-Prussian war by saying that the French and German ambassadors walked past each other one morning without raising their hats.

'I have now to give an account of his *military* history, and it's turning my hair grey. . . . I think next vac. I shall have to consider the question of whether I have any technique of composition left. Of course I have not been such an ass as to write anything just now, but you know I am always thinking out little harmonic and melodic corners, half unconsciously;—just as anyone always has something vaguely floating about in their minds. . . . The particular kind of musical thought I mean is no more to be dispelled by other occupation or by rest or by any nonsense of any sort than the power of thinking at all. . . . So I am afraid a great deal will have to depend on what I find out about my composition next vac. If there is any difficulty about the mechanical part of it after a week's beginning, well then I don't care if I get four x+ Collection papers; something will have to be done to keep my musical technique in order. . . . The 'cello sonata will be played on March 14th. It was partly looking at it that startled me; because I am *perfectly certain* I could not, if I had time, at present tackle half the difficulties I tackled in it. . . .'

The danger-point had been reached. Yet he was not by any means wholly absorbed in his own affairs: 'I am rather excited to find that a hare-brained and very well-meaning young man named Jardiner has a most remarkable talent for orchestration. . . . I think it's a pity the Musical Club doesn't occasionally find out something about its members.' And later: 'I've got Hadow to promise the next available opening for Jardiner's pianoforte pieces at the Club.' Playing duets with Ernest Walker at the Club was however *not* his idea of enjoyment. 'There isn't *room* for two performers on one piano' [certainly not for these two exuberant young men], 'and the audience loathe duets too. But', he adds, 'I want you to hear Walker's trio, which has some noble features. It is in the style of Brahms and Walker, but the form and texture of Schumann; a most singular combination, but just what one would expect from an original man, who knew all the works of Brahms, but had found out all he knew of form simply by experience.'

Plans of all sorts ran ahead in his mind. 'I want to get up a huge and exhaustive and terse lecture on the Sonata *Appassionata* and fire it off in Oxford next term. Make the blasphemers sit up a bit about the meaning of music and its contents. Farmer would find me an occasion to read it. . . . My latest raging themes for the Finale of F major violin sonata' [and there follow two new quotations from the man who was 'going to write no music this term'].

In the Easter vacation he was writing a book—the outcome of his idea of a series of essays on various musical subjects—'I work at present at "Music and its means of expression", of which I have finished the first chapter "On the position of Music in Art, and the true method of artistic criticism", and have begun the second "On Limitations".' He was struggling with a second draft of these chapters in July: 'It's the most trying piece of work I've done for a long time, . . . and the frightful long-windedness and frequent obscurity of the thing make it very unreadable.'

The summer term was not such a strain as the two previous ones—'The Master's lectures are beginning to assume shape and plan. It's awfully funny to hear the clever fellows who live on brilliance pitch into him.

'I am solacing myself at the end of the day by resting my jaded remains in the works of Bach. I take the first thing in Vol. I and the last thing in Vol. XLI, and the second thing in Vol. I and the last but one in Vol. XLI and so on. It ensures my sleeping well, and it's wonderfully improving to the mind. I calculate that when I begin upon my last term here I shall have just made my Bach reading meet in the middle, as it were, and so have covered the whole ground.' One wonders whether it ever did meet while he was at Oxford; it certainly did at some time of his life. Anyhow it gave him further plans for his book, for he writes a month later: 'I believe I can get quite an enormous stock of materials for my book out of Bach in a *new way*. He is always dishing up old material, and unlike Handel he always transforms it by very simple but very important changes; and I believe that if I can collate all the cases they will furnish me with a most important collection of general principles.' Details follow, concluding with the remark, in reference to the twenty-one extant Concertos, 'and there are traces in the Cantatas of the existence of at least four more [concertos]. I believe there is a systematic development in all these reconstructions and I want to work it out. Another thrilling thing is that we actually possess four or five big movements of the Markus-Passion in the shape of the *Trauer Ode*, the text of which is an *Umdichtung* of that of the *Markus-Passion*, which is evidently nearly as big as the *Matthäus-Passion*.

'All this is frightful shop to put into a letter, but I think you will allow it is awfully thrilling.'

In this state of mind he was apt to overlook the fact that his family not unnaturally liked to have some information as to his whereabouts. His mother wrote: 'We know not where either feather or bone of you may be, but I write nevertheless to wish you Many Happy Returns of your Birthday. A Mendelssohn volume which you ordered from Breitkopf and Härtel has come with the bill, 13/6, which we will present to you paid for a birthday present. When may we expect you home to receive it? And Echo makes the usual answer.

'A letter has just come from Duncan in scarlet ink. He asks us to excuse its being written with the "pen of the reddy writer". He says you are nowhere in particular, but that you may perhaps soon be at Englefield Green on your way home.

'Aunt Charlotte says she longs for the elections to be at an end, for the place is filled with vans and vehicles laden with the seven deadly sins in great triumph and glory.'

During this term Miss Weisse, alarmed by the distress of the previous months over the feared loss of technique, had endeavoured to persuade Dr. Parry to resume regular lessons with his former pupil—but without success. 'I am sure Donald is not likely to fall back at all,' he replied to her letter. 'His natural gifts and sympathy with what is finest in art are sure to keep him in the right path, even if he has to work out his own salvation without regular professional superintendence.' If Parry had seen fit to give some 'superintendence' it might have materially helped to smooth the rough passage of the last year at Oxford, by reassuring Tovey's anxious mind about his musical work.

A later letter from Dr. Parry to Miss Weisse reads: 'I gather that his work for Greats will not be pressed in such a way as to do any harm to his musical development. I should much like to see the Violin Sonata someday, and whatever little use I can be to him will always be a source of satisfaction to me.' It seems clear that Tovey longed at this time for the advice and guidance of the man for whom he had such affectionate respect and lifelong regard; and equally clear that Parry did not realize what some continued personal contact would have meant to his former pupil. The memory of his struggles without such a helping hand may well in later years have influenced Tovey's attitude towards young composers, who could always be sure of his ready response to any real need for guidance.

A situation of some delicacy had also arisen in connexion with his father and his work at Oxford, and a letter from Tovey to Miss Weisse is pathetically tactful: 'I'm afraid you said something about my reading with you which hasn't been taken very kindly at Worplesdon. . . . I think I ought to do a good deal of reading with Father, who can walk through textual difficulties as if they were a loose bead-and-bamboo door, and who has done quite enough philosophy to be of enormous use to me with Plato and Aristotle. I also most certainly ought to do a good deal of reading with you, as there are other aspects of Greats which you can develop in the same sort of way. . . . Please remember I don't know anything beyond what I gather from some rather poignant remarks of Father's.'

Later, 'I am trying to finish the Aristotle. It has been a bit harder this term because we have had to go much faster since the Greek is easier; but unfortunately I am in such a state that easy Greek and hard Greek are all equally Greek to me.— Father came up the other day and stopped the night; I managed a most successful little breakfast consisting of him and Mr Hardie (who blossomed out) and Mathews and one or two others.'

One of the disappointments in connexion with the Music Club this year was the discovery that both the *Goldberg* and the *Diabelli* Variations were down to be played by one of the college organists. 'I may be a bad pianist, but I *am* a pianist and I do understand those variations, and *I could have proved that an audience can be made to listen to them.* Old —— is a dear old bloke, but he will kill the faith even of Hadow and Walker in them. I'm really quite squashed flat.'

There were, however, compensations: 'Last Tuesday I played the Brahms G minor quartet with the venerable Deichmann, and Slocombe and Whitehouse. It was awfully funny because they all got excited, had the piano opened and ran away with me! Quite a relief after the everlasting dragging complaints of "Pianoforte too powerful". The performance was a bit coarse, but it was, for once in a way, vigorous. Deichmann has a big tone; though when he played the C major solo Bach sonata it was madder than the March Hare's tea-party, and would have sounded equally clear if played, on shipboard during a hurricane, on a double-bass. I haven't been "run away with" for *ages*; it quite cheered me up. And to be run away with by such a dear old walrus as Deichmann too; you can't think what a relief it is to get something fresh. Music sometimes seems to me to be going to sleep.'

Just at the end of the summer term he writes: 'That very nice and eccentric individual Maurice Baring wants to know whether I could go to Bayreuth this year, because he's got tickets and finds he can't! He offers me his tickets as a present if I can go.' Baring's companion was to have been Edward Marsh, who has recalled, in his reminiscences, his first meeting with Tovey and their subsequent trip together: 'In 1897 I was staying with Maurice Baring at Oxford, and in the course of a gay evening someone came into the room with a head under his arm from which an apologetic voice proceeded "Gentlemen, gentlemen, this is not the posture in which I should have chosen to be presented to you!" The head was then released from Chancery, and took its normal place at the summit of a lanky and loosely-built frame. I soon perceived that its owner was the beloved and respected and consenting butt of his circle.

'Later in the same year I had arranged to go with Maurice to Bayreuth, but his father, Lord Revelstoke, died rather suddenly and he offered the tickets to Tovey. . . . I was rather cross with Baring for not giving me the chance to choose my own travelling companion—but how wrong I was! If anyone could have made me a musician it was he.'

Baring himself has given a vivid picture of Oxford life in these days—describing the wonderful supper-parties in his rooms, with Belloc discoursing about the Jewish Peril and the *Chanson de Roland*, and Tovey playing Beethoven or his own settings of nonsense verse. When the parties became more lively and the high spirits of undergraduates found vent in hurling soda-syphons and other missiles around, Tovey might be found in a corner carefully explaining the intricacies of counterpoint to a Rowing Blue. In a letter to Ethel Smyth in 1902, Baring remarked that Tovey's intellect strikes him as 'tremendous', adding, 'I have absolutely unlimited admiration for his genius'.

Plans for work during the summer were many and optimistic: 'I shall have to write hard at the beginning of the vacation. I think I had better reel off the symphony and the concerto as fast as possible; and then settle down to Greats the rest of the time. I shall take Thicksides and Arribottle[1] to Bayreuth to cool me down between the *Ring* and *Parsifal*. I want to write essays to you in the vacation; you will be able to help me a great deal by pouncing on any inaccurate statements. *History* essays I mean; those are my weakest points. . . . I think it would be a

---

[1] Thucydides and Aristotle.

very good thing for me to get a good degree; but I foresee such an awful rush of repressed musical work as soon as I leave Oxford that I could almost have wished I had not to wait another year. . . . I'll write to Broadwoods about the piano. I don't think I'd better have one in my last year. There's too much to do and it would be no use trying to practise. The only thing I can do is to get a degree now. It will please them, though it really won't be any earthly use to me. . . . I've stuck trying to work out my analogy between tonality and perspective' [referring to his book].

'The day before yesterday I lost the letter I had begun. It has just turned up, so I continue it at the Bishop's party. . . . The party was interesting but tough. It was rather difficult getting Mother there, because there was some trouble about getting a vehicle and she rather rashly insisted on walking. So we followed a stream of bishops who were all, like us, an hour late owing to the disgraceful state the South Western gets into when Bisley or any other "gryte ochysion" is afloat. . . . We followed two bishops and a lady who seemed to know the way quite well, and who led us up a narrow lane into the park by a steep and rugged ascent with many a straggling root of gnarled oak to trip th' unwary foot; and eventually we came to a garden gate. 'Twas locked. The bishops knocked. No sound save the blare of an episcopal brass band from inside. Mother observed, "*The wedding guest here beat his breast for he heard the loud bassoon*". One of the bishops knocked again. Solemn voice from the top of a tree, "*Knock and it shall be opened*", and I caught a glimpse of an irreverent youth concealed in the foliage. At last Father found the front gate.'

The visit to Bayreuth was enormously exciting and stimulating; it was Tovey's first independent trip abroad. He stopped overnight at Bonn on the way: 'Very successful so far, *Meerestille und glückliche Fahrt*.'[1] He was probably then (as he certainly was later in life) one of those deceptive-looking people who have the air of being totally unable to travel safely for twenty miles alone,

---

[1] Mendelssohn's Overture.

but who have the undeserved knack of catching trains at the last moment, and arriving—if not in time, at least *sometime*—in an effortless way at the correct destination. 'The Beethoven house is most touching; and there are some wonderfully interesting sketches and letters. . . . I would write more, but I am in a healthy state of somnolence, enhanced by a night on deck (the sunrise was a most wonderful thing; I suppose Nature furnishes those spectacles every other day regardless of public attention. She is a very good model for artists in these little matters). . . . With my kindest remembrances to your hostess. . . . P.S. I hope I haven't miscalculated the date. But if I have, I doubt not your hostess will forward this; and that you will know which hostess I mean.' P.P.S. (on the envelope) 'I haven't miscalculated the date, but I see I very nearly miscalculated the address".

Two days after arriving at Bayreuth he dashed off the following on a *postcard*, the writing becoming more and more minute, and eventually winding its way round the edges until every scrap of space was filled.

This is very jolly. My room is very comfortable though somewhat surrounded by buildings, in spite of which, however, there is a very reasonable amount of light.

The *Rheingold* came off yesterday. It is certainly very beautiful, and the music represents in the most perfectly convincing manner what the libretto would have been if Wagner had been capable of writing decent grown-up poetry. The performance is very impressive too. Siegfried Wagner conducted, but the orchestra knew the thing by heart so he couldn't do much harm. There are only two persons who can sing, Marie Brema (whose voice wobbles terribly, but she sings in tune and like a great artist, and she is a splendid actress) Fricka is her part; and someone whose name I forget, who sang Froh yesterday, and who will sing Siegfried tomorrow. The others simply declaim anywhere within a minor third of the notes written. That is a mistake.

It is important to get the libretto, rot as it is, by heart, for it's quite impossible to catch the words from any of the singers except these two. But when you once really know the libretto the whole thing is easy to follow, and one can listen to the music with the greatest pleasure, except when the worst singers interrupt.

Wagner is the only Wagnerian whose music has repose and

breadth. It has those qualities in a degree to which only the greatest composers ever attain. I am surprised to find how much it impresses me, and how little it disturbs. Indeed it only sheds new light on older music; and after the *Rheingold* (which only took two hours and a half) I found myself quite fit to read the Beethoven D Major Mass through for the third time this week. These two impressions can exist side by side with no more difficulty than they make by the side of the impression of Cologne Cathedral. In fact you may take these as the most colossal extant specimens of three entirely distinct art forms; and why should they fight?

I hope you are quite well and that the irksome task of reports is easily and rapidly drawing to its end. I'm afraid I have all along misinterpreted your list of addresses. I punctuated the paragraph thereof wrong and so sent my scrawls to you where you hadn't yet arrived.

I hope you will be able to read this. It has drifted into a very queer arrangement indeed.

Bayreuth is not a particularly successful town. Nor is the theatre a thing of beauty either within or without. But the scenery is very fine; though not much better than at the Lyceum.

The weather has been cool and showery.

No room for more.

> Ever your affectionate,
> Donald Francis Tovey.

Other impressions followed: '*The Ring* is much too tremendous to describe while one's in the midst of it. . . . *Siegfried*, for instance, is a splendid structure if you don't look at it too closely. Analyse the words and the logic and you get more absurdity and Irish Bulls than you would expect from a twelve-year old child; but watch the scenes, the contrasts, and the tone and feeling of the whole and you feel as you do with a Mozart opera that you have great types of human character before you. . . . Certainty and suspense are the keystone to the structure of music drama; that gives the music time to work out broadly and symmetrically. Gluck's most perfect operas are *Orphée* and *Alceste*; and their libretti are remarkably like Wagner's in these qualities. Look also at *Fidelio* where everything is working its will at the outset and nothing is happening. This is not even a mere musical requirement although the music cannot do without it; it is characteristic of the most purely artistic drama as a whole. The first act of *King Lear* is a typical case; and *Oedipus Tyrannus* is still more so.

'However this is not Chapter 103 of my book! . . . By the way, at Mainz I picked up a treasure. If you knew your *Tramp Abroad* as well as a person of your breadth of mind should, you would remember the occasional Rhine Legends as translated by the Rev. Jarnham, B.A. Well, I never believed that the Rev. Jarnham existed outside the brain of Marcus Duplex until I SAW THE BOOK FOR SALE! I bought it! I opened it at the following:

THE LORE-LEI

I do not know what it signifies
That I am so sorrowful?
A fable of old Times so terrifies
Leaves my heart so thoughtful.

[2 more verses follow]

'One more quotation

The Blocksmount is a renowned stronghold
And produces only windy Lamentations;
There the Devil and Satellites is ever told
Expectorate their weirdly incantations.

'This book is even funnier than Tolhurst's *Ruth*.'[1]

Later, 'I'm off to Nuremberg in 20 minutes. *Parsifal* is wonderful, and wonderfully performed as regards orchestra. But (with the exception of Kundry and the small parts where the poor creatures are so contemptible as to learn to sing and act because they've no other claims upon the public) I never heard worse singing in my life. P——, who sang Klingsor, had only two notes; one was D flat and the other wasn't. Parsifal was Van D——. Very fat, and in the first act exactly like Tweedledum.

'Graal Hall the most magnificent scenery ever put on any stage. Blumengarten too tawdry for Drury Lane and absolutely grotesque. Wagner is such a colossal and reposeful musician

---

[1] An oratorio which in all seriousness incorporates some of the funniest settings of words that could be imagined.

that I have definitely come even to something like an admiration for the man himself.'

Later that year when he received the score of *Tristan* it 'shook him from stem to stern', said a fellow-student; 'he was found still putting on his boots two hours later'.

This was the foundation of an understanding of Wagner which came to be greater and more profound than that of any other musician of his day; and of a knowledge of operatic problems which bore fruit later in many penetrating essays and in his own opera.

The recipient of these letters (Miss Weisse), writing from an address at Hawarden, also had interesting news to relate: 'I had the most delightful day yesterday. We went down to the Castle, which is a fine perpendicular sort of bit of architecture, with a large terrace on the brow of a hill in an immense old park like Arundel. First I *did* play with Mrs Harry Drew. She is very musical. . . .

'Then we went out and joined Mr and Mrs Gladstone, perfectly *delightful* old people. No one has ever made on me the impression of a great man, a real man of genius, so much as Mr Gladstone. There was a Flower Show, and an immense crowd of people on the slope below the terrace, and he made a most delicious, humorous, sensible, sympathetic speech to them, delivered in the most wonderful way. Very old-fashioned and entirely in the grand style, and yet going straight to the heart and exceedingly funny in places. I had a great deal of talk with Mrs Gladstone who is the sweetest, cleverest, most unselfish old woman.'

September was spent at Worplesdon and was enlivened by a first visit to G. F. Watts, the painter, at Limnerslease. 'I've been so excited by my recent adventures that I really don't know how long it will be before I collect my wits again', said the letter describing this visit. He arrived late through being misdirected: 'Mr Watts came down the stairs and said "How do you do, Mr Tovey? I was just saying that unpunctuality is a very bad sign at the beginning of a young man's career." My heart was in my boots, but I summoned up courage and explained. I almost wished I hadn't, though it was very reassuring to be so instantly exonerated, for Mrs Watts expressed such regret at not having given me directions. . . . He asked some questions about Oxford and wanted to know whether there were any men likely to do some original work, literary or otherwise. . . . Then he turned to Belgium and asked about the colouring and the scenery there, and said various things about the skies in Italy and England. . . . He asked whether I had been to Bayreuth and he seemed to have a great interest in Wagner though he had never heard any. . . . There were a good many questions about music, especially about Bach and about the modern outlook. . . . He is especially fond of Bach and Beethoven because he finds their works embody *form* so clearly, which he takes as the highest and most accurate means of expression in art.

'Really I could hardly believe my ears at times. This astounding little old man with his extraordinary wizard-like appearance of extreme age coupled with the utmost freshness and vivacity, was continually dropping out, in the fewest and most lucid words possible, bits of musical philosophy and criticism that put the whole wisdom of all *Grove's Dictionary* to shame. . . .

'When after lunch he showed me into his studio, I felt much as if I were being shewn into Cologne Cathedral by the original architect of it. There was a huge picture of Time and Death, with Justice behind them, rushing straight forward, which I will attempt to describe later. . . . I am remembering bit by bit all that he said; but really it hangs together so closely that I can only get it into shape very slowly. He made me play a good deal, and also drew me out so much that I felt I was talking far more than was consistent with not being a bore; but as soon as I dropped a feeler on that point Mr Watts said, "Oh that's not at all likely". He evidently takes a *very* deep interest in music and has really an insight into it that makes me very nervous before him, though there never was anyone who had more of the art of putting people at their ease.

'Many, many thanks for the Brahms concerto (of which more

anon). . . . My own concerto is waiting for the assimilation of the Brahms and Mr Watts. I must let it grow a bit.

'Finding the narrative of Thicksides nearly as hard as the speeches, and possessing a crib for two books of Tacitus, Father and I are confining our attentions to Thicksides as being more important and more difficult. P.S. In spite of the disgraceful delay of this epistle, I have heaps more to say of the Wizard of Limnerslease.'

At a later stage in their acquaintance Watts expressed a desire to paint the young man, but the project was unfortunately never carried out. Watts in his old age painted a few portraits which were held to be very fine, although they did not attain accepted success, and it is certain that he saw something very remarkable in his young friend, and might have produced a notable painting.

5

TOVEY'S last year at Oxford was 1897–8, and he was well aware it was a crucial one; but from the impressions of the summer there had emerged afresh the notion of a violin concerto. 'It's eating me out of my senses', he wrote on 4 October, a few days before term began, 'it's so frightfully quiet and serious.'

Conditions were somewhat different this year as he was living out of College, and letters to Miss Weisse flowed freely at the beginning of term. 'Bray and Mathews and Cotterell are most ideally snug in their digs. The rooms haven't got a straight line in them, and are very nice. They are in the same house as Walker's.

'Trotter is up for a fifth year. Amery is hunting fellowships.

'I am already beginning to realise what it is to have a friend next door with communicable rooms. The experience is new, for my friends of my own year were scattered far and wide over the College. But the present arrangement is not only pleasanter but actually wastes less time. . . .' The friend next door was Hugh Godley,[1] who looked after him with much kindness during this trying term, even to the extent of valeting him when he became too fatigued to rouse himself in the mornings.

'How are you?' he continues, '*Please* be well. . . . You should neglect your duties more when you are exhausted. There aren't half-a-dozen people in England who stick to them half as hard as you do, and they are regarded as paragons of industry. . . . I shall have to go to Klondyke and bring back a million or two to bribe the British Parent to send its daughters to inferior establishments. Then you will *have* to take a holiday.

'I must talk a little nonsense sometimes. The sense that underlies it is too true and too serious to be put forward unadorned.'

[1] Later Lord Kilbracken.

On 20 October he writes, 'Many happy returns, as the minuet said to the rondo before it found out that it was a set of variations.

'My presents to you are always a little too like Edwin's present of an acre of linen to Angelina to make a set of dress-shirts with; but I console myself with the reflection that you really do want a Grote,[1] and I have picked up a complete one very cheap and so clean that I actually have the face to offer it to you. I will send it soon, but may I be so brazen as to look at it first, and send you the volumes as I get through 'em? This is very like Edwin, but it coincides—or rather, *and* it coincides with my work.

'I investigate Bach Suites every day after lunch. Mr William's rhythm holds water constantly. Of course it's only one of many, but it's a most important one. I wonder how much he knows of melodic organization. Probably an enormous lot. The suites are among the most astounding art products in the world. . . .

'I am writing an essay on "The nature and purpose of Logic!" Its nature is to confuse and its purpose to annoy. . . .

'I won't remark that Mr X' [his tutor] 'combines the facial contours of a gorilla and a toucan with the deportment of a hearse-horse. Such an observation would be unkind and so I refrain from making it. But he seems a very good sort.'

Things did not always go smoothly, however, and there were several occasions—all of them connected with musical matters—when the highly-strung youth showed irritation and anger. The first occurred when he missed a chance of playing with Kruse at a private party, and a fellow-undergraduate monopolized the violinist and played *all three* Brahms sonatas with him! At all periods of his life Donald Tovey was liable to sudden explosions of rage against whatever seemed to him wrong or unjust. These explosions could be very formidable indeed, but, while they appeared to shake him to the depths, they were always quickly over and he would be his usual serene self long before others had recovered from the storm. It was probably well for him that the

---

[1] Grote's *History of Greece.*

safety-valve was not too tightly shut down. After furiously re-counting the Kruse episode he adds: 'Did I ever tell you about C. F. Bell, the Ashmolean man; nephew of the P.R.A.; now sharing his rooms with Trotter and the possessor of a glorious double harpsichord? . . . When you come up I'll play you the *Goldbergs* on the harpsichord; and you shall see what a charm-ing person C. F. Bell is.' A letter to him from C. F. Bell said: 'I hope that you will consider the harpsichord as entirely at your service whenever you can come to practise upon it, whether I am in or out, but I hope even more that I *shall* be in, as it gives me unspeakable pleasure to hear you play.'

As the first term proceeds: 'I am getting along; a bit out of my depth but not badly. . . . Walker is to be president of O.U.M.C. next year. I am going to insist on his putting on my quintet. I have some themes for a future 5^{tet} in F sharp minor which quite frighten me. . . .

'I forget whether I told you about Richter. The programme was idiotically arranged, but the performance was splendid. The Brahms improved as it went on; the opening was too coarse and the strings in it drowned the wind. But by the beginning of the Scherzo the players had got their bearings, and the finale, which everyone says is impossible to play, might have been Handel for all the trouble it gave them. Tremendous!

'I had the misfortune to be rather off the rails and had to manage to put the bulk of my headache into Liszt's billionth Hungarian Rhapsody.'

Life was very crowded: 'Saturday is the date of Father's next lecture *and The Wasps* at Cambridge. . . . I think it would be a great omission on my part not to go to this lecture, when it is just humanly possible for me to get off and when all Balliol is going to *The Wasps*. . . . Bray has got a Taylorian for German. Most seasonable and beneficial to his spirits and energies.' A later letter describes Miss Bray's wedding, adding 'But it's horrid the way one of the grandest families there ever was has been scattered all over the world. No wonder Denys has moods.'

'The Club this term has so far been acute physical and mental torture to me', says a later letter. 'Only my benevolent wish to introduce freshmen and my having to play this week and next has been the cause of my going there at all. The performances, with the single exception of the first concert, have been *execrable*; Arbos included. He wasn't in good form, and was obviously too utterly handicapped by ——'s absolutely loathsome playing of the Brahms D minor. . . .

'December 6th seems the only date on which Farmer can bring off a sort of semi-private public performance by me in Balliol Hall of the *Goldberg* Variations. *Do* try and get up for that. . . . Pleeze forgive my muddles!'

The date was altered to 10 December, but circumstances nearly prevented this performance after all, as a letter dated 6 December discloses: 'Godley put me to bed by force (he is none too well himself, and the night before my cold got so heavy, I was very anxious about him indeed); and I had to spend Sunday in bed. It was particularly dismal as you will see from one of the accompanying programmes [of Balliol Sunday concerts]. . . . Fancy my missing playing our old friend, the first ensemble thing you ever taught me [Haydn Trio in A major no. 7]! . . .

'Of course I must be careful to be fit for next Friday' [the date of the *Goldberg* performance], 'as you will see from the third programme.

'The pheasant you sent must have been shot in Paradise. It is exquisite. Haven't they printed my programme well?

'This is a horridly stupid letter, and I'm in the depths of gloom because I lost my hair when that angelic Hugh Godley was badgering me and strumming on the piano.'

There is no record of how the performance succeeded. 'It was rather ticklish sending a programme to Dr. ——' (the organist who had performed both the *Goldberg* and the *Diabelli* Variations at the Musical Club at the invitation of Hadow in the previous term). 'But I explained that I was trying to do for my College Musical Society what he had just done for the Club. . . .

'I didn't tell many lies; and yet I think he ought to be pleased.

It's rather unfortunate though coming on top of Walker's definitely putting me down for the Beethoven *Diabelli* Variations.'
It appeared in retrospect that there had been some deliberate
intention of slighting Tovey in the matter of the performance of
the two sets of Variations, and relations with Hadow were somewhat strained for a long time.

He protested to Miss Weisse that he was better again, 'But, if
you don't mind, I shall come down as soon as I can. They seem
quite inclined to let me. . . . I certainly couldn't do a paper,
even on old ground like the *Republic*, in my present state of
stupidity. I can't understand what I read just now; the words
run in at my eyes and through my head without a hitch, but
goodness knows where they go to. . . .

'Godley has gone down. He has been simply too good for
words.

'A shy young man blustered into my rooms this morning
under the impression I was leaving them. If I have to, I shall be
profoundly grumbulous for the rest of my time here. There's
nowhere to go to.'

Writing during the Christmas vacation from Worplesdon, he
acknowledges Miss Weisse's present of Joachim's newly published violin concerto: 'The concerto is splendid and most useful.
Joachim will some day be recognised as the third greatest composer of the end of this Century. I know nothing outside Brahms
and the best of Dvořák that comes up to this. What it has not
got however is the *brilliance* of the work of the greatest composers.' After an account of various visits he had paid, comes the
remark, 'I am trying to do some songs. . . . By the time I get to
work next summer I think I shall find myself a stage further on.
I hope and believe that the days of extravagance and exaggeration were past nearly three years ago. . . . The violin concerto
shews signs of melting away'.

In February 1898 there is a rare mention of financial difficulties, which he was usually scrupulous to avoid: 'This is very
awful, and I'll try not to let it happen again. Shekels (50 of 'em)
safely to hand and Battells paid accordingly. Balliol is in a pack

of troubles. J. A. Smith has had to go down for his health, and there's no one I personally could spare less of my various Oxford tin gods on pedestals; the Master has just gone to Scotland to see his brother whose condition is dangerous; and Urquhart has gone to his uncle's funeral. I had to read my Collection papers like an essay. . . . I gathered though that I had got the main points right and that six questions would be enough for a Greats paper.' Then he goes on:

'It is a great experience playing with Kruse, but not so great as playing with Miss Wietrowitz, and it is much more expensive in time and temper. . . . I had to accompany a sonata of Tartini. In Balliol Hall the pianoforte is left at the left end of the platform in the afternoon, and the middle of the platform is occupied by the high table. Kruse taking this, very stupidly, for the usual concert arrangement, walked up and down the other side of these long tables and played his Tartini sometimes with his back towards me and *always* too far off to be heard distinctly in the echoing empty room. After a bit he shouted out "*My* time, not yours"; and came up very crossly, and subsided into good-natured and fatherly observations in German to *Ernest Walker* about my being very musical but obviously lacking experience in accompanying. I told him at once that I was good enough for Miss Fillunger, and that if he would play where it was humanly possible for me to hear him, I'd undertake to accompany him. I won't stand impertinence and unreasonableness even from a genius.

'Kruse didn't seem to believe what I said about the position of the piano for the evening, for after starting again where I *could* hear him (and making himself so intolerably captious that Walker began to sit on him too), he walked off into the farthest North again. However, I pottered about after him as well as I could; and of course it was all right in the concert.

'He was much nicer about the Mozart, which he didn't know, and he was very good company over the Brahms on Tuesday, and made himself very ingratiating. . . . My waltzes went off very nicely. . . .'

The question of the conditions of the Nettleship Scholarship and the problem of who was to be its second holder was occupying the attention of the authorities just then. 'I have just come from an exciting discussion with no less a person than H. H. J.[1] on no less a subject (started by him, too) than the probable fate of the Nettleship Scholarship. He very soon saw my point about the danger of sending a man here before he had finished the main part of his musical training. . . . H. J. wants me to talk to the Dean about it when Greats are over. Personally I should think that the Dean was the very last person who would believe what I told him; for he is undoubtedly disappointed in me, and thinks I don't know how to apply myself or to see my opportunities. However it's surely a detail to whom to talk. Joachim mentioned J. A. Smith as an alternative; he would, I think, be less unprepared to take me as a person of common sense. So would the Master.

'I am awfully glad there *is* some real understanding of the difficulties. H. H. J. was even more on my side than I expected. . . . He hoped I wasn't worrying about Greats;—that didn't matter a brass farthing etc., etc.

'I must conclude at once. *Can* you, oh *can* you send (*a*) Bach Vol. XIX, (*b*) Handel Instrumental Musik Vol. XL, (*c*) any parts (however incomplete, the rest being at Worplesdon) of Bach Concerto No. V (Brandenburg) that may happen to be in the fruit room? Angel!

'I have just read a cantata "Ihr werdet weinen und heulen" which is so overpowering that, though I thought myself pretty well case-hardened to Bach, I was quite knocked down by it.

'The Union is closing and the lights are going out!! To be continued.

Ewig dein, Donald Francis Tovey.'

Miss Weisse replied to this, 'The important thing seems to me to provide good and responsible tuition for the Nettleship Scholar in *music*. . . . And his "musical tutor" ought to be able

---

[1] Harold Joachim.

to tell if the sum of his activity in all directions represents the proper amount of work—whichever way it is distributed. As for you at present, it is now my great wish that you should do all you *possibly* can for your Schools.'

Others also were concerned about the Nettleship. Strachan Davidson wrote to Sir Walter Parratt: 'Thank you for your note. Donald Tovey is a man of first rate ability, but sadly hampered by ill-health. A certain dreaminess of temperament, and want of quickness in reading and writing are also drawbacks, but I imagine that these spring in the main from physical causes. His mind seems to me to be developing, but just as he is making real progress we fear that we shall be obliged to send him down, on account of headaches and lassitude. It is most provoking. I do not think that he has the art of managing his health, and when it comes to the Schools, it is quite probable that we shall see him in the 4th instead of where he ought to be,—in the 1st. Nevertheless I think that his selection has been amply justified and I believe that his career up here will prove to have been most profitable in its effects on his intellect and character.

'If all the Nettleship Scholars are as good I shall confess that the doubts which I entertained from the first of the usefulness of the Foundation are not justified by the result. P.S. I have shown this to the Master who desires to express his concurrence. . . .'

A criticism of a recital by Paderewski occupies much of a letter of 13 March from Tovey: 'I sat in the orchestra, very close to the piano. He looked far from well, and played with considerable effort, on the vilest of Erards, seating himself on a very low chair at such a distance from the pianoforte that his elbows became dimples and his legs as those of one who roweth in the Torpids. . . .

'The Waldstein Sonata was wrong from the beginning to the Prestissimo at the end. That was right, and it's the only time I've heard it so. But the rest was —— hiatus in MS, owing to spontaneous combustion. . . .

'A flat Polonaise—"The breaking of the Bride's China"; middle episode very fine. Three études; C major amazing, beyond praise; B minor (octaves) one of the most ghostly and terrific performances I have ever heard. . . .

'His own new minuet in A major. First rate. . . .

'Strauss-Tausig waltzes. Strauss is a genius. He was wiser than Tausig.

'. . . I stopped to the end, because obviously the fireworks are the thing to hear when the fine art is bad. But the first numbers distressed me greatly. Ill-health may make a genius play obscurely or feebly; it cannot be the cause of bad taste; and bad taste is very distressing in Paderewski because at his worst he has enough to make one listen to him, and no artist can have more than that. . . .

'I relieved my feelings next day by going to Sanger's circus. A genuine circus is worth fifty of those that go about masquerading as artistic entertainments, so after the illusion I sought the truth at Sangers. It was glorious.'

He went home for Easter: 'Many thanks for two delightful letters. There's no news here. Things goeth satisfactorywise.

'I have made a large hole in the Chronique Scandaleuse of Herodotus. Royal Reputations blasted while you wait. Terms (im)moderate.'

A projected holiday visit to Littlehampton was delayed by a sudden attack of cold: 'There isn't the smallest cause for anxiety about me (except that my fountain-pen is developing new theories as to where and when ink should flow). . . . The doctor seems to think I'm getting on well.' In pencil and with a few blots—'Here follows Swan's new theory of the spatial and temporal distribution of writing fluids.'

From Littlehampton later he writes, 'I confess that the disgust of stuffing myself with premature knowledge is getting worse and worse. . . . It is very revolting to realise for instance what a wonderful writer Herodotus is,—in the same process in which one realises that one's work is abominably hasty and superficial. . . .

'I think I am covering the ground; though I heartily wish the examination was at the bottom of the Red Sea. Except as part of the University machinery my going in for it is the most idiotic thing I know of.'

While still at Littlehampton he received a letter from Strachan Davidson:

'Dear Tovey,

I am shocked to find that you have not put down your name for Greats either personally or through a Tutor.

'It is now too late for the regular entry and you must have a Schedule Suppletoria which will cost you two guineas extra. "Peccatum est mortale, quia debemus bene respicere."' 'This is truly awful! isn't it?' writes the culprit on the back page; 'I sent the biz off with a telegram to explain address and delay.'

During the week of examinations he wrote to Miss Weisse:

'14 June 1898. Greats has not altogether satisfied me!—by which I mean that I'm very far from sure that I have satisfied the Examiners. . . .'

'15 June. Trotter writes to me very pressingly to help him pull through a very comical scheme of his at Liverpool; and, as I certainly owe him a good deal more than I can repay, I am, strange to say, firmly resolved to go there tomorrow and pull it through. . . . The "ploy" will set me up a bit; for I am still very tired and am not so fresh to enjoying "Oxford without work" as I expected. Moreover my book is in a stage where Trotter can give me an enormously helpful shove. . . .[1]

'On Saturday I return to a don's dinner here; and on Monday we meet over the 9th Symphony. On Sunday I'm playing the horn trio.'

A later letter (undated) completes the Oxford picture: 'Viva simply awful. Examiners all kindness and sympathy. Gave me a translation paper in the morning,—to pull up my scholarship, the Master thinks.

'No sooner did I set eyes on Greek than I just got absolutely bewildered of course. Headache, such as I have often had to-wards end of term. . . . Nothing alarming, simply what often

---

[1] *The Language of Music*, of which he had just completed three chapters.

happened in Collections and also in Greats itself. Quite natural to them as meddles with things too high for them. Explained to Examiners who allowed me whole morning for translation,—and told me to come and be viva'd in the afternoon! . . .

'Began viva tolerably well but soon lost my head completely and couldn't remember the simplest facts. Examiners quite understood, and at last asked me very kindly if I thought I should recover myself. I thought it very unlikely, so they let me go, and I trotted back to Balliol and went fast asleep. Weather simply boiling.

'There's nothing the matter with me now, and there wasn't anything to speak of then, except that it is some time since I could tell Latin from Greek when I saw it, and will be some months before I can do so again. The Cairds were simply astonishingly kind, and devised every conceivable way of making things look encouraging; but it was never possible to get rid of the tantalizing prospect of passing in the "philosophy" group only.

'However, shortly after I got here the enclosed settled matters "in the most satisfactory way possible", and there's no more bother. It's a most extraordinary sensation being firmly established the right side of the gulf—not even in it—but actually across it.' The 'enclosed' was the announcement that he had been awarded a Third.

Mrs. Caird wrote to Miss Weisse: 'If you had seen the crushing headache under which your poor boy had to work in the Schools yesterday, you, who know so well what that means, and what it takes out of him, would probably have shared his own lowest expectations, and hailed a Third Class as a marvellous success, won under such collapse. We could not help hoping against hope that the strong impression made in some of his papers might avail even so far as getting a Second,—but as Examiners for the most part judge, it was likely quite a vain hope. It is clear that the strain of Exams. is not for him. . . .

'Mr Caird has just seen two of the Examiners, who say that in their opinion, some of your boy's philosophy papers were *the best in this time. . . .*

'For the first time *two* women are in First Class.'

An authentic account of the dilemma of the Examiners is given by Mr. Frank Howes:

'Tovey got a third in Greats (Literae Humaniores) and the following story was told to me by Sidney Ball, Fellow of St. John's, who was one of the Examiners in the year Tovey sat for his Finals. Greats, the final classical school, consists of papers in ancient and modern philosophy and in ancient history. Translation from the original Herodotus, Thucydides, Plato and Aristotle, Livy and Tacitus is also required. Tovey characteristically sent up two enormous and quite outstanding answers—one in the Plato paper and one in the Ethics paper, but neglected the set books and made no showing in history. The Plato answer dealt with the nature of Art, which Plato discusses in the third and tenth books of *The Republic*, and Tovey illustrated what he had to say on the aesthetic problems involved out of his own musical experience. The other question with which he dealt fully was on immortality.

'When the five Examiners came to collate their results with a view to awarding classes to the candidates, the philosophers put forward Tovey as a clear first-class. The historians however were outraged that anyone who had virtually ignored what is a prescribed part of the examination syllabus should receive a first, and refused to agree. The philosophers pressed their point but when the historians proved obdurate, they said "Very well, then, we'll give him a fourth-class", which they regarded as being at any rate more distinguished than seconds and thirds. Again however the historians refused to concur, arguing that if the candidate was really as good as the philosophers had at first asserted, he was at any rate worth a higher rating than a fourth. The historians won the day and the compromise of a third-class was finally assigned to him.'

The musical impression which he left at Balliol is sufficiently indicated in a letter from Farmer to Miss Weisse, not long after he had gone down:

'It does me good to hear about Donald. God has given him a

terrible power. In all my many years of experience I have never come across any one, with the exception of Brahms, so blessed. There is breadth and purity in his character and his music. He must in time become a blessing to England, both by his compositions and his writing about music. I could do nothing for him at Balliol but love him and give him opportunities to play in our concerts. Only goodness knows how thankful I am that the Nettleship Scholarship has been stamped with such a great advantage. I shall not live to see another Donald.'

'His whole career at Oxford was incongruous', wrote Sir Denys Bray. 'In Greats, for instance, no one knew whether he was going to get a First or get ploughed. He was inclined to look back on his years at Oxford as a waste of time. I doubt it; it gave him his first introduction into the *Strom der Welt*, and made him rub shoulders with men of his own age but very different ideas, many of them forceful personalities.'

Whether or not the headaches from which he suffered so acutely during the examination were symptomatic, Donald Tovey celebrated the end of his Oxford career with an attack of appendicitis, from which his recovery was slow.

The two years which intervened between the end of his Oxford days in midsummer 1898 and the beginning of his public career in the autumn of 1900, were probably the happiest months in Donald Tovey's whole life. He was free at last to devote all his time and energies legitimately to music.

After being nursed back to health by Miss Weisse, he spent September with friends in Arran, doing a little pleasant sailing and recovering his energies, sketching the Clarinet and Horn Trio ('terribly gloomy, but compensatingly romantic'), and overhauling the first chapters of his book. From Arran he went to Biggar to stay with Dr. Dickson at Hartree. 'I am practising, with some success methinks, most of the morning', he wrote to Miss Weisse; 'Chopin studies (all the Chopin in the world is here) and corners of Beethoven sonatas. I think my tone is getting more under control; and I can do your patent 4th finger shoot now without the least difficulty. The only thing that is still always wrong is "the elbers sir"!... Did you see the I. C. S. list? Bray is 16th, higher than the three men he always will regard as cleverer than himself; and Dale is at the top of all!' Old Mrs. Weisse stayed at Hartree also for a few days, and together she and Tovey played nine Mozart concertos. But the severe old lady did not entirely approve of his methods of practising, and reported this to Miss Weisse, for his next letter contains a detailed account of what he is doing and why: 'I am practising all the 3rds and 6ths and shakes in the world, there's such a lot to be done with them that I find my three hours doesn't take the subject in nearly completely. . . . 3rds and 6ths and such monstrosities are most undoubtedly *quite* as useful to me in the way of sheer tone-production as scale-passages or anything else of a character that I could read fluently at sight nowadays. Certainly the effect on my actual playing is already perceptible.'

There follows a fearsome list of the studies he is working at and 'corners in Pfte. literature, at present somewhat subject to the influence of my programme for the evening', for he was always asked to play to the company after dinner, and was always willing to comply.

'I hope', he continues, 'you will not be too horrified to hear that I fired off op. 106 at Dr. Dickson and household the day before yesterday. . . . As for playing at large and from score I cannot with all possible scrutiny find that it does any harm.'

A fortnight later he writes: 'There are two rather jolly, but limited old maids staying here, and my practising is somewhat in abeyance for a while. But I have done a most tremendous chapter, tracing the whole growth of an art from the nature of artistic limitations. Not a historical sketch, but a logical one; and I'm shewing how circumstances modify it. I've hit on a gorgeous way of keeping the argument together without losing the discussions which arise from it. That is, by cutting off the discussions and grouping them in a set of essays at the end. Thus Book I, Part I, Main Arguments (5 chapters); Part II,

Essays and Illustrations on points raised in Part I.' This book was never finished, but it formed the basis of most of his later writings; and the exhaustive way in which he thought out so many musical problems in these early years bore fruit in the extraordinary concentration of the *Encyclopædia Britannica* and other masterly articles.

An invitation came for him to stay at Cambridge with the Newalls in November, and the above letter concludes 'Please tell me what to do about dates, won't you? I should *like* to get as long as possible at Cambridge if it's reconcilable with duty'. He was intensely anxious to browse in the Pendlebury Library at Cambridge, which was far more comprehensive than any collection of music that Oxford possessed. But the 'duty' that by this time he felt he might be neglecting, was that of doing a certain amount of teaching and lecturing at Northlands to help to pay his way. The lectures were, however, fixed for the following spring. 'Would you want mine to be historical?' he asks Miss Weisse. 'I could do that, with preparation; but I personally think that historical lectures are the bane of modern art-criticism.'

From Cambridge he wrote to his mother, 'I am getting a good deal of work done which I much enjoy—reading Wagner, theorising and practising.

'Tell me (*a*) Duncan's address and (*b*) whether there are any aunts, great aunts, second-hand or first-hand cousins removed no times or many times, or any other appurtenances whatever situated in this region and requiring attention, and if so how many and of what fitin' weight.

'I think my degree day is the 8th and I am playing at Balliol on the 26th and 27th of this month.'

He was not to be prised loose from Cambridge to attend concerts in London which Miss Weisse thought he should hear. 'I am just getting into the hang of things, and would very much value any way of avoiding rushing about, which always rather muddles my head. . . . Meanwhile here there are opportunities for equipping myself some ten times as rapidly as I could by any number of concerts. . . . I am finding that the importance of the particular things Wagner knows is simply incalculable; not of course to a composer of sonatas and such, but as a study in the aesthetics of instrumental technique and tone, and above all, the metaphysics of tonality. But it is not easy, and it wants going at awfully regularly, especially if one's to practise decently too.'

In the spring of 1899 Miss Weisse was anxious and uncertain as to how and when it would be wise to launch the young man on the London musical world, a world which glittered at this period with brilliant virtuosi of every instrument. His hands, in spite of her massage, were evidently not yet flexible enough for all his purposes, and he went for treatment to a Swedish masseur. Miss Weisse thought of Schumann and his damaged finger and became alarmed, but she was assured by Donald that 'the masseur treats my hands as if they were eggshells; and tells me that I don't gain anything by stiffening them as I do.' For a tall man Tovey had not a large hand, and he had a very moderate stretch.

Plans were going forward for concerts at Northlands in May and June. These were to include two little-known Bach cantatas and were to be accompanied by analytical programmes; but, on second thoughts, 'Don't you think', he wrote, 'that we could keep the full analytic programme for our more public performances of these concerts? I can't help thinking it's more suited to a full London public. The present sketch will do nicely to send round as a prospectus.'

Joachim was in London early in spring and Miss Weisse arranged that Tovey, who was much too shy to make such a move himself, should play some of his own compositions to the great man. 'I played the first two movements of the quintet, which he seemed to like very much; but he said that there were too many full-closes, which make it seem as if it began over again so often. Then he went on to point out how Brahms' latest tendencies are so much more towards compression than his earlier ones—evidently taking the line that that is an improvement. . . . So I produced the violin sonata, which he promptly proceeded to play with me, and, inevitable hitches apart, for all the world as if he had written it himself. . . . It answered its purpose, and shewed him that the sprawling in the quintet was under pressure of more direct and definite material, and that when it comes to compression I can do that too if I use rather abstruse and undramatic material. . . . He likes what he heard of the quintet better than the violin sonata.' [Joachim *did* like the quintet and spoke highly of it to Stanford.] 'He asked me where I was and what I was doing; so I told him I was at Englefield Green trying to get some pianoforte technique, and sketching my trio and concerto. He is optimistic about my playing; but I believe he is rather easily satisfied with pianists, isn't he?

'I don't know how far he is really clear about what I'm doing. I'm almost sure he thinks I'm getting my things played and published and making myself well-known in the ordinary sort of way, and am in the centre of a Young-England musical circle. Which is certainly not the case. And there was neither time nor fit occasion to explain that, by "working by myself", I meant not only working without tuition but seeing no fellow-students.' The isolation, into which by circumstances and by his own nature he was at this time impelled, set up a barrier which in later years he never succeeded in surmounting.

He was at this time sketching the concerto for violin—which was never finished. Miss Weisse wanted Joachim to see it, and tried to pull strings, unknown to Tovey, with the not unnatural result that misunderstandings arose. Fortunately no real mischief was done, but Miss Weisse did not learn the lesson that it was dangerous to be too managing, and that even an artist so helpless in furthering his own cause knows very well when the time is *not* ripe to put his work forward. Nevertheless, some degree of 'managing' was necessary, even essential. 'Whenever we wanted to know anything about Donald,' said one of his contemporaries, 'we wrote to Miss Weisse. She looked after his affairs, answered business letters and kept a note of his engagements.' And it was not mere laziness which made him acquiesce gladly in this arrangement. No doubt he was rightly dubbed 'absent-minded', and behaved in the way in which the absent-minded do, but his mind was concentrated during every waking moment on the one thing which to him represented reality—music. His faculties were stretched to the utmost to penetrate to the heart of its problems in the most comprehensive way, as an executant, as a composer, and as a theorist. One aspect of any one of these three forms of musicianship is generally enough to fill any man's career, but his was a truly cosmic view of art. No wonder letters from Balliol asking if he would play on such and such a date escaped his notice, in spite of a desperate Secretary's plea, '*Let us know*. LET US KNOW. ONLY LET US KNOW'. No wonder also that the Secretary plotted revenge, when a last-minute telegram merely said 'put down what you like'! Arriving at the Hall Tovey said, 'What *am* I playing to-night?' 'Here is the programme,' said the Secretary with delight, handing him a list carefully chosen from the more obscure classics. And Tovey sat down and played them!

There was a second violin sonata which 'got aground in the finale; but', adds the composer, 'I shall send *both* to Dr. Joachim for his birthday'. Later in the same letter he remarks: 'I've just read Beethoven's 4th Symphony with a feeling of absolute novelty. Ever since I took up the question of *rhythmic* terseness and rapidity of phrase, the whole of classical and modern music has become more vivid. In the 4th Symphony the contrasts between short phrases and long suspenses on single chords are half the staple of the dramatic and formal expression of the work, and are emphasized in a way that no other work shews so clearly. You can unlock Beethoven's rhythms if you take the 4th Symphony as a key.'

A great occasion was the Festival of Meiningen in October to celebrate the unveiling of the Brahms memorial. Tovey's Cambridge friends were there, and many others, along with Sedley Taylor, H. P. Allen, and Edward Dent—all three of whom found Tovey rather overpowering; but—as Professor Dent later wrote—'Tovey was never conceited at any period of his life; he displayed his learning because it was all so new and exciting to him, and because he wanted his friends to share the joy of it. . . . Jealousy was an emotion which he simply could not conceive.'

To his contemporaries he appeared to be in the 'innermost ring'; but if so, he was too shy to make much headway. 'Have you got your missive to J. J. off?' asks a postcard to Miss Weisse. 'I didn't like to raise the point with him without preparation. I have had "how-do-you-do" glimpses of him, but to-night I must try to get to the point.' The point was a proposed concert in the following June at Windsor, but this did not materialize.

About Steinbach he was enthusiastic: 'the most amazing conductor I ever dreamt of. Flies into three pieces with a strong electric spark at the *fortissimos*, but never loses clearness or lets the orchestra mistake his meaning.' He adds, 'You would have been delighted with Borwick's playing of the Mozart A major concerto; so dignified, so Greek-god-like, and with the most marvellous orchestra in the world.'

In the following August (1900) he was again staying at Hartree, where he was always so happy. 'Here I be. Train an hour and a half late, but they sent a special from Symington, as four irate passengers were clamouring in pursuit of pleasure and doonrecht deevilry at Peebles.

'There are burglar's tools and strawberries here, but no hectographs; so please forward when convenient.

'Kind remembrances from the Doakter.'

He used the hectographs to make copies of short sixteenth-century works from Dr. Dickson's extensive library, for the use of the girls at Northlands. These were afterwards printed as the *Northlands Singing Book*.

Preparations were in train for his first public concerts in the autumn. The programmes included both pianoforte solos and chamber music, introducing works of his own in this medium; and he was writing his first series of analytical programme-notes. These gave him endless trouble because of the compelling necessity for him to state musical facts clearly and comprehensively in the intractable medium of words, and in a form that the layman could understand.

'I am doing all I can to get my programmes ready,' he wrote to Miss Weisse on 9 August, 'both practising and analysis.' But a fortnight later, discussing the question of printers, he said 'If this meets your view, I'll send them to Over at once (i.e. when ready)'; this must have sounded ominous. 'I want the *circulars* to mention where the programmes are to be had. They're a mighty fine feature, Madam. I think the sooner they're out the better.' This was an admirable idea, but *never*, during the whole of his life, were his programmes out in time, that is to say long enough in advance of the concert for the public to read and benefit by them. He could not finish them except under compulsion.

'My preparations are, I think, flourishing,' he writes the following week, 'though they are mighty heavy and I sometimes get a bad day in which this

seems to fall to bits, and my hand to be no size whatever, and my writing quite unreadable and stupid.' But the next letter cheerfully announces, 'My bad days disappeared, since the discovery that the difference between this

and the unholy original is inappreciable, especially when you give the original now and then! It's only a question of time, and there is lots of time'. [Fatal statement, which he often made.] 'I am making a monstrous last and final improvement to the coda of the first movement of my quintet'—the result of that was of course the inevitable rush to get parts ready for rehearsal.

6

'MR. DONALD FRANCIS TOVEY's Concerts of Chamber Music', with which he made his bow to the world as pianist, composer, and writer, were given on four Thursdays in November 1900 in St. James's Hall. Associated with him were old colleagues of the Northlands concerts —Miss Fillunger, who appeared at each concert, four fine wind-instrument players, Malsh, Draper, Borsdorf, and James, the Kruse quartet, and Miss Maud MacCarthy.

Through her well-known and exclusive school, Miss Weisse had many contacts with wealthy and fashionable members of society in this the last year of Queen Victoria's reign, and Tovey had many friends of Oxford days who were very willing to support with their presence his first concerts. Miss Weisse records, 'St. James' Hall filled, to my surprise, more than I had ventured to think.' The artist's room was crowded with many distinguished people after the performance, but possibly the concert-giver got the greatest pleasure from his father's delight:

'Dear old Don,

It was a joy to see you and witness your great success and hearty reception last night. I did not intrude upon your bower wittingly, I was only in search of an analytical programme; *you* called me in. I had no notion I was in sight of such august presences. But, man, it was gran'!'

Innumerable press-cuttings give evidence of conflicting opinions among the critics. An article over the initials H. A. S. in the *Westminster Gazette* says, 'Not for some time, certainly not since the appearance of Mr. Ernest von Dohnányi (whom he resembles in more than one respect), has a young musician of greater promise come forward than Mr. Donald Francis Tovey, the brilliant young Oxford composer, whose first concert at St.

James' Hall must emphatically be reckoned the event of the musical week. Perhaps, indeed, in future years the date may take on significance considerably greater. For all his youth Mr. Tovey comes before the musical world as a musician of quite unusual attainments. As a pianist he gives evidence of a musicianship which innumerable players of greater note might give their ears to come by; as composer he translates that same musicianship into works of indubitable charm and interest; while as author of the analytical notes—a regular volume of them—which he sprung on Thursday's audience,—he proved himself further a writer on musical matters of quite unusual capacity and erudition.'

As a pianist he was received generally with approbation at the first concert, and the 'deep poetical insight and fine tone-graduation', remarked upon by *The Times*, struck many critics. On his compositions (the trio for piano, clarinet, and horn, and two duets for oboe and piano) there were sharply divided opinions. 'The themes [of the trio] are quite original,' says *The Times*, whose critic then was Mr. Fuller-Maitland, 'and their disposition for the unusual combination of instruments shows the hand of an accomplished tone-painter. The slow movement is a set of lovely variations on a beautiful theme.' The finale appealed to the *Manchester Guardian* critic as 'the most attractive part of the trio; it is full of melodic charm and possesses to a remarkable degree the rare quality of concentration'. The *Sunday Times*, however, finds that he had achieved 'little beyond an unconscionably dull imitation of Brahms', and the *Pall Mall Gazette* is more severe: 'Mr. Tovey's playing, we must confess, did not attract us any more than did his compositions. A great deal of his trio is far from agreeable, though not void of cleverness.' His career at Oxford, instead of at one of the Colleges of Music, was suspect to some critics. 'The crying need for the general culture of musicians has long been one of my favourite texts;' says a writer in *The World*, 'but I am bound to confess a doubt whether an English University is the best place for a musician now. . . . There is danger lest a music scholar should become a sort of hybrid—a musician among undergraduates, an undergraduate among musicians. Mr. Tovey takes himself a little too seriously.' This reflects the substance of much of the adverse criticism over years to come, and was the line of attack to which its victim was most vulnerable, and which occasioned some of his bitterest remarks about critics.

But it was the programme notes that really set the fat in the fire. He had already had articles on musical matters—such as 'Performance and Personality' published over the pseudonym 'Tamino' in the *Musical Gazette*. This venture of programme-notes, however, was another matter. If they had been available in advance, as he had so optimistically hoped, much hasty criticism might have been obviated; but a critic finds it hard to retract his words after they have appeared in print. These and later analytical programmes have now achieved fame and the early criticisms have therefore a curious interest. The *Manchester Guardian* was favourable: 'The analysis of the various works on the programme, both new and old, was so attractive to read on account of its penetrating insight and admirably lucid style, that it proved rather a disturbing element to the industrious listener. But anyone who took the trouble to read it at leisure after the concert must have found it a really valuable addition to musical literature.' Not so the *Daily Telegraph*: 'We are among those who doubt very much the use of the peculiarly dull method of analysis which Mr. Tovey brings to bear upon the works on the programme.' The *Pall Mall Gazette* is in *no* doubt about it: 'We may as well begin by saying that it would have been far better if the programme had never been published.' And the *Sunday Times* remarks: 'These notes are not exactly calculated to aid the comprehension of his own somewhat complex and obscure productions, though, curiously enough they may throw a flood of light upon the hitherto misunderstood intentions of a master like Chopin.'

The author of the notes had attempted to forestall some of this criticism in an Introduction, but in spite of this, his modest way of dealing with his own works by means of quotations and a précis, undoubtedly, as *The Times* said, 'went far to create an impression that the trio was a feat of musical erudition and nothing else'. Furthermore those critics whose methods and knowledge were somewhat superficial were nonplussed at being expected to assimilate the analytical essays, and felt slightly aggrieved at having their ignorance laid bare—'the long and weighty essays', wrote one of these gentlemen, 'are said, by those who like analytical remarks, to be full of ability'.

The final paragraph of Tovey's Introduction to the programmes is amusing: 'Berlioz remarks in his *Traité d'instrumentation* that a sound, insignificant when heard singly, such as the sound when the butt-end of a rifle strikes the ground at "order-arms", becomes brilliant and attractive if performed by a thousand men simultaneously. I am sure that the public will forgive me for reminding them that the truth of this is positively venomous in the case of an audience turning over the leaves of programmes with smartness and precision in St. James' Hall. The present programmes are printed on soft paper that turns noiselessly.'

At the second concert he appeared only in the capacity of pianist: 'Plainly this is a young man to be reckoned with', says the *Westminster Gazette*. 'It may or may not exactly be a case of "Hats off! A genius!" [Schumann's famous welcoming words to Chopin.] Time alone will determine that point. But of this young musician's commanding ability there can be no manner of doubt. . . . He may not indeed possess the technique of a Busoni or a Rosenthal, but his playing possesses many less common qualities by way of compensation. . . . Mr. Tovey, in short, is hardly likely to make a *virtuoso*, although his playing alike in the Brahms, the Beethoven and the Schumann was brilliant in the extreme. But many *virtuosi* might hear his playing with advantage—and benefit by reproducing the depth of feeling. the broad and luminous phrasing, the poetry, the insight, the warmth and the reticence which are its most conspicuous qualities.'

The Brahms–Paganini Variations made something of a sensation. He played the first set—always a *tour de force* for any performer—and when it was evident that he was going to be encored, Borwick, who was sitting with Miss Weisse in the hall, turned to her and said, 'What will he play as an encore?' 'As I know him', replied Miss Weisse, 'he will play the second set!'—Borwick's whistle of astonishment could be heard all over the concert-room—and he *did* play the second set.

The *Manchester Guardian* in writing of this performance and that of the same work given by Busoni a short while later, points out that while there was no comparison in the technique of the two, 'there were some passages, such as the wonderful variations in the major key in the first set, where Mr. Tovey seemed to penetrate deeper into the heart of the music than the great *virtuoso*, and to draw from it a profounder and more soul-stirring expression'.

One week later, in the third concert, he produced his pianoforte quintet. 'A work full of fine ideas carried out with astonishing ability,' proclaimed *The Times*, 'and yet one in which mere erudition is never allowed to predominate. One or two of the themes strike the hearer as not particularly original, but their working-out is masterly, and so interesting that the circumstance is easily overlooked. . . . It was excellently played by the composer and the Kruse quartet.' But the *Daily Telegraph* was of a completely different mind: 'that the Quintet played yesterday engaged agreeably the ears of a single listener we cannot believe.' The *World*, which had disapproved of the influence of Balliol, remarks: 'The Quintet shows more traces of individuality than the trio we heard a fortnight ago, and that individuality is strong, manly and healthy. But Mr. Tovey *will* do his utmost to conceal it beneath a mask.'

The composer's programme note on his own work, containing an extravagant number of musical quotations and a cut-and-dried analysis, again seriously misled many critics, especially those who were not really knowledgeable enough to follow the letterpress. In truth, it was a *very* unfavourable way of introducing new works to the public, and the cold and impartial statement of facts was bound to look academic on paper. But it was the only alternative he could see to 'hurling my works at the audience with a tacit implication that they are either so much more impressive than the great classics, or so bad that analysis is superfluous'. It might have made a great difference to his career, particularly as a composer, if the tag 'academic', had not thus early been fixed to him by many both in musical circles and in the press.

The final concert included the violin sonata which had been shown to Joachim as a contrast in style to the quintet. The *Manchester Guardian* was enthusiastic about it; *The Times*, while complimentary about the whole concert, found the sonata 'solid and rather severe'. There certainly could be no doubt, however, at the conclusion of this series of concerts, as to the extraordinary amount of attention they had attracted.

The *Musical Standard* sums it up. 'The appearance of Mr. Tovey has been hailed in some quarters with an amount of laudation which might do him harm, were he not, as I am convinced, a musician of modesty and sense; he has elsewhere been spoken of with a severity which I trust will not discourage him. His reputation in Oxford is well-known. Now he comes to London, a new Schumann,—pianist, critic and composer. His concerts have abundantly shown that he is not only a learned and cultured musician, but that he is profoundly in love with his art. Music is to him no casual mistress indeed; evidently she is the partner of his life, in whom his whole being is entwined.' The writer is impressed by the programme notes, and concludes, 'The catholicity of his taste is one of his strongest points; his devotion to Bach and Schubert cannot blind him to the worth of Weber's *Invitation à la Valse.* For having introduced Schubert's *Viola* and three solo cantatas of Bach at his concerts, he has my most cordial thanks, and I look to him with confidence to undertake the task of raising the standard of musical appreciation, while he from time to time enriches the literature of music with illuminating and suggestive commentaries, and brings out editions of forgotten or unvalued works.'

Finally, the *Musical Gazette* in an article headed 'A New English Musician' (December 1900) states: 'Very probably no other English musician has ever leapt into fame so instantaneously; and it is certainly no light thing to be compared to Mozart in *The Times*, and to suggest to a writer in another important paper Schumann's famous welcoming words to Chopin. And quite possibly no one has ever made quite so versatile a first appearance. . . . Mr. Tovey's four programmes were models of their kind. There can be no doubt that a more superbly equipped all-round musician has very rarely, if ever, come before the English or any other public, and his future career will be watched with the keenest interest. Unless all indications prove false, Mr. Tovey's will be one of the greatest names in English music of the twentieth century.'

A letter of 20 November says: 'Dearrr Mswicy [a mispronunciation of Miss Weisse's name, which was a long-standing form of affectionate address],

'I'm so awfully sorry; but I really have rather been run off my feet, and have got rather excited and tired.

'I wish you could have heard my quintet. Rehearsals were only moderately promising, but the Kruse quartet rose to much more than the occasion, and it was the first time I had a real approximation to something like what the thing is.

'My lecture—thanks to care in preparation, went splendidly. Op. 101 went very well on Sunday.'

The lecture—on Brahms' *Tragic* Overture—and the concert were given at Balliol, and as they came between the third and the fourth of his London concerts, it was not surprising that he was tired.

In December he went to Vienna. His mother, who was by then a complete invalid, wrote to Miss Weisse:

'Dear Sophie,

We had a very kind letter from Mr. Fuller-Maitland. He says, "I think you may well be proud of your son's success, for it is genuine and decisive." . . . Also Mrs. MacLean writes, "My son met Mr. Fuller-Maitland after one of Donald's concerts and said he was most enthusiastic." We *were* so sorry to be absent when Donald was with you. I suppose he is off to Vienna.

'Shall we see him before he goes? And will Miss Fillunger commend him not to take cold?

'With love, and if Don is there put a pen in his hand and tell him to write.

'Yours affectionately, Mary Tovey.'

He took a pencil in his hand on the way to Ostend 'A bord du paquebot, Prince Albert.

'My attitude during the voyage has been that of *Reserve*. My nautical proclivities are as yet undeveloped.'

(These proclivities developed considerably in later years, and when he went to America on one occasion in one of the giant liners, he asserted that the ship rolled in perfect eight-bar rhythm, so that when practising, his stool receded from the piano, and he continued to play mentally, being returned to the keyboard so punctually that he could continue without a break!)

A small diary kept by Miss Weisse at the beginning of 1901 tells the tale:

'*Jan. 11th* Donald returned from Vienna; very well. Enjoyed himself very much and was I think much appreciated. We came down to Northlands together [for the spring term at school].

'*Jan. 21st* Death of Queen Victoria.

'*Feb. 2nd* Donald to view the funeral service of the Queen from the organ-loft in St. George's Chapel, Windsor. Very bad cold again.

'*Feb. 13th* Very honourable and agreeable letter from Mandy-czewski suggesting that Donald's quintet should be played by the Tonkünstlerverein in Vienna. Cold better; took himself off to Vanstone [his cottage at Englefield Green]. Donald working at a new string quartet.

'*Feb. 25th* Donald to Edward Speyer's, Ridgehurst.

'*Mar. 9th* Sort of musical party—Hugh Godley came for the night. Donald to lunch at the Cornishes with H. G.
'*Mar. 11th* D. started for Berlin.
'*Mar. 18th* Concert with Joachim in Berlin, Bechsteinsaal.

And so the pattern of his life was set—travelling, playing, composing, writing endlessly; tireless in every musical activity and prodigal of his energies.

Sir Walter Parratt was anxious about this and wrote to Miss Weisse: 'I rejoice greatly over Donald's well-earned recognition. Parry also is delighted. My own fear is that Donald will at first keep some blank days for storing of energy and development of ideas, and then he will allow the importunate public to encroach upon his fertile leisure. He must *not* play at 40 concerts before Easter. The last time I heard him signs of fatigue were evident.'

The concert in Berlin was given at Joachim's suggestion; he wanted Tovey to play the *Goldberg* Variations there, and said he would also appear himself at the same concert. An appearance in Berlin was a *sine qua non* for any young artist in those days, and Joachim's belief in Tovey and his affection for him were now fully established. When the young man knocked on the door of his study in Berlin, a deep, gruff voice answered him 'To-bee, or not To-bee?'

The Bach Variations created something of a sensation in Berlin, where, incredible as it seems, they had not been heard within living memory. The critics regarded the playing of such a long work by heart as a feat, but also were unanimous in praising the great beauty of tone and the clarity of the performance.

Dr. Warre-Cornish wrote from Eton to Miss Weisse: 'I must write a line to say how truly delighted I am and we all are to hear of Donald's splendid success in Berlin. It is a real triumph both for him and for you, who have been so splendidly *propositi tenax*, when you have had "safe advice" to the contrary from so many people, myself among them. Your training, as well as Donald's genius, has brought it about, and you must feel very happy at the results of so much patient and loving faith in him and music. I am glad to think, too, that though Joachim's friendship is worth a great deal to anyone who is happy enough to possess it, Donald has not climbed into fame on his shoulders.'

The programme was repeated in London in May 1901 at the first of Tovey's series of summer concerts, with the like result. 'Throughout one hardly knew whether most to admire the virtuoso or the musician,—the justness of the conception or the brilliance of its execution. In short the whole performance was a triumph' (*Westminster Gazette*). The *Pall Mall Gazette* had some reservations: 'He has all the sentiment and all the spirit of that which is best in music, but he has not quite got the physical power to produce effects which storm the nerves and enslave the emotion.' One wonders where such effects should have been produced in the *Goldberg* Variations.

In contrast to all the others, the critics of the *Morning Post* and the *Sunday Times* were bored, the latter writing: 'I suppose the feature of the afternoon was Mr. Tovey's revival of Bach's famous *Goldber* Variations. . . . But what a pity to waste time and money on printing the turgid stuff which he glorifies by the name of "Analytical essays" and worries the hearers withal! If Mr. Tovey must relieve his soul by writing this appreciative nonsense, let him do so by all means. But why burden his audience with it, like a prosy and wearisome Ancient Mariner?'

Joachim, who was almost 71, now accepted no engagements to appear in England except with his quartet or as a soloist with an orchestra, and the *Manchester Guardian* was touched by the exception he had made in favour of Tovey. 'The combination of this young and interesting musician with an older and so well-founded an artist was in its essence extremely pathetic. One travelled back in memory to the days when Joachim himself was consorting with the great musicians of his day, himself a lad praised and encouraged, and one felt how beautifully he had read the lesson of his youth in returning the example to a young man of the present generation who is, we are certain, destined to be worthy of his beginning. . . . When one considers that Mr. Tovey not only played the *Goldberg* Variations note by note with perfect accuracy but that he also rendered the emotion of every passage with exceedingly fine distinction, even a hyper-critic has reason to say that a really engrossing musical genius has swum into our ken. . . . The analytical programme is, in its own way, a work of admirable talent. The English of it is nervous, significant and equipoised.'

'After an hour with Donald', said Joachim about this time, 'I feel as if my head were on fire. I have never seen his equal for knowledge and memory.' At the Leeds Festival of that year, when Elgar's *Enigma* Variations were first produced, Joachim wanted one day to rehearse the Brahms concerto at his hotel. There was no score available, but Tovey sat down at once at the little upright piano and played it from memory without a flaw. 'Of all the musicians of the younger generation that I know', wrote Joachim to a friend, 'Tovey is assuredly the one that would most have interested Brahms.' It is curious that he never did meet Brahms, although he was so often in Germany before the composer died in 1897.

In criticizing the next London concert, when Beethoven's formidable *Diabelli* Variations were the main item on the programme, the *Westminster Gazette* observed with truth, 'There is, indeed, danger of overlooking Mr. Tovey's very distinguished powers as an executant by reason of his capacity in other directions. Certainly if Mr. Tovey had come forward as pianist alone his gifts in this respect would probably have attracted much more attention. He is a player of the most accomplished order.'

If at this stage in his career he had put himself unreservedly into the hands of one of the big musical agents, there is little doubt that he would soon have become an 'International Celebrity'. There is little doubt either that, if he had ever submitted to it at all, he would soon have broken loose from the narrow confines of a virtuoso's life. His view then was the same as that expressed more than thirty years later in writing to a brilliant young 'cellist,[1] who, after having been one of his best students

[1] Peggie Sampson.

at Edinburgh University, was completing her training in Paris:
'The experts, including quite musicianly ones, always find it
their duty to make their pupils concentrate upon technique: so
that their ideal is Paderewski, who maintains that no virtuoso
can keep up a larger repertoire than twelve pieces. He is probably right in thinking that nobody can take more than twelve
pieces on one and the same world-tour, but world-tours are an
obsolescent and barbarous form of concert-giving.' This and
similar expressions of opinion have been construed by ill-disposed
persons as meaning that Tovey despised technique. Nothing
could be more outrageously untrue. He was an expert in the art
of practising and in showing others how to practise, though not
many could discipline themselves to his degree of mental and
aural control. Technique was a means to an end: 'Take care of
the *sound* and the sense will take care of itself', he used to say,
while at the same time pouring vitriol on the slick 'trade-finish'
of fashionable virtuosi who had never penetrated beneath the
surface of the music.

Something began to go wrong, however, with his second
series of London Concerts: indeed there had been some signs of
hostility in advance. 'Mr. Tovey threatens three concerts in
May', says an unidentified press-cutting. When, therefore, the
chief item of the third concert proved to be the *Hammerklavier*
Sonata, some critics felt that this was too much of a good
thing—and said so. The London public wanted to be amused
and thrilled by virtuoso pieces, not to be expected to concentrate on serious listening, certainly not for three concerts in
succession.

There were other difficulties too. His father wrote:

'My dear Don,

This morning after service, Mr. Gerald Balfour and Mr.
Alfred Lyttelton who were at our church, both expressed a great
wish that some of your concerts were in the evening. Mr. Balfour
says it is impossible for a Member to be present at 3 in the afternoon because that is Question time; and Mr. Lyttelton equally

complains that a barrister cannot get away at that time. They
were both *most* enthusiastic.'

His agent did not serve him well in this respect, for next
season he found again that he could not book the hall for evening
dates.

A further concert, given in June with Kruse, clashed with a
recital by Ysaye and Busoni, and called for adverse criticism on
account of the all-Brahms programme, which consisted of the
three violin sonatas and some songs; again the general public
was not ready for this kind of thing. Indeed it was not a good
programme, and on this occasion Tovey's enthusiasm outran
his judgement, which was usually very sure in the matter of
programme-building.

His career had passed beyond the point when Miss Weisse
could guide him and advise him wisely; and he was entirely un-
fitted by temperament to keep afloat in the concert world of
London, although he could have done so quite easily in the
utterly different musical conditions of Berlin or Vienna. Miss
Weisse had behind her the record of many years of successful
organization of concert-giving of a semi-public kind, but this
experience was of little use for the purpose of London concert
business and the attraction of engagements thereby; the various
agents she employed were probably quite unable to persuade
her of this. These agents most likely despaired of Tovey also; he
had a perfect genius for failing to turn his opportunities to
worldly advantage, and it was not until many years later that he
learned how to allow for the frailties of the listening public without in any degree lowering his own impeccably high standards.
Furthermore, the nature of these concerts of his second season
easily misled agents into thinking that he was not open to accept
engagements on a less exalted level, and press-notices, good and
bad, added to this impression

In August Miss Weisse and Tovey went to the annual Cecilia-
Verein Festival at Ratisbon, which was designed to 'encourage
a taste for pure Church music by means of model performances',

largely of works of the sixteenth and seventeenth centuries. Many years before, Tovey had been thrilled to hear the music of Palestrina 'come alive' for him at Ratisbon. He could always hear a score on reading it, but the countless beauties of vocal 'colour' of the early period remained quite neutral even to his wonderful imagination until the first overwhelming experience of a real performance. His enthusiasm was then such that he covered many sheets of manuscript paper copying out works which were unobtainable in print.

On this occasion, however, he took part in the music-making, giving a concert for the benefit of the building-fund of the Church of St. Cecilia. Sir Walter Parratt was also at the Festival and gave a recital on the new organ in the church, and an account of this in the English press said: 'The impromptu part taken in the festival by Sir Walter Parratt and Mr. Tovey, and the unstinted praise bestowed on both of them by their audiences and by the Ratisbon press, left a very pleasant impression on the little group of English-speaking enthusiasts who attended the Cecilia-Verein.'

In 1900 Donald Tovey met Edward Speyer and from 1902 was closely associated for nine years with the concert ventures of this remarkable man with whom he maintained a lifelong friendship—marred only by a short breach in 1911. Speyer was 61 in 1900 and came of a long-lived stock. His father had known Mozart's eldest son, and he himself remembered at the age of 5 seeing Mendelssohn. The Speyers were on terms of friendship with Clara Schumann and with Brahms, and heard the memorable first performances of many of Brahms' works. They were also, of course, intimate friends of Joachim.

They had settled at Shenley in their spacious house, 'Ridgehurst', which, in the course of the next thirty years, was visited by all the famous musicians of the day, and where was amassed with loving care one of the finest collections of musical manuscripts in the country. Tovey was frequently consulted while this collection was in the making. In response to one inquiry regarding the authenticity of a few pages, he wrote: 'The Bach

MS. is either autograph or by his wife; the bar-strokes are rather too long for the stave, which I remember is almost the only difference between his wife's writing and his own.'

The 'Pops'[1] came to an end in 1900, Mr. Chappell retired, and Mr. Speyer founded the Joachim Quartet Concert Society, for the purpose of renewing the annual visits to London of this famous ensemble; these began in 1901 and continued until 1906. The concerts were run by a business committee, but the musical control remained solely in Mr. Speyer's hands, with a secret 'Shadow Cabinet' of two—Leonard Borwick and Donald Tovey—to advise him. This arrangement worked well for a bit, but was eventually productive of much trouble and distress.

Plans were in train for Tovey's own autumn concerts when his father wrote, in September 1901:

'Dear Donald,

I do wish you would be more careful to keep your correspondents *en rapport* with you. It is a constant worry, and at this present moment I am neglecting my own correspondence in order to remedy your neglects if possible. If you don't like writing to us, at least don't make our existence a complete burden after this fashion.'

But the culprit was on holiday in Arran, and was completely immersed in new compositions which he hoped to bring forward.

Miss Weisse heard from him occasionally: 'The Coda of the String 4^{tet} was a holy terror. I had to sketch it *fourteen* times after I got to Hartree. . . . I don't believe I have been awake for one hour in the last 18 months without making a new device in part-writing or instrumentation, except when playing. And I find now that reading scores, or rubbish, or most things doesn't stop the process at all. It merely supports it. I'm beginning to get used to it and hope soon that it will no longer distract my attention from other things. This last year there's no doubt I've been half-asleep, and I really think this is the reason why.'

[1] The famous series of concerts started by Chappell in 1859 in St. James's Hall.

When the concerts took place, programmes had to be re-arranged because the pianoforte quartet was not ready for the first concert, though it turned up in the third; while the string quartet had got temporarily stranded and a new pianoforte trio appeared in its stead. This was bound to invite hostile criticism. Some critics also took exception to the repetition of the *Goldberg* Variations and his own pianoforte quintet, both of which had been included in the spring series of concerts.

Three concerts in Vienna and four in Berlin followed at the turn of the year, and he nearly missed the first one owing to a bad attack of bronchitis which delayed him *en route* in Bonn. Writing to Mr. Speyer on his return to London Tovey remarks, 'There is no doubt whatever that it is on engagements that I must depend now. The Vienna and Berlin concerts are, in fact, my last luxury of the kind: it will be some time before I can do anything so independent again.' The concerts, however, had been thrilling: 'Joachim had promised me in Leeds that he would fill in the names of the other artists for my Berlin concerts; so I sent him my programmes without any definite idea that he and his colleagues would consent to play themselves. However he not only played, but left the programmes unaltered. . . . He was tired after a long day when we had our first rehearsal, and I felt rather glum when he found he didn't like my 4^{tet} then. Next morning we had another rehearsal when he changed his mind so completely that I was almost more upset than the night before. He himself is very suspicious now of signs of his own old age; but I'm sure all the young people I know, including myself, are old fogies by the side of him.'

Most of the critics in Berlin were enthusiastic, but one writer disapproved entirely of the performance of the Brahms Horn Trio: 'I was really pained by the brutality with which Tovey treats his instrument. Was he completely unconscious of the enormity he was committing in raging away at a mad pace when playing with Joachim, who had condescended to assist him?' At the bottom of this notice Tovey wrote: 'Fragment of a dialogue at rehearsal—

'_J._ "I say, you know, this really is too slow. Don't you like it faster?"

'_T._ "Well, I'm very glad; I've got used to playing it with violinists who are afraid of the quavers, but I should be only too delighted to go faster." (We do so.)

'_J._ "That's better. I don't know whether you feel it yet, do you? Brahms used to take it still faster himself." (We do so!)'

This same critic writing of an orchestral concert a few days later said of another English musician: 'The first part of the programme closed with a Concert Overture entitled _Cockaigne_ by Edward Elgar; it purports to describe scenes in the lives of the people of London. Someone, who knows the country and its people, remarked, "Only an Englishman can write such unpalatable stuff!"'

7

THE visit of the Meiningen Orchestra to London in 1902 was one of the most successful of Mr. Speyer's concert-giving enterprises. There were five concerts—given on successive days; Steinbach conducted, Donald Tovey wrote the programme-notes. When he undertook this task he sent Mr. Speyer a copy of the programme-book for one of the Richter concerts with devastating marginal notes by himself and the remark, 'Of course I can't make analysis *easy*; but I had rather be unread for difficulty than for uselessness.' In limiting the Meiningen programme-notes to the same dimensions (thirty-eight pages including musical illustrations) Speyer had in mind not merely reasonable motives of economy, but also the adverse criticism which the length of Tovey's notes for his own concert programmes had aroused in some quarters the year before. But it was a hard task to keep such a writer within set bounds. 'I'm doing the utmost I can for the practical aspect of the matter,' wrote Tovey, 'but if the requirements are for something that I think an altogether inadequate and misleadingly superficial treatment of such music I can only confess myself entirely the wrong person for the work. I don't think I can do any better within my limits; and though I haven't the slightest doubt that the critic of the *Athenaeum* and other academics will say half my work is "padding", I think that this need not worry either you or me.' The truth was, however, that the hostile criticism of the *Athenaeum* on his *Goldberg* Variations essay still rankled. Like Joachim, he was abnormally sensitive to press criticism, in particular to criticism which showed misunderstanding of his motives.

A few days before the first concert Mr. Speyer received a characteristic letter enclosing final proofs for the fifth concert programme: 'I regret to say I greatly miscalculated the length of this. It seemed to me shorter than the others, but I overlooked the fact that I wrote it with a different pen that made my writing smaller, and it turns out to be the longest of all.

'I am very far from content with the whole piece of work; and I fear it has been a sore trial to you, none-the-less since you have been so very patient and kind about it. I would give anything to be able to have done it more shortly and clearly; but I am more than ever convinced that no analysis at all is infinitely less mischievous than a short one, and that these things of mine are difficult from *over-compression*, in spite of all the critics say about "diffuseness".' (This is true of all he ever wrote for publication.)

'I have to play a big programme at Cardiff tomorrow, and two others on Saturday and Monday, and I'm half-dead and wholly idiotic, having written a big motet,[1] Alice Pollock's wedding-march, and scraps of my concerto, besides practising, teaching, proof-correcting (at which I fear I am no good), learning Italian and swearing; anything in fact but sleeping!'

Mr. Speyer thought highly of the programme-notes and sent them to all the prominent musicians of his acquaintance. 'I haven't, I confess,' wrote Tovey when asked, 'remembered about sending them to Uncle Jo. As a matter of form I should be glad that he had the programmes of course; but I don't expect they will much interest him. He has had such experience of musical metaphysics (what with Wagner and Liszt and the eternal jabber of their disciples) as may well give him a distaste for them! However he mustn't be left out.'

Musical London was at this time divided into two antagonistic camps—the classical adherents, who were followers of Brahms and Joachim, and those who were in revolt against tradition. The visit of the Meiningen orchestra revealed clearly this cleavage, and the controversy became increasingly bitter in succeeding years. A long article in *Musical Opinion*, written under a pseudonym, attacks the audience on the grounds of

---

[1] *Offertorium in Festo Sanctorum Innocentium*, performed 1902 at St. James's Hall by the Fillunger Quartet.

snobbish enthusiasm for a foreign orchestra and neglect of the Queen's Hall and Philharmonic orchestras—compared to which, it states, 'The Meiningen orchestra is quite second-rate'. Then, under cover of enthusiasm for Steinbach's warm and romantic performances of Brahms' symphonies (which, he claimed, were the real success of the concerts), the critic proceeds with a venomous attack on Joachim and his followers, in particular, Tovey: 'In this country Brahms' music has attracted a curious clique of worshippers who are not happy unless they are dull. Secretly ashamed of the emotional appeal of music, they have hailed Brahms as the representation of pure musical thought which can only be grasped by those who have not too much blood in their veins. . . . The scores of the master make a Brahms specialism easy. They delight a mind such as that of Mr D. F. Tovey who wrote the analytical programmes for these concerts. He is the kind of musical analyst who finds an unholy pleasure in noting the diminution or augmentation of a theme on its repetition, and an addition of a new counterpoint sends him into chaste ecstasies of delight. . . . Brahms, in short, has become the refuge of the half-educated in music, who find it easy to analyse his complexities on paper.'

This ill-mannered and unjust onslaught, and even more the attacks on Joachim, whom he venerated both as an artist and as a man, laid the foundations of the hostility and distrust with which, to the end of his life, Tovey regarded music critics. To a man so generous-minded, the attitude of a section of the press towards a great player, whose technical brilliance was admittedly waning with the years, was unforgivable. The circle with which Joachim found himself surrounded in England did, without doubt, contain the usual number of musical snobs and half-baked 'intelligentsia', whose misplaced enthusiasm can do real harm to the reputation of a great man; but there is venom in Francis Toye's sneer at the 'Joachim stained-glass window clique'.

Another attack on the Meiningen programme-notes came from the *Star* and was based on different grounds: 'Mr Tovey, who had written excellent analytical programmes, rather came to grief in his appreciation (or mis-appreciation) of Strauss' *Don Juan.* . . . His remarks seem to show a complete want of sympathy with the aims of the so-called "advanced" school, and even a misapprehension of the principles on which their music is based.' Time has proved otherwise; it is evident now from this analysis that Tovey had grasped the nature of the new music long before the self-styled enthusiasts for the modern school. No one with a 'misapprehension' of the music could have written: 'In less poetic hands we should expect the climax and end of the work to depict the fatal duel in which Don Juan practically recants and expiates his ruthless life by throwing down his sword at the critical moment of the fight,—but for Richard Strauss there is yet more significance in his dying words "Es war ein schöner Sturm, der mich getrieben".'

Tovey was out of sympathy with some of Strauss's later developments. He detested the fact that a musician of Strauss's calibre should stoop to cheap and sensational effects, and that he should not only tolerate but encourage the type of propaganda in which his followers indulged. He relieved his feelings by writing—for purely private consumption and on thirty-six stave manuscript paper—a parody of *Also sprach Zarathustra.* This parody, which was only a fragment, was entitled *Also sprach die Reine Vernunft,* and is prefaced by the following 'Programme': 'Till Eulenspiegel teaches the Mastersingers of Oxenford the chromatic scale. The grave members of the Guild condemn him to death. He is promptly hanged; but his more promising disciples sing a solemn dirge, and having successfully tested their grasp of the new scale by treating the dirge in twelve-part canon in the twelve keys, they give free expression to their emotions, until, terrified by a Voice from the Future, they flee in disorder, leaving the problems of their art unsolved.

'(Visual effects, such as are suggested in the score, ad. lib. and in any quantity. Amongst other possibilities I suggest "umbrellaphones" to open with the crescendos.)'

The years from 1902 to 1914, when he was appointed to the

Reid Chair of Music in Edinburgh, were stormy and difficult ones in Tovey's life. They were years of constant and varied— too varied—activities, alternating with a considerable social round. He had many wealthy and devoted friends with whom he was exceedingly popular, and week-ending at one great country-house or another was of very frequent occurrence.

But the cause underlying many of the difficulties with which he found himself beset was, unhappily, his domestic circumstances. He was still living in his cottage 'Vanstone', near Northlands—as yet not financially independent, and conscious in every fibre of the inestimable debt which he owed to Miss Weisse's devotion. The success of his début had led Miss Weisse to believe that in a few years' time he would be a world-famous pianist—as, in other circumstances, he might indeed have been. She also believed that he would soon make his mark as a composer—a reasonable belief, frustrated by the fact that his flow of composition now became slower, and that he frequently failed, owing to other claims on his time, to have a promised new work ready for performance.

The inability to consolidate his position, the fact that he was and remained unpractical in so many matters and so careless in looking after himself, was a source of great anxiety to Miss Weisse, but it is tragic that this anxiety should have caused her to become more and more possessive in her attitude. As time went on, his nearest friends repeatedly urged him to break away from her and from Northlands, but although her jealousy and interference often caused him unhappiness and even the loss of some friendships, he could never bring himself to deal such a blow to one to whom his gratitude and affection remained lifelong. The happy relationship was, however, irretrievably marred, and the strain was at times very terrible.

The pianoforte concerto—dedicated to Miss Weisse—had its first performance in St. James's Hall in November 1903 with the Queen's Hall Orchestra under the conductorship of Mr. Henry J. Wood. 'My concerto went very well', wrote the composer to Mr. Speyer. 'Wood proved a really wonderful interpreter and there wasn't a single point in which he did not anticipate my most detailed and least obvious intention.' It had an almost uniformly unfavourable reception; 'without a touch of inspiration or breath of emotion', says one critic. Many of his fellow-musicians were of quite another opinion; 'a composer who writes a concerto like Tovey's Op. 18 is to be reckoned with', said Stanford.

The *Manchester Guardian*, among others, was now severely critical of the programme-notes: 'He printed in place of the usual analysis an essay on the classical concerto which is an extraordinary mixture of extremely able and interesting criticism and the most startling narrow-mindedness. . . . His total misapprehension of what is called the modern spirit in music is simply astonishing.' The work received a second London performance three years later under Richter's conductorship. On this occasion Queen Alexandra paid a surprise visit, arriving in the hall just as the concerto was beginning. While mentioning that the composer received an ovation, the press notices go on to relate that Tovey had not observed the Queen's arrival, and was acknowledging the applause, when his attention was drawn to the fact. He then made an exaggeratedly deep and awkward bow to Her Majesty 'which caused considerable merriment'. When the concerto was published by Schott, Parry, writing to Miss Weisse to acknowledge the present of a copy, remarked 'I hope Donald gloats a bit over it. There is something rather romantic and mysterious about a full score!'

Although the enormous success of Tovey's début as a pianist was not followed by a dazzling career as a virtuoso, the number and variety of his concert-programmes between 1902 and 1914 is extraordinary. In 1902 Joachim gave him a glowing introduction to Richter, but this did not bear fruit until four years later, with the second London performance of his pianoforte concerto already mentioned and a performance in Berlin.[1] His shy and modest fashion of presenting the introduction did not at

[1] Tovey liked to repeat to soloists at rehearsal Richter's remark to him at rehearsal: 'Have you a vish? *Come on,* I am not touchy!'

first make any impression on the great conductor, who thought that a pianist who had chosen to make his first appearance with such unusual works as the *Goldberg* and *Diabelli* Variations was not likely to want to play any of the more popular concertos which might be a box-office 'draw'. This misapprehension was one which Tovey found difficult to dispel, and he wrote some years later to Miss Weisse, who was on a visit to Germany and had been seeing Steinbach on his behalf, 'My concerto can wait. But can't Steinbach get the Committee to take me as a player? I'll offer them *any* Mozart, Bach, Beethoven, Brahms or Schumann concerto: or even Chopin, Weber or Tschaikowski. I am more or less within memorizing distance of 65 concertos.' Steinbach *did* take him as a player; and in the following year also as a composer.

Joachim's interest and encouragement never failed: 'Stanford writes to me with great praise of your concerto', says one letter; 'So does Mandczewski about your trio, to my great delight.' He presented Tovey with the manuscript of his own transcription for orchestra of Schubert's *Grand Duo*, a gift which gave great joy. 'As an interpretation of the orchestral possibilities of Schubert's original it is absolutely perfect', wrote the recipient to Miss Weisse; 'One or two points (which Schubert would certainly have done just that way) in the use of trombones are altered in red pencil, with a note in Uncle Jo's hand-writing "Von Johannes[1] geändert".' On another occasion, writing to Tovey on his birthday, Joachim says, 'My heartfelt good wishes for the 17th. I am sure there can be nobody who takes a greater interest in the day than myself'. This is evident also in a letter of introduction to Buonamici.

'Cher collègue et ami,

Permettez-moi de vous présenter un de mes plus estimés amis, le musicien hors ligne Donald Tovey. . . . Il joue le piano en maître, commandant un immense répertoire, et il a une connaissance inouïe des œuvres de nos grands maîtres, soit Opéras,

---

[1] Brahms.

Oratorios, Symphonies etc. etc. Je crois que vous serez étonné de ses ressources artistiques, comme je le suis toujours de nouveau, quand j'ai la bonne fortune de le rencontrer. — Vous verrez!'

'Mon cher Maître' [came the reply]

Je vous remercie beaucoup de m'avoir fait faire la connaissance de M. Tovey. Il est véritablement extraordinaire, d'une rare valeur musicale, et d'une bonté unique. Et quelle mémoire, mon Dieu!'

The Diamond Jubilee of Joachim's first appearance in England was celebrated very splendidly by a great reception and concert in his honour in the Queen's Hall on 16 May 1904. Sir Hubert Parry read an address and Sir Arthur Balfour (then Prime Minister) presented Joachim with his portrait painted by Sargent. There was a musical party for the Joachim Quartet at Northlands in the previous week. Robert Bridges was present at this party and wrote a sonnet in honour of the great violinist. His permission was asked to print this on the programme for the Queen's Hall ceremony. Writing to thank Bridges on behalf of the committee, Tovey remarks that Joachim 'made his first London appearance as a boy of 13 and played what the critics considered a "thankless work, rather trivial and more curious than beautiful"—Beethoven's violin concerto, under Mendelssohn's conducting!' 'I knew nothing of the Jubilee,' wrote Bridges in reply; 'I was merely prompted to write because there seemed an opportunity, when I met him among his friends, of my expressing my lifelong admiration and gratitude. . . . I wish the sonnet was better, but it contains what, or some of what, I wished to say.'

The Speyers had a house-party at Ridgehurst during the week-end preceding the presentation; among the guests were the Balfours, John Morley, Watts, and Tovey. The old artist, Watts, died a fortnight later, and Tovey had great plans for writing a large choral work in memory of him. 'I have for at least five years', he wrote, 'been thinking out the possibilities of the last chapter of Ecclesiastes—every word straight through beginning "Remember Thy Creator",—for male-voice 6 part chorus; to end (in spite of certain notes of strength and of facing the facts) in darkness thus [musical quotation]. And so straight on to the 55th chapter of Isaiah, nearly the whole, with the principal weight on "For my thoughts are not your thoughts" and "for as the heavens are higher than the earth"; and a big fugue on the verses about "So shall my word be".' This project unhappily remained unfulfilled.

The Balfours gave a 'Joachim party' each year for the great violinist. After one of these Arthur Balfour wrote to Tovey: 'I send you two books of mine which bear upon conversations that we had together at Fisher's Hill last Sunday. Please, in accepting them from me—as I hope you will—do not suppose that I want you to read them: but you may care to look at Chapter 2 of *The Foundations of Belief* and at the article on Handel in the Collected Essays. Your playing last Sunday was a source of endless delight.'

Lady Betty Balfour was also a staunch friend and supporter, and organized over a number of years a series of concerts in Woking at which Tovey played. 'To my thinking,' she wrote to Miss Weisse at this period, 'his solo playing is now greater than that of any other artist I know.'

Many years later in 1927 Arthur Balfour, who was then the Earl of Balfour and also Chancellor of the University at Edinburgh, paid a visit to the Music Classroom to hear a rehearsal of the Reid Orchestra; there was apparent, not only the sincere mutual admiration of two distinguished men, but also a curious resemblance between them—hard to define—a kind of identity of outlook. It seemed as if both had the same grasp of fundamentals, the same far-seeing tolerance in essential matters, the same touch of the quixotic and chivalrous in their characters. In acknowledging Tovey's letter of condolence after her brother's death in 1930, Lady Betty wrote: 'I am glad you realize what a true friendship A. J. B. gave you. He admired you wholeheartedly—and what a joy your playing gave him that last time at Whittingehame! I used to long that you lived near here during his long illness. . . . To the last music was his favourite form of expression.'

Donald Tovey's teaching activities were not confined to Northlands. His three successors in the Nettleship Scholarship, F. S. Kelly, Tom Spring-Rice (later Lord Mounteagle, 'one of the nicest of Donald's friends'), and Ferdinand Speyer all received a certain amount of coaching from him. When the question arose of Ferdinand Speyer (son of Edgar Speyer) trying for the Scholarship, Tovey wrote to the father:

'Balliol seems to me a place where everything is done to draw the best out of a man.

'I think there are four distinctly musical musicians in Oxford, Walker of Balliol, Hadow of Worcester, Allen of New College and Harwood of Christ Church, a fine Musician and a charming man, but hopelessly mild and too vague to influence anyone. Hadow is splendid company and stimulates thought, though his blaze of general culture is not always so sound as it appears. Walker I have never known to be superficial, and he has been profoundly influenced by Lewis Nettleship, whose mind must have been one of the most truthful and sympathetic that has ever been known. Allen seems, from what I have seen of him, to come in some respects rather near to being a great man.'

Frederick Septimus Kelly was Tovey's immediate successor as Nettleship Scholar, and was not only a musician but an athlete of note, winning (among other distinctions) the Diamond Sculls on three occasions. The friendship which grew up between the two men lasted, with many vicissitudes, until Kelly's tragic death in France in 1916. After completing his years at Balliol Kelly went to Frankfurt to study the pianoforte with Engesser and composition with Knorr. Tovey paid him a visit during his first year in Frankfurt (early in 1904) and wrote home to Miss Weisse: 'Enjoyable as Berlin was, I am much the better for a few days here where I know no one except Kelly. Berlin is not a place to rest in, even if I treat it as if Uncle Jo were the only living inhabitant; and that I could not do, though as a fact I saw him everyday.

'I must stop over Saturday, because Uncle Jo gave me a letter of introduction to the Direktor Scholz (his greatest friend here). Knorr is, I think, a really great man. Kelly is very comic; hugely nice and horribly afraid of my disgracing myself before his spiritual pastors and masters. He looks after my diet (which he has found out)—and, as to music he is, apart from Knorr's really splendid teaching and example, inspired by a proselytising hatred of all the things *I* ever told him not to do—such as heavy basses,—and is shocked at my laxity about such matters in my songs. I fear he is sometimes pained at the difficulty he finds in taking the conceit out of me.

'But it's really most remarkable what a difference Oxford and Eton makes. After even the very nice younger generation one finds in certain places in Berlin, Kelly produces an effect not so much of a return to one's native land as a coming into a larger world. His interest in his newspaper, and in people, and in whatever musical technicality or artistic impression comes his way;—all these things have a certain unprovincial quality added to them and a kind of co-ordination which makes it impossible for him to say anything superficial, however much he may give himself away. Knorr says he has never seen anyone grasp the technique of contrapuntal writing so quickly; but he doesn't know for certain whether Kelly has a real talent for composition "as we have just begun".

'I believe Kelly will feel miserably void of ideas for the next two years or so, and I spend half the time here ramming into him that he must never get into the blues about that but plod along without ideas, even if Knorr himself loses interest. I'm afraid Kelly must think me awfully patronizing; but he has his revenge in trying to cure me of my slowness and hesitancy of speech and my arrogant dogmatism. . . . If only he tides over the next two years he will become a real composer, and he is pretty certain to be a great player.'

Writing to Kelly that summer Tovey remarks that the press, with the exception of *The Times*, is against him, but that so long as they are also anti-Brahms and anti-Joachim, he really does not care, except for the influence critics have not only on concert-agents ('who know nothing') but on conductors ('who ought to know better'). 'However', he continues, 'it really hasn't begun to concern me yet: greater musicians are no further on than I, though they are much older. And certainly I have nothing to complain of in the attitude of other musicians to me. . . .

'At present I've more teaching than engagements; and I must wait till it's the other way round. Fortunately teaching suits me; in fact, if your pupils get on visibly before your very eyes there's danger in it: for it flatters your vanity to Be an Influence in Other's Lives. . . . Still, I do think that a young artist "whose nerves would never stand the torture of teaching" had better compete for a scholarship in Valetudinarianism.

'I have now got four lessons every Monday afternoon at that school at Ascot where Dorothy Usborne is. The head-mistress is *Ur-komisch*—butter in a lordly dish isn't a circumstance to her. The pianoforte (apparently the best in the school—which is an enormously expensive one) is more atrocous than any I ever saw that professed to be in playing order: but that is going to be changed before long. I never realized before what a long way a lordly independence goes with a certain type of Superior Person at the Head of an Educational Establishment. This particular one was so flabbergasted at my not only showing no eagerness to teach Dorothy Usborne there (it's about 8 miles off, and I've no time and it was much easier to send her to me at Miss Weisse's as before)—even with one or two others, but also at my writing the plain truth that I couldn't even go over to see her about it,—well, as I say, she was so flabbergasted that she came over to see me.'

In an effort to stimulate Kelly's work in composition Tovey initiated a kind of musical correspondence whereby the two exchanged—at erratic intervals—canons (to be solved by the recipient) and waltzes for pianoforte duet. The plan was to compile a set of waltzes, each composer contributing one alternately. In September Kelly wrote: 'The first vivid effect your waltzes made on me has not abated and I don't know to which I give

the palm. . . . I have done my E minor and D minor. The latter
is obstinate and keeps harping back on to one phrase. Your A
major is quite a masterpiece for its range. . . . The F minor is a
splendid penultimate and I am rather up a tree to give you all
the splendours it promises,—it was rather a mean trick of you
to play. . . . Knorr is delighted with the lot, and says my con-
tributions have quite set his doubts at rest as to my imagination
—but I only hope it will last. I was interested to hear you have
Goodhart Rendel as a pupil. I was always told he took the cake
for pure talent.'

This pupil, who eventually became Slade Professor of Fine
Art, said of Tovey many years later: 'I made him a disappointing pupil—I have only realized how disappointing by retrospect. I was very fond of him, and grateful to him, but I could
not understand his point of view nor benefit by his method of
teaching. He was quite right when he said in the end that what
creative knack I had would be better employed in architecture.
. . . I remember chiefly his impracticability and intolerance. Also
his fun and charming companionship,—no-one could forget
those;—but I was very young and he much less adaptable than
he afterwards became!'

'Our Waltzes are most successful', wrote Tovey to Miss
Weisse, 'I shall join mine on to the old ones and send them to
Schott. I feel as if it would be purely ridiculous ever to give
Kelly advice again'—as an earnest of which he then asked Kelly
to correct the proofs of his pianoforte concerto. The combined
waltzes were never published, but a few years later a set of sixteen by Tovey appeared under the title of *Balliol Dances*, dedicated to Ernest Walker and F. S. Kelly. Kelly's appear in the
list of his compositions as *Waltz Pageant for Pfte. Duet* (1905–11).

Tovey was also full of plans for collaboration with Kelly in
future concerts and in the post-graduate training of Nettleship
Scholars, but, he wrote to Miss Weisse, 'I have only begun to
realize that his wealth is a difficult thing to get over. He is very
sensitive and will be awfully distressed if he finds any difficulty
in understanding my attitude towards him on that score'. Tovey

was sensitive too; Kelly's enthusiasm cooled, and a projected holiday in Italy in spring 1906 failed to materialize. Finally, came a disastrous week-end with the Kellys at Bisham, when Tovey lost his temper over some songs by Cyril Scott, and Kelly, losing his temper also, made it clear that he thought Tovey was wasting his time over such doings as the Northlands concerts and teaching. With incredible folly Tovey appealed to Miss Weisse to save the situation. 'Whatever happens,' he wrote, 'Kelly must not be allowed to lose sight of us. And that's where your diplomacy—i.e. your perfectly natural grip of the situation, comes in. I can do no more, but you can get hold of his sister. . . .'

To both the Kellys, Tovey was sincerely attached, and the misunderstandings and estrangement of this year were embittered by the fact that Kelly resented Tovey's feelings for his sister. In the unstable emotional condition from which Tovey was suffering as a result of Miss Weisse's continued endeavour to mould his life, frustration had a serious effect on his health and spirits. The more he tries to analyse and explain Kelly's motives and character in letters to Miss Weisse, and his own in letters to Kelly, the more clearly does it appear that there was a real clash of temperament between the two young men, and that the younger was afraid of being dominated by the older— a fact which evidently never entered Tovey's mind.

The friendship was patched up in the autumn and on the occasion of a private concert at Sandringham on Queen Alexandra's birthday in December, Kelly was invited to play the *Liebeslieder* waltzes with Tovey in place of James Friskin, who was ill. The rehearsals, however, caused friction; 'I won't have him play hard and cold,' wrote Tovey, 'and we have already set each other's backs up.'

Some years later in this fluctuating friendship (March 1909) Kelly wrote,

'Dear Donald,

I've just got your letter and am so keen to see you that I lose no time in answering it. Any night or nights (the more the better) you can come here I shall be delighted to see you. Don't go to the Cohens but come here as I am sure you will enjoy yourself more. . . .

'I should like to discuss with you the advisability of your taking a room in London for the purpose of giving lessons. There is a good deal to be said for it. . . . Lady Betty [Balfour] has written about the Woking concerts and very kindly asked me to go and meet you there which would be great fun.'

In the following year Kelly played Tovey's pianoforte concerto at the celebrated Petersfield Musical Festival, which—commencing in 1900,—was the first of its kind in the country. Tovey's first connexion with the Festival was in 1904, when he conducted the closing concert. In 1905 the conductors were Miss Craig Sellar (later Mrs. Alexander Maitland) and Donald Tovey, and the soloist was Miss Fanny Davies. In 1910, Dr. H. P. Allen conducted 'and brought [says the press notice] his celebrated Oxford orchestra augmented by wind players from the London Symphony Orchestra. The male voice choir rendered Grieg's *Recognition of Land* with Mr. Adrian C. Boult as soloist. . . . We were given the welcome opportunity of hearing Mr. Donald Tovey's pianoforte concerto superbly played by Mr. F. S. Kelly, and at the close both pianist and composer received ovations'.

Two events of great consequence took place in 1905. The first was the invitation to contribute the main articles on music to the 11th edition of the *Encyclopædia Britannica*; the second was the ripening of a casual acquaintance with the poet Robert C. Trevelyan into a deep and lasting friendship, and Tovey's proposal that they should collaborate in writing an opera. With these two considerable projects on hand, in addition to concerts and teaching, one would have thought that Tovey would hesitate to accept any other work, and it is a mark of how over-driven and unpractical was his way of living, that in the following May he signed a contract with Methuen to write a book on Beethoven. This work never materialized, but the fragment

Beethoven, published after his death in 1944, consists of the early unrevised chapters—written before 1910, and *retyped* in 1936 when he had thoughts of rewriting and completing the book.

Letters from Miss Weisse to Mrs. Trevelyan shed light on the stresses and difficulties of these years, although due allowance must be made for Miss Weisse's inveterate habit of exaggerating. Writing in August 1905 from Brighton, where Tovey was staying with her, Miss Weisse outlines the round of visits which he has to pay before coming to stay with the Trevelyans at their home, 'The Shiffolds', in September and adds, 'I know you will take care of the dear fellow for me and would let me know if he is not all right. I am so miserable when he is out of reach! How selfish I am: pray forgive me'.

In June 1906 she writes: 'Donald is slaving away at the *Encyclopædia* up to the verge of his strength. . . . About Saturday —do entreat Mr. and Mrs. Roger Fry to join you in staying for supper to meet Mr. and Mrs. Ed. Speyer who will be staying here. . . . Then about your kind invitation to Donald, would September do after all? Since I have been a little less well it has been settled that he is to take me out to Nauheim, and he may I think be in Germany all August.'

Miss Weisse was determined to keep in close touch with Tovey this summer because of his continued despair at having broken the friendship with the Kellys which had meant so much to him. Her fear of brain-fever may not have been without foundation; the combination of overstrain and emotional distress was dangerous. But it seems almost as if she were anxious to keep him away from all his English friends. Her next letter to Mrs. Trevelyan is from Nauheim in August: 'I have heard accidentally that Donald is certainly to play his concerto again at the Gürzenich in Cologne this winter,—and they want him to come to Mayence too to do it. I confess I am greatly pleased. English concert authorities won't have him, so there is some consolation in finding Germany seeking after him.' Still at Nauheim on 2 September she writes: 'It is shocking that you have not heard from us and that you are still in the dark about Donald's plans. . . . All the month at Nauheim I have been able for nothing and Donald was very unwell. The doctors are beginning to be anxious because since Christmas his pulse has never been more than 54—and then when he was getting better and arranging to be in Ireland (visiting Lord Mounteagle) his plans were suddenly changed owing to the urgent desire of Joachim and of the exiled Royal family at Hanover, of all odd things, that he should spend a week with them,—which I am thankful to think he really has enjoyed.'

Letters to Miss Weisse from Tovey describe this visit in great detail: 'I got a room in the hotel, while J. J. went off in the Queen of Hanover's carriage to his Maierei (the Queen's villa is so small that not only her guests but the Princess Frederika live in the farm-house below). Then I took a walk after tea up a big wooded hill overlooking the lake. Imagine my amazement and horror when I found on my return a letter from Uncle Jo saying what a pity I was out as the Duke[1] invited me to stay and I was to have come to dinner at 8.30 with my luggage! . . . So I made great haste and sacrificed the completeness of my packing to the completeness of my costume (as I found next morning when I had to telephone for my waistcoat) and arrived in good time after all. . . .

'The most striking personality here is undoubtedly the Duchess, sister of Queen Alexandra, with whom one really does see the way in which royalty, and more especially female royalty, pulls society together. . . . The Duke is very kind too. . . . He is a very typical figure such as one has so often seen caricatured that one feels rather touched at finding that the type goes with such good-nature and such evidently genuine fondness for nice things like Bach and Handel.

'But the most touching figure here is the Queen of Hanover. She is 88, and, like the Duke of Meiningen, she can't hear music now, because she hears discordant noises with it. But she is extremely kind and very lively; full of interesting memories. . . .

'I had to get into evening dress (as an available substitute in

---

[1] The Duke of Cumberland.

this country for a frock-coat at all times of day) in order to lunch
with the Queen. The daily programme here is, breakfast in my
room; playing with Uncle Jo—or rehearsing, lunch with the
Queen, some visit or excursion, and then about 7.30 music here
before and after dinner. . . . Schloss Cumberland is heraldic
rather than artistic; but the Villa Hanover is bristling with
objects of bigotry and virtue, and is very bright, and, I think,
harmonious.' Joachim made Tovey sing 'Harry and the Hornets'
(a Wagnerian skit to a comic text) one evening when the serious
business of music-making was over. It was such a success that
the aged Queen asked next day to hear it, standing close by the
piano and laughing all the time.

'You'll see,' continues this long letter, 'if I just catalogue the
events, how difficult it is to get time for writing. . . . It isn't very
easy to send messengers with telegrams and things from this
place as it is a good walk from the town, and one doesn't like to
ask to use the private wire:—otherwise of course I would have
kept in daily communication with you as I would have done if
I had been in an hotel.'

Miss Weisse rejoined Tovey after his visit to the Schloss Cumberland and accompanied him to Ireland, whence eventually
she wrote to Mrs. Trevelyan regarding his long-delayed visit to
'The Shiffolds': 'I hope it is all clear about Donald's reaching
you. I confess it cost me a great deal to leave him in Ireland
yesterday, and do what I will I cannot shake off the feeling of
apprehension while he is in this discouraged and suffering
condition.'

8

AFTER a break of six years the regular series of Northlands concerts was resumed early in 1905. During the two previous seasons Tovey had kept himself before the public in London as a performer and composer by means of his own ventures at the Grafton Galleries and Bechstein Hall; these were mainly chamber-music concerts and were accordingly costly. The few London engagements and numerous but scattered provincial engagements, which were all that he, as a new player, could hope to get without the backing of a powerful impresario, were not sufficiently remunerative to justify the continuance of independent concert-giving in London at a loss. The return to Northlands was therefore originally dictated by prudence; but the concerts, which continued without a break from 1905 until 1914, were in respect of artists and performance as remarkable as any given in London during the same period, and the most famous musicians of the day collaborated with Tovey in the well-known music room at Englefield Green.

Many of his friends, however, were not happy about the semi-private nature of this concert-giving, and at the instance of the Hon. R. D. Denman[1] an influential committee was formed which 'invited Mr Tovey to give four evening Chamber Concerts during March 1906 in the Chelsea Town Hall'. It was hoped that, were the committee to remain a permanent body, 'it would exercise a real influence in the encouragement of English music'. These concerts established themselves and were continued with varying success until 1913, during which time Tovey produced a wide range of interesting works, many of which were quite off the beaten track of the average concert-giver.

The collected programmes include the Fantasia and Six-part

---

[1] Later Lord Denman.

Fugue from *Das Musikalische Opfer* and most of the solo cantatas
of Bach; the two Brahms clarinet sonatas, with Mühlfeld, the
great clarinettist, for whom Brahms wrote these works; two remarkable concerts with Hausmann comprising all Beethoven's
works for 'cello and piano; three equally remarkable concerts
(spaced throughout the 1910 series) in which Tovey played all
the pianoforte works of Brahms. On the occasion of the appearance of the famous German clarinettist, critics were unanimous
in agreeing that the greatness of Mühlfeld's playing was fully
equalled by that of the pianist; for the rest, opinions were
diverse and contradictory, even with regard to the music, dis-
missing, for instance, Dvořák's greatest chamber-music work, the
F minor Pianoforte Trio, as 'not in the great Bohemian's most
inspired vein'.

There were other friends who were concerned lest Tovey
should be either swallowed up in the musical jungle of London,
or unduly tied to the narrower confines of Northlands. In October 1906 he received a letter from Edward Hilliard of Balliol:
'Dear Mr Tovey,

'As you are doubtless aware there is at the moment a movement on the part of old Balliol men to endow and benefit the
College. A generous benefactor influenced by the example of
others has just endowed two Jowett Fellowships. Doubtless inspired by this example an admirer of your work has asked me
to submit to you the following proposal.

'In order to give you more time for original composition and
critical work he offers £300 a year for the term of three years to
be of use to you. The donor makes no stipulation as to the way
in which you should use your time, this he leaves entirely to
your own judgment. He, however, subject to what you may
think best, suggests that "your musical influence would be of
great value to the College and University of which you are a
member, and that he would consider his scheme to have more
far-reaching results were you to find it possible to take up your
residence, for as much time as you found it convenient yearly,
in Oxford itself." . . .

'I hope I have made it quite clear to you that the donor wishes you to be quite free in exercising your discretion, nor does he want you to be prevented from taking pupils or giving concerts. He believes you capable of producing really good original work if only you have time for it.'

An immediate reply from Tovey accepts this proposal as 'an honour and a responsibility', and yet, for an unknown reason, the scheme came to nothing. This was one of the first, and the most serious, effort on the part of his friends to set him free from the domination of Northlands. To one with his fatal gift of seeing everybody else's point of view, however, the situation was too complex to be easily resolved. There was, moreover, some truth in Miss Weisse's pronouncement—made on another occasion when it was urged that he had no leisure for composing—'For Donald, freedom from all other work or routine would mean first deferring work, and then working against time in a way that constitutes a danger impossible to exaggerate!'

In the spring of 1907 the Joachim Quartet came to London for the last time, but without their leader, who was taken ill at the last minute and was unable to travel. Gradually it became evident that Joachim would not recover, and Tovey went to Berlin early in August to see him; but his old friend was so weak that he was only allowed to see him through the open door of his room. The great violinist died on 17 August and was mourned by hosts of friends and music-lovers of many countries, but by none more sincerely than by Donald Tovey.

If he inherited much of the spirit of Joachim, Tovey also fell heir to the hostility of that section of the London press which had always been anti-Joachim, and two years later *Vanity Fair* delivered an astonishing attack headed

'The Most Holy Kingdom of Tovey.

'Mr Donald Tovey, notwithstanding his comparative youth, is undoubtedly one of the most learned musicians in Europe. But to me he is interesting primarily as a symbol; for there have gathered around him a band of the elect—few in numbers, but not devoid of social importance—who have founded a sort of monastic order, holding themselves haughtily aloof from the rest of the musical world, despising their enemies and praying for them with about equal earnestness.

'These reactionary purists have enthroned Mr Tovey as their King and their Pope. His authority remains unquestioned. His infallibility is established by divine right of the Joachim succession.

'Now the capital of this State is, of course, at Oxford (where else possible?) but from time to time we heretical barbarians in London receive missions to convince us by personal example of the hopeless levity of our ways. . . . At the present time there is a nunciature extraordinary established in the Chelsea Town Hall, where every Wednesday the Great Man himself instructs us how to play Beethoven, Brahms and Mozart.

'As a severely intellectual interpreter of the classics the Great Man might deserve his reputation if he had the least idea of how to play the pianoforte. . . .' The critic is less severe about his compositions—'of his two new String Quartets I only heard one and it gave me genuine pleasure'—but he proceeds to imply that the works are purely derivative, and concludes: 'In the meantime we are all glad to welcome the Tovey "settlement" in Chelsea, and we shall watch the progress of events with interest. After all, London *might* reform Oxford. Oxford has reformed us so often!'

The Joachim Concerts Committee came to an end with the death of Joachim and was succeeded in 1908 by the Classical Concerts Society under similar auspices; Borwick and Tovey, in the capacity of musical advisers, were shortly joined by Kelly. Mr. Speyer sent Tovey a draft of the proposed programmes for the first season, opening with a concert by the Klingler String Quartet. 'This seems nice,' replied Tovey. 'I only wish we weren't beginning after all with the most exact conceivable imitation of a Joachim programme; and I should not be surprised if some people felt strongly about it, while some d—d fools are sure to make *laudatory* remarks in the worst possible

taste, thereby putting Klingler into a false position. . . . Do
please, if you possibly can, persuade the quartet to come a week
later so as to begin the series with a new kind of programme.'
His advice was taken on this occasion, but in later seasons he
often had cause to complain that decisions made by Mr. Speyer
on his advice were either overturned by the other two members
of the 'Shadow Cabinet' without consulting him, or frustrated
by the actions of the concert agent. No doubt his colleagues also
had cause for complaint, for his inefficiency in business matters
was incurable.

The whole method of running the concerts invited trouble,
for the distinguished Committee merely served to pass accounts,
and in no way controlled policy or programmes. The concert
agent who was employed by Mr. Speyer was concerned to make
the concerts 'pay', and adopted methods—such as starring
Casals on the posters without even mentioning the other artists
who were appearing with him, and beating down the terms of
reputable artists—which aroused Tovey to wrath. It was not
always easy to get Tovey to reply promptly on the matter of
programme details, but when his sense of justice was touched
in matters concerning the status either of other artists or of himself, he made no bones about expressing his opinion in letters of
ten and twenty pages to Mr. Speyer. 'I have no hesitation in
saying exactly what I think about the agency question. I had
rather write it than say it by word of mouth; it looks worse in
writing, but it makes me so indignant that I can't talk of it without raising my voice: and then it looks as if I had merely lost my
temper. On paper you can take it as a mere statement of facts.'
He *had* lost his temper. He believed—possibly with reason—that
this agent's policy was to introduce as many new artists as possible in London through the medium of these concerts and to
take a special commission from them for so doing. Moreover, he
had given concerts himself with the same agent and had found
that, although the hall seemed full, the takings were less than
those at Northlands! The vexations of these matters of business
were a constant source of irritation.

His opinion of new artists was frequently sought and was given, as this report on a singer shows, in lively and illuminating style:

'Dear Mr Speyer,

  '(1) Voice very fine

even in the exceptional bracketed notes outside its normal compass.

  '(2) Intelligence first-rate, of a more or less material range.

  '(3) Diction first-rate, with a faint trace of Berlin Cockney which an arch platform-manner (to me the most insufferable thing in the world) does much to accentuate.

  '(4) Imaginative use of vocal colour really *geradezu genial.*

  '(5) Taste—runs excessively to witches and mousetraps and is kept within bounds rather by diplomacy and intelligence than by nature.

  '(6) Rhythm, very nearly always first-rate—but *Waldesgespräch* proved too much for it. I thought at first that, like Casals, she was going to preserve the right movement through dragged-out tempi by means of her command of tone—but the dragging got the upper hand, and reduced the excitement to mere Formidable Personality. . . .

'The Learned Pig who accompanied her is probably an essential part of the works. We must get Hamilton Harty if she doesn't absolutely insist on her own man—whose tone and temperament are brainy but (to me) ugly.

'I am afraid she will, so to speak, act any decent chamber-music off the platform. Don't laugh at me when I say, in confidence, that I think it would be just as well to take Frau Schumann's view of some of Brahms' texts in selecting songs for her. . . . There's a bad, cold, hard streak in her art which fools will call passion because it happens to be destructive of passion. It's not for nothing that she ends her programme with the

Mausfallensprüchlein. I like cats, but they mustn't pose as Human Frailty, presume on my charity, and then expect me to worship them.

'Against this I have to set the indisputable fact that she made the whole merit of Loewe's Faust-scene manifest at once. . . . The composition is almost impossibly simple in texture and subtle in style—but by the time she had sung it straight through from beginning to end it might have been Schubert at his best. . . .

'Well, there you have all my pros and cons. What I dislike is not easy to define though I do dislike it intensely. The merits, on the other hand, seem to me to leave astonishingly little room for criticism—barring *Waldesgespräch*, which I'm sure you and Mrs Speyer would never expect to hear sung quite as you would like. If you want that done properly you must have it done at home.

'Auf Wiedersehen.'

Tovey's position in relation to the Classical Concerts Society became increasingly difficult. 'The Brahms C minor Pfte. quartet oughtn't to be at the end of the programme,' says a letter of April 1910, 'and it would suit Borwick fifty times better than Fanny [Davies]. I suppose Kelly doesn't approve of the way I play it.' Mr. Speyer suggested that Tovey should discuss the programmes with Kelly, but he refused to do so. Kelly, who had not yet made his London début, had resumed his study of composition with Tovey, and was also due to play his pianoforte concerto at the Petersfield Festival in May. 'He has been extremely critical of me lately,' wrote Tovey, 'and his lessons in composition have been almost a contradiction in terms.' Tovey's own playing about this time was very unequal; none knew it better than he, and Kelly's criticisms were none the less unwelcome because they contained a grain of truth.

Inevitably Tovey's Chelsea concerts and the Classical Concert Society came into conflict. 'The fact that the whole executive committee of the C.C.S. consists, with set purpose, of personal friends of mine, only makes my position more intolerable', wrote

Tovey, who had come to realize that the Committee was power-less, and that the suggestions of the concert agent and others now carried more weight with Mr. Speyer than did his own. 'Unfortunately we lack the personal object of a Joachim quartet to keep controversy and confusion of aims and ideals out of the question. My own influence is exaggerated in theory and report, and is inadequate in practise. . . . Foreign artists who are intro-duced to me as to a person of appalling authority and power, soon find out that the position the Society gives me in public is an evidently inferior one, . . . and the remonstrances of my friends, including a member of Committee who has since resigned, have not the smallest effect in inducing the Society to refrain from giving a new series of concerts [in 1911] at a season and on a week-day that seriously inconveniences my own concerts.'

He did not immediately resign, on the quixotic ground that Borwick, who had just completed a successful tour of Australia, was not yet back in London, and that he did not wish to do any-thing that might wreck the Society while its 'main pillar of support' was absent. The final break followed shortly afterwards however. In the following year (1912) Mr. Speyer, who was now 72 years of age, also resigned; he was followed by Kelly as chairman.

The friendly relations between the Speyers and Tovey were clouded for a very brief length of time; even Miss Weisse's bitter letters to Mr. Speyer did not effect a serious break. The end of the chapter was written in 1937 in a telegram from Tovey to Mrs. Speyer: 'Greatly moved by every chapter of *Life and Friends*.[1] Hope I have acquired more wisdom since days so generously described. Letter follows someday. Donald.'

Interwoven with all Tovey's other affairs, from 1907 until 1918, was the lengthy task of composing the opera *The Bride of Dionysus*. His friend and librettist, R. C. Trevelyan, gives this account of the early stages of the undertaking:

'Though I had already several times met Donald Tovey, I did

[1] Edward Speyer's *My Life and Friends*, Cobden-Sanderson, 1937.

not become intimate with him until he came to stay with us at
'The Shiffolds' in the summer of 1905. On most afternoons he
and I went for long walks together on Leith Hill, Donald strid-
ing along at five miles an hour, talking the whole time, I listening, and occasionally interposing with an attempt to short-circuit
his argument, which would often wander away for an hour or
more through distant regions, but would always sooner or later
return, enriched, to his original theme. At first this discursive-
ness would bewilder and sometimes irritate me; but I soon became used to it, and learnt to let him go his own way, much to
my own profit. His theories and illustrations ranged over the
whole of musical and literary history; and though he sometimes
forgot how sadly ignorant I was of music, that did not seem to
matter much; for it was the general principles of creative art
with which his mind was full. I seem indeed to have learnt more
from him than from any other theorist about art, and that perhaps because he was, in a sense, so little of a theorist.

'The day before his visit came to an end, we had hardly begun
our afternoon's walk, when he suddenly turned to me and asked
whether I would consider the idea of writing the libretto of an
opera for him. He had been reading an unperformable verse-
drama of mine, called *The Birth of Parsival*, and beneath its
shortcomings had divined a not impossible librettist. No moment
of my life has ever given me so pure a pleasure. I was already
not a little bewitched by the spell of his genius; and it seemed
to me, and still seems, an almost incredible good fortune that he
should have thought me worthy to collaborate with him. It was
an act of faith on his part, which little that I had so far done
could really justify.

'The rest of that day's walk he spent in explaining to me his
notions of a satisfactory libretto, and in pointing out certain
dangers. What he was most concerned to impress upon me was
the necessity of clearly distinguishing the relatively prosaic
recitative passages, the business affairs of the drama, from the
more lyrical and melodic parts; and above all of seeing to it that
there should always be a sufficient dramatic and theatrical

reason for every change from prose to poetry, from recitative to melody. He gave as a warning instance the climax of the first act of *Fidelio*, as to which he wrote later on that "the music bursts into the middle of a prose dialogue, and continues the subject thereof, without any discoverable reason".

'Though he envisaged a more or less Wagnerian treatment of the words, he did not intend to carry realism so far as to exclude vocal *ensembles* or choruses, as Wagner had done in a large part of *The Ring*. For the rest, he wished to give me a free hand in the use of any metres I liked, whether blank verse or lyrical. But as we had not yet chosen a subject, he could not for the present go beyond such general considerations. Shortly afterwards he wrote "As to rhythms and assonances:—*don't consider the music at all*. I'm more and more convinced that it's the business of the English composer to learn how to sing the English language; and that it's not the business of the English poet to spoil his verse to suit the incompetence of the English composer".

'A few weeks after he had gone, I had set to work on that oldest of operatic themes, the story of Ariadne, Theseus and Dionysus, complicating the simple drama of desertion, that had appealed to Monteverdi, by bringing in a vindictive and self-righteous Minos, and explaining the hero's fickle conduct by making Phaedra and Theseus fall in love with one another in the first scene, before Ariadne's humanity and resource had awakened a disastrous gratitude and admiration in Theseus.

'When I brought Tovey my sketch of the first Act, he at once saw the possibilities of the subject, especially of the as yet un-written Dionysian finale; but he was quite rightly critical, not of the language or of the lyrical passages, but of various weak-nesses of construction and undramatic redundancies. His own innate sense of drama was far more powerful than mine; but fortunately I had the good sense to find this out very soon, and to accept or adapt a large portion of his suggested alterations or additions, which were almost always designed to heighten or enrich the dramatic situation, and were seldom concerned with verbal phrasing or euphony.

'While I was still writing the first draft, I used from time to time to go to Northlands in order to show him what I had done, and consult with him as to how to continue. Usually we had no more than an hour or two, of which every minute was precious; but Donald, whose sense of non-musical time was very defective, would often exasperate me by plunging into long discourses that threw only a remote light on the business in hand. Once, I remember, when we had less than half an hour left, he suddenly jumped up and rushed to the piano, seized a full score of Cornelius's *Barber of Bagdad,* and in order to illustrate some theoretical aspect of opera-writing, started playing the second Act, singing all the voice-parts. It was a marvellous performance; but I could take no delight in it, and sat fretting while the minutes passed until I had to rush off to catch my train with half my questions and difficulties unsolved.

'In those early days, before the libretto was finished, he was naturally still dubious as to how it would turn out, and very critical of its imperfections. He was too honest to praise my work until he saw clearly what it would amount to; and sometimes both his silences and his criticisms were so discouraging that I began to fear that it was going to be a failure. But as soon as he had read the libretto as a whole (which I sent him in July 1907), and had realized its musical possibilities, his attitude changed entirely from doubt and reserve to excitement and even enthusiasm. He at once wrote me an immense letter of thirty pages, headed "July in general" from which I quote these passages:

' "It will be a large undertaking, for I know this will be a full-sized opera indeed, and I have grave doubts as to whether my intention of trying to do it with a pre-Wagnerian orchestra will be really feasible. However I shall know all about that by the time I've made a sketch (in black and white, so to speak, i.e. on two staves like a pianoforte arrangement) of the first act; and if it can be done for a small orchestra, it shall.

' "P.S. (three days later) I have been on the move and have

carried *Ariadne* about with me and think better of it the more I
see of it. Moreover I have (without waiting for your consent)
even showed it to one or two people who think it very fine;
though I fear their opinions may be a little biassed by my inability to conceal my own excitement and hopes.

' "However I have meanwhile read it in more detail and take
this opportunity of sending you my first notes."

'Then follow nearly twenty pages of suggestions, many of which
we adopted in whole or in part, though some proved to be unnecessary. He then continued:

' "I think you have chosen a splendid story, and in spite of my
croakings, you have pulled it through all the difficulties which
frightened me, and you have produced a play that cries out for
music, and is utterly unlike any opera-book, Wagnerian, pre-
Wagnerian, post-Wagnerian, Italian, German, Russian, French,
or British, that has ever been seen.

' "I shall very soon be boiling over with themes and contrasts.
Already I've a terrific heroic row ready for Theseus's first entry.
By the way it is significant that all the beginnings of musical
ideas I have so far had are concerned with those points that are
most entirely yours; and I think you will soon find that, in spite
of the patience with which you have received and adopted my
suggestions, there really won't be anything in the whole which
you have not made your own. That's why I have no hesitation
in sending you all this screed of details; because I know that, if
you can't make of them something better than I thought possible, you would long ago have refused to go on."

'That was indeed a very generous way of putting it; for without
the numerous major and minor improvements, which, until the
final score was completed ten years later, he was continually
suggesting, and which I embodied in libretto language, the play
would have been a somewhat loosely constructed affair, and
many of its dramatic potentialities would have remained imper-
fectly realized.'

The correspondence between composer and poet—for Trevelyan could write his thirty-page letters also—would make a fascinating text-book for students of opera. Showers of letters followed the completion of the libretto. 'Dear Poet, I was at Worps yesterday and read *Ariadne* to my people. It was delightful to watch my father's relish of its classical spirit and detail, and to find him getting excited at every point where one can foresee a fine spectacular or dramatic effect. He confirmed my impression that Minos needs filling-out and preventing from being an abstraction of ogredom. But he made me feel also that probably a good many of my other scruples may be meticulous. Still, I think it does no harm to mention them.' (It took nine more pages to do so.) 'One more carp and I am done. I'm full of themes and possibilities, but I'm hampered by a difficulty in getting over the first line of all. I quite see that in an opening of which the beauty largely depends on its extreme simplicity it is immensely difficult to make any alteration. But if I *could* have some other first five words than "Slow, slow yet more slow" I should be able to get an idea of the first notes (and hence of the overture and its relations to the 4th Act, which at present is shrouded in mystery to me). I'm tormented by the frivolous impressions and fears of the words sounding partly like an address from the stage to the conductor and partly like a catch-word for critics. . . . I don't object to the word "slow"—it's absolutely necessary: but I wish I could begin with "Dark ship" so as to hit the aural eye (this expression is copyright) with a colour at once instead of a tempo direction. . . . Don't be alarmed and think that I am going to be like this over every other line. . . . It only stumps me because it's at the very beginning.'

A few days later, having received the alterations from the poet, he wrote (aboard Lord Rendel's S.Y. *Zingara* off Ryde): 'Another thing I think one is apt to overlook is that it's just at the critical situations that simple and few words have most weight, especially when they are set to music. For example, I propose, with your permission to bring the curtain down on Act II with nothing but "Her shadow did I deem thee? Oh blind, blind"—*sotto voce*. I don't think Theseus has a word more to say.' This is characteristic of the remarkable way in which he saw all the protagonists as *live* people, and profoundly understood their human reactions. The fact that all the characters emerge on a noble and lofty plane is the natural outcome of the collaboration of two artists so well-matched in generosity of understanding, sensibility of feeling, and unshakeably high ideals.

Very soon after the libretto was finished Tovey urged that it should be published separately as a play, saying that this would also help its career as an opera. 'The following extract', continues Trevelyan in his account of their early collaboration, 'will make clear what he conceived to be the relation between verse-prosody and its translation into musical form: "You must be prepared to find musical emphasis very different from that of prosody. . . . You see, your verse technique aids the rhetoric and resists wrong emphasis, and *vice versa* (pun unavoidable); and in so far as music does the same it will run parallel with the verse in expressing the words. But even where, as in my sketches for the first act, it seems (owing to its unusual rapidity, which I shall not be able or willing to keep up) to retain your verse-rhythms, really the one thing it doesn't express is verse-technique. You, knowing your own verse, may be able to recognise it in the music; and of course the music gives your emphasis, or fails to do so on pain of misrepresenting you; but only in the most formal lyric moments can it give the impression of your *lines* where the sense crosses them.

' "Hence, in the more dramatic passages I shall very possibly make fairly full sketches in which I may omit words without always consulting you: on the assumption that your version and no other shall be printed apart from the music—without any comment; and that my version shall only appear in the scores—also without comment. Comment would only draw attention to what no one would notice, and all would take for a real difference of opinion. Of course if any of these liberties spoil the sense or tone of your poetry, I will revoke them; but you will find in such passages that no question of prosody, however alarming it may really be without music, has the least weight when the passage is sung in dramatic style."

'When I became familiar with his setting of my words, I did not find, at least in the more lyrical passages, that he ever distorted or obscured the essential poetic rhythm. Of course, as he said, "for dramatically musical purposes blank verse is prose;" but although he often imposed upon my blank verse musical rhythms which had little relation to the prosody, there were many occasions when he retained and gave full value to the metrical form and phrasing.

'It is difficult for me now to think of my words in dissociation from his music. Though he made them so completely his own, his imaginative understanding of them could not have been more perfect. It is not only that he exactly expresses whatever poetry I had intended the words to convey, but his music transfigures and raises them to a far higher dramatic and lyrical plane. Except occasionally in quite minute details, I never found myself raising any objection to his musical treatment of my poem.'

The essentials of the music and the general plan of the work all took shape in Tovey's mind during that summer of 1907. When he was in Berlin in August, just before Joachim died, he wrote proposing a division of the opera into three—instead of the original four—acts, and suggested also the title by which it was finally known, *The Bride of Dionysus*. But it was not until a year later that he wrote—again from the S.Y. *Zingara*, with the heading 'floating in the neighbourhood of Skye, where it rains angoras and terriers'—'The 1st Act is practically finished in what I call a declamatory sketch: viz., a sketch of the mere voice parts.' After an extremely interesting and enormously detailed account of how he has treated it, he continues: 'My theories as to the possibilities of musical form in modern opera are vastly enlarged and changed. To me, musical form is as much a gain in realism as in anything else; it is a resource, the mastery of which in purely instrumental music enables one to move with every kind of speed (Wagnerian as well as rapid) but gets rid of much Wagnerism that will, I am increasingly certain, some day appear as archaic;—e.g. the abnormal exaggeration of every pause in Wagner's sentences—which nearly destroys the value of his really dramatic silences. . . .

'Still, I am driven to despair when I come on any of Wagner's great outbursts of music. His business-technique no longer impresses me . . . but the climaxes he reaches after half-an-hour's ingenious style-twisting; the situations, reached by methods of schoolboy complexity, to be expressed in music of classic sublimity; and the sort of planetary orbit in which the music spins along while the curtain is down or while the Norns are spinning; —these things seem to me as inaccessible as the 9th Symphony.'

A brief postcard to Mrs. Speyer next day is headed—'On the High Seas, living on Coffee and Rolls, especially Rolls.

'I hope to arrive on Sunday morning. . . . I shall bring a sketch of the 1st Act of *Ariadne* and I shall be a ghastly bore with it.' The beautiful language of the libretto was his main source of inspiration, but these brief holidays aboard the *Zingara* may well have helped to stimulate the invention of some of the loveliest music of the work.

'The only line I don't know how to set in Act III', says another closely written postcard to Trevelyan from the yacht, 'is your favourite "Beautiful in pied fawn-skin"—which I am most truly sorry to say *will* keep filling my irreverent mind with the alternative "or very superior in red morocco", to the total inhibition of any adequate idea for a vocal melody. I have fought with this prejudice for years, and am no better now than I ever was.'

After hearing the musical sketch for the first Act Trevelyan wrote to Tovey: 'It is strange how many things that seemed to me rather uninteresting in the text, get interest and importance and even quite new meanings I had not thought of, when they are set.' He then sends new lines for the finale of Act III. Ensemble passages proved something of a stumbling block to the poetic mind, as he had already pointed out at an earlier stage: 'From a purely literary point of view there is something a little comic about an operatic ensemble, which of course is anything but comic as opera. Anyhow there must be a tendency for the quality of the verse to become second-rate. However I don't mind. Your encouragement is a great help to me to go on trying to do new things, but however pleasant it may be to get such encouragement, it is not quite fair on you, since any I can give you must be much more a matter of faith than reason and criticism.'

Another letter from Trevelyan makes interesting reference to proposed changes in the impressive scene in Act II which opens in the Labyrinth with the captives descending into its shadows through a great door at the back of the stage: 'I see also that you are right in cutting out the Chorus "O tomb of death" at the beginning of the scene. If in the literary version I wanted to keep it, I should be rather tempted to put it back where it was originally intended, that is before Minos's long speech and while the captives are descending the steps. After the opening of the doors some little time would naturally elapse: we do not want the guards to hustle them down brutally, and Minos would not begin his speech till they were all well inside and downstairs and the door ready to be shut. In the musical version this interval would no doubt be filled up orchestrally, but in a purely literary version, it might be a good thing to have this chorus here, so as to indicate a decent, almost ritualistic, introduction of the victims, and not a brutal *dégringolade*. Minos's speech would contrast better with that possibly than with a mere shuffling of feet and whispering etc., which would I think suggest itself to a reader. However it does not much matter, but I always fight hard for the life of my condemned passages—on principle.'

The passage was restored to its place later and combined with a chorus of guards in a splendid ceremonial march. The addition of this chorus was incidentally the only occasion on which Tovey gave his librettist a musical theme and asked him to write words for it.

It had been with 'delight and relief' that Tovey found Miss Weisse sympathetic to his plans for writing an opera, and enthusiastic about the beautiful libretto. But after two years she realized that it was going to take much longer and occupy much more of his time than she had imagined, and that, moreover, his other work was suffering. The simple plan of dropping other activities in order to concentrate on such an important piece of composition was never regarded as feasible by either of them; it might possibly have defeated its own end, for Tovey was a man who always must drive himself to his utmost in order to produce his best work.

On Christmas day 1908 his mother died in her sleep, rather unexpectedly, after an attack of bronchitis. Although he had lived so little at home, Tovey was much attached to his family; his mother's death was a shock, and he felt it his duty now to devote some time to his father. In January they both went to stay with the Trevelyans. Miss Weisse was greatly alarmed— anxious about his health ('he is in what seems to me a perilous condition of nerves', she wrote), disapproving of his father's easy-going ways, jealous of his friendship with the Trevelyans, but also rightly conscious that a man so exceptionally equipped as he in mind and temperament still needed much care if his health and his work were to be maintained. It was a difficult problem for her, and the wisdom which she had so often shown in his upbringing began to fail her now, when his life seemed to be following lines so different from those which she had foreseen. She was *determined* that the ambitions which she had for him should be fulfilled.

The Chelsea concerts, which now ran weekly on Wednesdays, began for the season on 20 January 1909; on 19 January, Hausmann died in his sleep in Vienna. This was a fresh shock to Tovey, to whom Hausmann represented the last link with Joachim, and with whom he was to have given two recitals in February. 'Hausmann's love for the young Tovey—both as a musician and as a man—touched me deeply', Miss Weisse once said in recalling early days. 'After they had rehearsed together for the first time, I came in as they ended, and, Tovey having gone, I asked Hausmann about the rehearsal. He said "Das war gar keine Probe; er hat gespielt, und ich habe vor Thränen kaum sehen können um mitzuspielen".'[1]

Arrangements this year for the Northlands term were formidable; there were two series of lectures, on Tuesday and Thursday afternoons of each week—the Tuesday series being given by Roger Fry on *The Imaginative Content of Painting* and the Thursday series by Tovey on *The Orchestral Works of Beethoven*. Every fourth week there was a concert instead of a lecture. There was also the series of Woking concerts, arranged by Lady Betty Balfour, every Friday in February. This meant that Tovey had to play or lecture—during February at least—on every Wednesday, Thursday, and Friday, with, more often than not, a completely different programme each night. It was during this month that the scurrilous article, 'The Most Holy Kingdom of Tovey' appeared (see p. 123).

Miss Weisse's diary this spring contains the following entries (the complete list is much longer):

'*March* 5–7. D. F. T. to Lampeter. [To see his aunt and cousins in Wales.]

'*March* 9. Mr. Fry's last lecture, D. F. T. to Fisher's Hill [Lord Balfour's home] Mar. 9th and 10th.

'*March* 13–14. D. F. T. to Crabbet Park.[2]

'*March* 15–17. D. F. T. to Mr Kelly's.

'*March* 18. D. F. T.'s last lecture—and at 7 p.m. Oxford and Cambridge Musical Club.

'*March* 21. D. F. T. at Haslemere [concert].

'*March* 27–29. D. F. T. to Ridgehurst [To visit the Speyers].

'*March* 31. Newcastle [concert].'

Clearly no one could maintain perfect concert technique— to say nothing of writing an opera—under such pressure.

---

[1] 'That was no rehearsal; he played, and I could hardly see my own music for tears.'

[2] This was the house of Wilfred Scawen Blunt, poet and Egyptologist, whose passion for the East was such that he often wore full Arab dress at home. His charming wife was a granddaughter of Lord Byron; his daughter married Neville Lytton, the painter—a friend of Tovey's.

During Easter 1909 Tovey spent a fortnight in Holland with the Trevelyans and laid the foundation of his lifelong friendship with Julius Röntgen, his wife (who was Mrs. Trevelyan's sister), and his lively family. His first meeting with the Dutch composer had been in 1899 when, on his way home from Germany with Miss Weisse, he visited Amsterdam to hear the Joachim Quartet, and Joachim had brought his shy protégé forward to play at an evening party. The friendly, happy atmosphere of the Dutch home, where music was the natural means of intercourse, was a very congenial one; and there was also some blessed leisure to discuss points about the opera with Trevelyan. 'I long to see you and to thank you for the good his Dutch visit did to Donald', wrote Miss Weisse to Mrs. Trevelyan after Tovey returned; adding, however, 'though even already I think his work on *Ariadne* is beginning to tire him again a little'. A shower of postcards from composer to librettist—obviously written in the highest spirits—indicates that, far from tiring him, the opera was threatening again to absorb all his interests—and this was just at the beginning of the summer concert season.

One of the features of this season was the début of Joachim's nieces, Adila and Jelly d'Aranyi. When they, with their older sister Hortense (an excellent pianist), came to settle in London after their uncle's death, Miss Weisse showed them great kindness; they often stayed at Northlands, and were helped and coached by Tovey. The younger sisters, now on the threshold of their great careers, were 'in love with everyone, and everyone in love with them'. They came completely under the spell of the English musician, so beloved of their uncle, who 'made them sit up and practise like one o'clock', and who looked at times so finely handsome and at times so like a nervous schoolboy.

The d'Aranyis afforded an excellent pretext for keeping Tovey at Northlands—and Miss Weisse insisted that it was of critical importance that the girls should work with him. She bitterly resented the suggestion that 'The Shiffolds' was the only place where Tovey could really work at the opera; in any case she wanted him to put it aside for the time being. 'I hope more than

I can say', she wrote in the summer to Mrs. Trevelyan, 'that he will *practise* the piano regularly again. It is absolutely urgent that he should—though he is not nearly well enough yet for me to worry him by telling him how much important people are saying to me about the obvious evidences of his not doing so;—they don't spare me—and I hear it only too clearly myself in his playing.' She schemed, therefore, in a fashion which she probably regretted in later years, to get him to Germany that summer —well aware that there must be some very definite reason to make him go. 'It is so delightful', says her next letter, 'that Schotts have bought three more of Donald's things today! I do hope his visit to them will come off successfully'—he could not, of course, afford to refuse to go to see his publishers in Germany. Unhappily there is every reason for believing that Schotts did not on this occasion buy the works, and that Miss Weisse arranged for their publication. It was a cruel deception, for Tovey had set his face against publishing his works at his own expense —believing that, if they were worth while, publishers would take them. It was some years before he ascertained the truth about these transactions, and it hurt him deeply. But Miss Weisse believed that the end justified the means—and the end was the preservation of her beloved adopted son's career as a pianist and as a composer.

He did succeed in spending part of August at 'The Shiffolds', working on Act II of the opera. Early in September Miss Weisse wrote to Mrs. Trevelyan from Munich, where Tovey had joined her for the Brahmsfest: 'I have heard two numbers of the *Ring* and *Parsifal* and a performance of the Ninth Symphony which made me ache to hear Donald conducting it, . . . of course I am *eagerly* looking forward to the second act of Donald's opera. I only hope I may hear it several times. As far as I know I have only heard the first act once all through. I often really have not time during the terms at Northlands, and I have seen practically nothing of Donald for the last eighteen months. We *must* arrange that when next he is working at it, you and Bobbie must come to us. It will be a great thing to get it finished and out of the way.'

The most important event of the autumn was the first public association between Donald Tovey and Pablo Casals—two of the greatest musicians of their generation. The first concert was given in October at Northlands when the beautiful *Elegiac* Variations for pianoforte and 'cello, which Tovey had written in memory of Hausmann, were performed for the first time. A second concert followed in Oxford, and the collaboration between the two artists proved so congenial that two concerts were arranged for the next London season. The concerts with Casals in the autumn of 1909 were probably the happiest and most stimulating musical experience in Tovey's life since the last occasion on which he had played with Joachim, and they marked the beginning of another long friendship between two musicians who held each other in the highest esteem.

The constant interruptions to the work on the opera began to tell more severely on the librettist than on the composer, and matters reached a crisis in the Christmas vacation of 1909, when Tovey failed to fulfil a promise to visit the Trevelyans because Miss Weisse had made other engagements for him. It is indeed a measure of the great belief which both the poet and his wife had in him, and of their generous and affectionate understanding both of his nature and of his circumstances, that the friendship and collaboration did not there and then break down for good. When Tovey realized how serious the situation was, he endeavoured—at what cost one can only guess—to make it clear to Miss Weisse that she must no longer interfere to such an extent in his affairs.

He wrote penitently:

'Dear Poet,

I'm very sorry indeed that things have fallen through thus. It is perhaps rather more difficult for me to steer my course than you might imagine; but I will try and not inconvenience you again by making vague plans I can't execute.

'Meanwhile unless you wire to the contrary I shall descend on you tomorrow for the afternoon. I have a new fiddle sonata

on a plan which in several respects has not been done before.'
[Mrs. Trevelyan was an excellent amateur violinist.]

'As soon as I know when I shall have to be in Germany for
the Darmstadt Kammermusikfest I will make some plan for the
next holidays in which (if you will once more lend your aid)
there shall be no indecision.'

But his own extremely 'defective sense of non-musical time'
perpetually obscured from him the length of the gaps which
intervened between one period of absorbed composition and the
next—gaps which were so very trying to Trevelyan, who found
it difficult in the intervals to concentrate on other work.

He spent Easter at 'The Shiffolds'. 'I hope so much now that
the opera will be achieved', wrote Miss Weisse to Mrs. Trevelyan
—having capitulated completely for the moment; 'we need a
new beautiful thing so much and it will be good for Donald to
get a steady pull of work and forget other things.' The 'other
things' were the first serious clashes with the Classical Concerts
Committee, which had shaken him deeply and roused that
furious anger which Miss Weisse rightly believed to be so bad
for his health, precipitating the most distressing attacks of
nervous eczema.

His playing had recovered its old form during the spring, and
the two concerts with Casals in June were so immediately successful that a third was arranged at the beginning of July.
'Together Messrs Tovey and Casals make a fine pair of concert-
givers', said the critic of the *Daily Telegraph*. 'Their ensemble,
spiritual no less than physical, is beautiful, and the reverence of
their performance undoubted and genuine.' The feature of the
second concert was the first performance of the *Elegiac* Variations in London, where they made as great an impression as
they already had done in Oxford. As a result of these concerts
the Classical Concerts Society engaged both players for the first
concert of the autumn series.

Tovey was to spend August and September at 'The Shiffolds',
but illness, occasioned by the nervous strain of the past six
months and precipitated by a chill, delayed his arrival. Miss

Weisse departed reluctantly for Germany to take her annual *Kur* at Nauheim, masking the jealousy which she could not overcome with a very real anxiety for Tovey's health. Occasional references are made to the opera in his postcard correspondence with her; it had progressed as far as the beginning of Act III, and some of the previous material was being scored. '*Ariadne* is gaining enormously by scoring', he wrote in September; 'and I shall not do any more sketching except in isolated difficulties as they come. I intend now to score all the musically important places and then to make a continuous score in which the connecting links will be done *currente calamo*. Otherwise I don't see how I shall ever face the strain of 1,000 pages of scoring. How the deuce Wagner got through eleven such works, libretti and all, plus two wives and a million vitriolic controversies, the Lord only knows.'

'During his visits to us', says Trevelyan's account, 'while I was writing and revising the libretto, he always brought with him the full score of several operas, which he used to play through to us in the evening, singing all the voice parts, and producing for the sopranos a quite effective falsetto. Among these operas, I remember, were *Figaro*, *The Magic Flute*, and *Die Entführung*, *Fidelio*, Cherubini's *Médée* and *Les Deux Journées*, Gluck's *Orfeo*, Méhul's *Le Jeune Sage et le Vieux Fou*, Weber's *Der Freischütz* and *Euryanthe*, Cornelius's *Barber of Bagdad*, and Verdi's *Otello*. His pretext was my education as a librettist; but it was also very characteristic of his way of approaching and solving a new and difficult artistic problem, that he should thus play through so many operas of all kinds, some of which he already knew almost by heart, learning from them all the time, as well as enjoying them and sharing his enjoyment. Though he never played to us the whole of a Wagner opera, or of Verdi's *Falstaff*, he was continually reading them to himself, always, so he told me, trying so far as possible to read them at the same tempo as if he were conducting them.

'It was quite different in the early days of his first orchestral sketches. He would then sit for hours in a room by himself, apparently browsing in volumes of the *Encyclopædia*, or in detective stories and other "illiterature", as he called it. But his mind must have been working musically all the time, struggling with obstinate problems of invention and design. When these seemed insoluble, he would go out for long solitary five-mile-an-hour walks through the woods, generally returning with some of his difficulties peripatetically solved.'

A good deal of correspondence ensued between Tovey and Trevelyan in the early autumn, before the activities of the winter season totally immersed him. The opening of the last scene gave the composer a great deal of trouble:

'Dear Poet,

I am now approaching the Satyr's song—with dread. The second stanza I have already got into a shape sufficiently musical to do as a prelude before the rise of the curtain; a *tour de force* of almost idiotic difficulty which I would not repeat even for an annuity sufficient to maintain me all my life in cultured ease with a licence to marry whom I chose whether she liked it or not.

'But the first stanza is XXXNABLE!!!!'

A comparison between the words of this song as they appear in the opera, and as they appear in the printed play is of great interest to students of literature and of music alike.[1]

Miss Weisse's diary for October reveals how completely other claims once more supplanted those of composition.

'*October* 1910 *Tue.* 11 V. H. H. [Victor Hely-Hutchinson, who as an exceptionally talented child of 8½ years of age had just begun to have lessons from Tovey, at the instance of Sir Hubert Parry and Mr Spring-Rice.]

Wed. 12 Classical Concerts Society with Casals:—rehearsal in the morning at Bechstein Hall. [This concert was an immense success and there was a crowded audience.]

Thur. 13 Concert with Casals at Northlands—Princess Christian came.

Fri. 14 Casals staying here.

[1] Tovey's compression of three lines of the poem into one enabled him to write one of the most shapely and beautiful melodies in the whole work.

Sat. 15 Casals and Donald left—D. to madrigals at Oxford, Casals to the Speyers.

Sun. 16 Balliol Sunday Concert. D. played Suite of Bach, *Wandererphantasie* etc.

Mon. 17 D. returned. Fräulein Phillipi here [a notable singer].

Tue. 18 Music in evening—Bach, D.'s Variations, Beethoven Sonata op. 102 for pfte. and cello. Princess Christian, Princess Victoria, Fräulein Phillipi here. Casals with bad cold.

Wed. 19 Casals and D. to London.

Thur. 20 Mary's Wedding [Mrs Desmond McCarthy]. Party at Lady Bath's.

Fri. 21 The children's play and fancy-dress ball.

Sat. 22 M. Geoffroy Déchaume for dinner—later Casals back from Haslemere.

Sun. 23 Casals left for London.

Mon. 24 Went to London Symphony Concert evening—D. in morning to Hugh Godley and Mr Denman.

Tue. 25 D. back from London. V. H. H.

Wed. 26 D. to Windsor and London. Classical Concerts Society Concert.

Thur. 27 D.'s lecture 4.30—most admirable. Mr Kelly here for his lesson.

This autumn saw the completion of one of the great tasks which Tovey undertook in 1905, for the eleventh edition of the *Encyclopædia Britannica* was then published. The articles on music were hailed as being among the most notable in the whole work.

After a brief visit to his father at Christmas Tovey went to Mainz for the first three weeks of the New Year, to stay with Herr Geheimrath Strecker, senior partner of the firm of Schotts. He resumed work on the opera there. 'For the last two months', he wrote to Trevelyan, 'I have been suffering from a most disquieting inability to tackle anything whatever—a thing I'm quite accustomed to in fits now and then:—but it has really got to be pretty bad this last year, especially as it coincides with most depressing feelings about music in general. I really do think the present time to be about the worst period in musical history since the 17th century. . . . However, I think I've got over the worst of it, and if I can get a successful bit of work done now, I expect I shall be all right again. Then perhaps in summer we can arrange to get the last act done together. *But* do, oh do, if you possibly can, put in an occasional week-end at Northlands. I shall have to sit pretty tight next term anyhow: one of the things that really doesn't answer with me is doing as much running about as I did last term—if only because it knocks my practising to bits.' None the less he never could realize that there were limits to the amount of work which even such as he could undertake. Sir Walter Parratt had long ago foreseen this, but his warnings had gone unheeded.

The problem about which Tovey and his librettist were exercised with regard to the last act was that of presenting Dionysus in a really convincing fashion—no mere *deus ex machina*, but the inevitable climax to Ariadne's tragedy, and the appointed means of her apotheosis. Tovey always had a vivid sense of the visual aspect of opera and of the relevance of stage 'business', and he was full of suggestions and schemes—and quite as ready to make fun of his own suggestions. 'I shall have to make Dionysus visible before the climax; otherwise his invisibility will become a bore. The thing to think of is a gradual diorama effect:—I believe that the Keeper of the Home for Lost Cats in Chester is considered rather an authority on the subject. A Dionysiac smile might appear in the sky'—(Ariadne has already mentioned the 'smile of dawn')—'to be gradually surrounded by the rest of the smiler.'

The visit to Mainz was stimulating. 'I've heard a good many operas', says another postcard. 'Within a radius not twice the size of London are four provincial towns, Darmstadt, Mainz, Wiesbaden and Frankfurt, in which you get a much-better-than-Beecham opera every day, and pay five marks for the most expensive seats. The singing is curate's eggs—(when the eggs were opened the birds began to sing) but the orchestra, conducted by nobody in particular, is most respectable and could be made into anything you please. So much for German institutions. Of course it doesn't pay,—but it is considered as much a necessity as the electric light, the churches and the tramcars. Imagine Salisbury and Winchester with institutions of this kind!

'I think the whole performance of *Lohengrin* was many times better than the one we saw ages ago at Munich', he wrote also to Miss Weisse. 'One thing struck me very forcibly. You remember the childish place before the last scene, when the nobility and gentry of Antwerp blow trumpets on horseback all over the stage. Well, here (as the Geheimrath explained to me, simply because the Mainzer Droschkenpferd suffers from stage-fright) they do this with the curtain down; and the effect is first-rate. The passage happens to be well constructed musically, and it's a blessed relief to be able to listen to it without being bothered by a set of rampant chess-men charging into a frightened chorus. And they chose exactly the right moment to raise the curtain, viz., when the key of the king's trumpets is reached, and the excellent theme that pulls the passage together comes to its third and last statement. The moral is that the prospects for my *sinfonia-eroica* between the Labyrinth scenes are decidedly good.' (This refers to the episode of the slaying of the Minotaur by Theseus, which occurs while the scene vanishes in complete darkness, the orchestra illustrating the incident meanwhile.)

Herr Geheimrath Strecker thought favourably of Tovey's opera, of which he had already seen early sketches. But Miss Weisse still had her doubts, and if she discounted Tovey's hopeful prediction that it would be finished by the summer of 1911, events proved her to be right.

9

THE decision of the Classical Concerts Society to run a spring series of concerts on Wednesdays from January to March 1911, debarred the Chelsea concerts from their accustomed dates. Tovey was greatly vexed about this, and although he was engaged to play at three of its concerts his relations with the Classical Concerts Committee became increasingly uncomfortable, until he finally severed his connexion with it in the following summer.

The spring term at Northlands involved, besides concerts, a series of important lectures on the B minor Mass (which were remembered vividly by Lady Barlow). In spite of the distraction of other work, however, the opera continued to engage his attention, and correspondence with Trevelyan—mostly on postcards covered with minute writing—was very lively for a few months. Miss Weisse could not but admit that Tovey showed renewed vigour, but she had lost what faith she had in the opera, and was now convinced that the proper thing to do was to get *all* his completed works published as soon as possible, so that his recognition as a composer need not be further delayed. To that end she was—without divulging the real basis of the business to Tovey—in touch with Willy Strecker, son of the Geheimrath, and at that time London representative of the firm of Schott & Co.

During Easter Tovey was again in Germany, and Miss Weisse wrote to Mrs. Trevelyan: 'I wonder if *you* know how the opera is going on? I get more and more anxious as half-year follows half-year and there is nothing to show for it. I feel it is almost impossible to know what I ought to do. A struggle for existence would *perhaps* have made Donald put out more of the kind of work he is best fitted to do—far more probably in his case it would have destroyed him. However, if only this thing is drawing towards completion I shall breathe freely again—for I never have the least doubt of Donald's real greatness as an artist and would do everything in the world that is good for him to back him up. He is playing quite splendidly. . . . Of course he cannot help knowing that I mind the apparent loss of these five precious years very much—though I am hoping it is only apparent. . . .

'He is seeing a good deal of Miss Kelly I fancy just now, and has written a few songs for her. How I wish a *lovely* planet could be created to receive the Kellys both, and leave Donald in peace in this dark vale. Though I do like what little I know of Miss Kelly so very much that if *only* she were poor and would marry him and help on his work, I should be the happiest "Schwieger-mama" possible.'

Concerts during the summer season involved a number of appearances with Casals, and the Chelsea series now took place in May, coinciding unfortunately with the opening of the London 'season' and being somewhat eclipsed thereby. A house-party at Northlands after the concert on 11 May included Casals, the Röntgens, the Trevelyans, and Adila and Jelly d'Aranyi. Gatherings such as this suggested to Miss Weisse her next project on Tovey's behalf—namely, the building of a convenient house for him in the ample grounds of Northlands. (This was completed in the following year.) Among other visitors to Northlands during May and June 1911, were Mme Noordewier, the Dutch singer, M. Fleury, Harriet Cohen, Hugo Bell (brother of Gertrude Bell), and Yvette Guilbert and her husband. Miss Weisse's diary also notes: '*June* 23. To view Coronation Progress.'

As soon as his concert engagements were over Tovey plunged into work on the opera again. Term at Northlands was not yet over, so he could only pay flying visits to 'The Shiffolds', showering postcards of suggestions, alterations, and requests on his librettist between whiles; one of these is labelled 'No. 4 of to-day's issue'. A casual impression of this protracted correspondence would be that this was the fussiest way of handling a libretto, but in truth the manner in which Tovey worked over every single word and detail was characteristic, 'I can only set what I *know*' he said over and over again, and that meant that he must understand every possible implication in each situation and visualize exactly the action on the stage. He knew, too, that he was very fortunate in his librettist: 'Another of my finicking suggestions which please forgive', says one card: 'It helps my *Auffassungsvermögen* to make them and doesn't in the least oblige you to adopt them.' In Trevelyan he found a poet of the same artistic temperament: endlessly patient in seeking exactly the right word and the right rhythm to express truly that which had been conceived in the white-heat of inspiration. But to have to do this through the medium of the penny (or rather halfpenny) post *was* trying.

It is not surprising that Mr. Hilaire Belloc received no replies to the letters he wrote to Tovey during June. He endeavoured to get an answer, as did so many others, via Miss Weisse: 'Dear Madam [he wrote],

'Some time ago I wrote to Mr Tovey suggesting that he should send me the score of the music that he has written to illustrate my Children's Verses. These settings of his are very much admired and quoted, but they have never been published. If published, both he and I, I think, could make a considerable sum.

'I wonder whether you would be kind enough to let me know your views and his upon the matter?'

Miss Weisse was in no doubt about her views, but it is unlikely that she was able to give Belloc Tovey's views at that moment. However flippant he might often appear to be in his correspondence with Trevelyan, he was then in no mood for *The Bad Child's Book of Beasts*; the songs had never been written down, and he was not in the least inclined to spare time to do so. How unfortunate it was that the suggestion came at the wrong moment, for the clever and amusing songs are now completely lost.

Other things of this kind—like the music for *Sylvie and Bruno*, and what Lady Fisher calls the 'perfect tune' for 'You are old, Father William'—*had* been committed to paper years before for family performances at the Warre-Cornishes, but the scraps of paper vanished with the schoolroom 'properties'. A setting of

'My aged Uncle Arly', in an incredibly neat hand, is the only manuscript which survives in evidence of these witty offshoots of Tovey's genius.

Tovey's plans for spending the rest of the summer with the Trevelyans were suddenly complicated by an invitation to visit Casals in Spain in September. Much as he wished to get the opera finished, the stimulus of further contact with the greatest artist he had known since Joachim was too precious to forgo entirely. Early in September, however, a terrible epidemic of cholera broke out in Catalonia and the Spanish visit was abandoned. Casals and his wife, Guilhermina Suggia, were able with some difficulty to get out of Spain, and Tovey paid his promised visit to them in Paris later in the month.

'Chère Miss Weisse [wrote Mme Casals],

Ces quelques lignes pour vous dire le bonheur que nous éprouvons d'avoir la visite de Monsieur Tovey; nous passons des heures délicieuses et je sens le besoin de vous le dire. . . . Nous avons avec sa visite une belle récompense du temps que nous avons perdu en Espagne à cause de ce terrible choléra, mais j'espère que l'année prochaine il viendra chez nous à S. Salvador, et pour plus longtemps.

'Mon mari a des projets de donner des concerts avec lui à Barcelona, à Wien et à Paris cette saison. Ce sera pour moi un bonheur de les entendre autant que possible ensemble. Et bien, chère Miss Weisse, soyez tranquille, nous veillerons sur lui.'

On his return from Paris the preparation of manuscripts for Schotts perforce occupied much of Tovey's time and attention, and Miss Weisse's plans for the publication of his chamber music began to bear fruit in October, when Strecker reported that he had just received the manuscripts of the sonata for pianoforte and 'cello and of the pianoforte quintet. A month later he sent Tovey the proofs of the clarinet sonata along with the two arrangements of the same—for piano and violin, and for piano and viola, which had been made by the composer. But Strecker was not happy about the enterprise, and in January begged

Miss Weisse to let Tovey know the facts: 'You will remember', he wrote to her, 'that I was from the very beginning of the opinion that he ought to know, and that it would be much fairer for you to get the credit of what you are doing, and for us not to be put in the wrong by it.

'I disliked bringing out all the previous work without paying him a copyright fee which would adequately correspond to the artistic value and the enormous amount of work and time which he had put into them, but it lies in the nature of the works that the sale will be very limited, especially at first, and it was because of our strong conviction of the artistic merit of his works that we undertook the publication. . . . While our interest in Donald is stronger than ever, we have had such an enormous amount of new enterprises and capital investments, that we shall have, for the next few years, to employ our entire printing establishment in carrying out certain works in our general publishing line.

'You and I were both of the opinion that it was of the utmost importance for Donald's career that his works should now be on the market, and within the reach of every artist and performer, and it is only by bringing out as soon as possible a certain number of his most important works that the world can recognise his position as a composer. . . . By your kind assistance we shall avoid losing valuable time and missing the right moment.

'These considerations were what guided us when our arrangement was made, and I am sure if you explain this to Donald he will see the position, and cannot possibly feel hurt in any way in his artistic pride.'

It was, of course, too late for any such explanation; Miss Weisse knew that only too well and over-rode all Strecker's objections. Proof-correcting and the overhauling of manuscripts meanwhile held up work on the opera once again. 'When I get through Phaedra's scene', he wrote to Trevelyan, 'I shall overhaul my last pianoforte trio before tackling the rest. Then I hope it will go with some zest.'

In November 1911 Tovey played the Brahms B flat Concerto

in public for the first time with the London Symphony Orchestra, under the conductorship of Sir Edward Elgar. A few years earlier Elgar had written to Tovey asking for a copy of all his analytical essays, adding that, as he was representing every English composer by one score in his library, he would like also to have a copy of Tovey's pianoforte concerto, 'or any other work you consider more representative'. In acknowledging the essays, on characteristically large and handsome note-paper, Elgar added 'they will be bound at once with 24 pages of "nice" (horrible word) writing paper for your index'. The performance of the Brahms Concerto was the only occasion on which these two English musicians collaborated in public. The combination was not a particularly happy one. 'On the one hand', says *The Times*, 'we had Mr Tovey whose view of Brahms is entirely the introspective one of the scholar, and on the other Sir Edward Elgar who seemed to lack confidence in combining the orchestral music and the solo instrument.' In regard to the music of Brahms they were indeed poles apart. The critic also complains that the pianist's tone was thin in the climaxes and lacking in colour, though he praises the slow movement and finale. This was a concerto which in later years Tovey made peculiarly his own, and no one who heard his performances in Edinburgh could ever forget the magnificence of his playing.

A recital with Casals for the Classical Concerts Society two days after the Brahms performance was followed by another (with, of course, a different programme) the next day at Northlands. This was succeeded immediately by the first of four weekly lectures at Oxford, and so the familiar round began again. It seemed, however, that this autumn Tovey began to feel that he was treading in a groove—indeed in an ever-narrowing groove—which must always circle around Northlands. He was still vexed and sore at his break with Speyer and the circumstances of his quarrel with the Classical Concerts Committee—although he continued to fulfil such engagements as they offered. London was stifling him, and he longed for the more stimulating contacts of continental musical life.

He spent some weeks at Christmas with friends at Cannes where, although proofs might follow him and practice might be necessary, it was possible to relax some of the accumulated tension. The opera, of course, went with him, and he spent some time writing part of the final scene of the last act, which had hitherto only been sketched, and was now 'getting on like a house on fire'.

Trouble which had been brewing over Victor Hely-Hutchinson's lessons came to a head during this holiday, and Tovey received a letter from Sir Walter Hely-Hutchinson telling him that the Headmaster of Heatherdown had issued an ultimatum to the effect that either Victor's lessons with Tovey must cease or the boy must be withdrawn from the school. This school was only six miles from Northlands, and the Headmaster, whose letters show him to have been an incredibly conceited and arrogant prig with a narrow pedagogic outlook, hated Miss Weisse whole-heartedly and did his utmost to discredit Tovey in Sir Walter's eyes. With characteristic rashness Tovey had put himself in an awkward position. The Headmaster had refused after the first term to send the boy to Northlands for lessons, and Tovey had agreed to visit Heatherdown once a fortnight on condition that young Victor's work was supervised meanwhile by the school music master, who was also supposed to be present during Tovey's lessons. These conditions were not carried out by the school, and the fact that Tovey had occasion once or twice to cancel a lesson because of a concert engagement was made the grounds of complaint.

Victor Hely-Hutchinson was a very remarkable and talented boy and Tovey was aware of this, but he was determined not to play the part of 'an exotic music-master' at Heatherdown any longer. In his reply to Sir Walter he remarks: 'If my proposal about weekly visits to me on Monday afternoons seems to you or the Headmaster a large demand on Victor's school-time, I would remind you that at any school, preparatory or public, he is bound to race to the top of every form and remain for two years unoccupied as head boy: while on the other hand it will be quite easy to keep him occupied with the higher branches of composition till his school-days are over. . . . Meanwhile it is extremely important that his pianoforte playing should be taken in hand: it is far behind his composition in refinement and sensibility, and if it is allowed to run riot it will be a most enervating drain on his whole organisation, and will go far to spoil his ear. It is not a question of whether it is desirable for him to be a great executant:—nothing will stop his facility from asserting itself. What is quite certain is that it will do him no good unless it is brought under conditions of absolute accuracy. I am ready to go to great inconvenience in so important a case, if I can only get a proper handle over it; and I would therefore sacrifice my weekly day's teaching in London. More than one fixture a week I cannot possibly undertake; but if it's a choice between Victor and half-a-dozen amateur lady pianists it's no choice at all.' The Headmaster's efforts to discredit Tovey failed entirely, but Tovey thereafter gave young Victor lessons in holiday-times and cemented a lasting friendship with the family and with his pupil.

A real break in the groove was provided by a visit to Budapest in February 1912 to give a recital with Casals. 'He seems to have given such satisfaction', wrote Miss Weisse to Trevelyan, 'that they immediately asked him to play again in an orchestral concert on March 2nd. So there he is, and I think in very good spirits. They give him quite *large* monies, and he is seeing people and shaking off some of the parochial worries of London.' In the orchestral concert he played, with Casals and Enesco, Beethoven's Triple Concerto, a neglected work for which he had a particular liking, and which he could make completely convincing.

He stopped in Vienna *en route* for Budapest and wrote to Trevelyan: 'With fountain-pen and thirty-six hours of railway I found it possible to get quite a good grip of *Ariadne* again, and I hope to be on the threshold of the finale in the course of my return journey. . . .

'Yesterday—a performance of *Faust* (first part) in a small theatre. I had no idea it could be made so effective and coherent.

And, crikey! what a tongue Mr Goethe had! Absurdly interesting to compare his effectiveness with Gounod's and Berlioz's; and I, in my *ungebildet* professional way, began to note the thousand and one ways in which things on the stage can be infinitely more moving without music. . . . My respect for Goethe as a dramatist has gone up immensely. . . .

'From the progress in Mozart's operas I have already learned that the connexion between one scene (or aria) and the next is only the first step in vitalizing the drama: e.g. when I first read *Idomeneo* I thought it worthy of Gluck as music-drama, plus all Mozart's musical greatness. And I put its ultimate ineffectiveness down to the libretto. As a matter of fact the libretto isn't half bad; and what had impressed me as so dramatic in the music was the fact that the beginnings and ends of almost every item were dramatically inspired. *But* inside each number is a whole set structure of undigested concert-music in which the form has no rhetorical force. . . . I'm beginning to see now that perfection of form, desirable as it is, is never historically or aesthetically prior to rhetorical fitness: in fact it is rhetoric on a vast scale. Get the rhetoric to ring true and the truth brings logic and inevitability into the whole structure, while the rhetoric forces the surprises and contrasts into the foreground, and so makes the whole work true to Nature, in which facts are never presented in their logical order.

'Bow-wow. Similar instructions may be had from the same firm in six grades of which this is No. 2. To be taken twice daily before meals.'

He often made fun of himself like this, when he felt he had been dogmatizing too freely.

The libretto of the opera was now in the printer's hands, and it was published as a play early in summer. 'I've just seen the review in the *Nation*', Tovey wrote in July, 'excellent for both of us—I don't see how it could be better. How very well done and arranged. If there's one thing I envy it's that kind of skill in essay-writing.'

During the months of February and March of that year Kelly

made his long-delayed début in London with three recitals, two
of which took place while Tovey was abroad. Tovey's resignation from the Classical Concerts Society had, of course, meant a
fresh rift in his friendship with Kelly, but he was none the less
anxious for the success of Kelly's first London appearances. On
his return he wrote to Trevelyan 'Thank heaven I've heard
from Hugh Godley (to whom I wrote in great agitation from
Budapest) that Kelly's second concert was nothing like what
Miss Weisse's account made of it; . . . sympathy for misfortune
is the deadliest weapon a self-deceiving hostility can forge. . . .
If I had been sure of my ground I certainly would have gone to
hear him yesterday; but, with all Miss Weisse's bitterness towards him, there was too much chance of her having been fairly
right for me to take the risk. Most of the papers seem to be fairly
good, but it is very unfortunate that the only really bad criticism
comes from the *Westminster*, which has recently taken to standing
up for me:—so I suppose it's now my turn to be suspected of
having "got at" the Press! Lord—what a world we live in!'

This letter disturbed Trevelyan considerably, for it showed
how dangerously the stresses of the past five years were reacting
on his friend. In spite of his scrupulous dislike of interfering in
the least degree with the affairs of other people he felt obliged
to remonstrate. 'I am glad', he wrote to Tovey, 'that you take
a hopeful view about Kelly's concerts. No doubt the second was
less well attended than the first, and very likely he played pro-
portionately less well. But I am sure nobody would suspect you
of having "got at" the *Westminster*, neither Kelly, nor anyone
else. Of course you only meant it as a joke; but it does show a
state of mind that is a pity. . . . I have a feeling that however
trying Speyer's, or anyone else's, conduct may have been, even
taking the worst view of it, and however desirable it now may
be for you to be rid of the Classical Concerts and give yourself
up to your own concerts under better auspices,—that all the
same you do not take things quite in the best way for your own
happiness and peace of mind, nor ultimately for your own energy
and health as an artist. To allow hostility and injustice to em-

bitter one, or unreasonably to affect one's peace of mind, is to allow it just the triumph over one which it does not deserve. Bitterness, even apparently justified bitterness, seems to me more and more the greatest evil in life, at least of those evils we are able to some extent ourselves to control. . . . I do not know how to say what I feel at the right time, and in the right way, and when I write it, like Balaam's Ass, I can only preach. But I would not mind your likening me to that animal, so long as that would make you see the angel of the Lord standing in the way.' Trevelyan also dreaded the way in which Miss Weisse worked herself up into unreasoning states of hostility and jealousy, and the extent to which she still could exert influence over Tovey.

During this spring, very fortunately, another new friendship entered Tovey's life. Young Adolf Busch came to London to play the Brahms Violin Concerto under Steinbach. He went to stay at Oxford with the Denekes,[1] and Tovey was invited to meet him. 'The friendship between him and Adolf was established as soon as they had played half-a-dozen sonatas together', writes Miss Deneke. 'One night the two sat up till the early hours of the morning going through Adolf's MSS. songs: the next day Adolf poured upon me his amazement at Donald's insight. Another day Donald started the opening tutti of the Beethoven Concerto hoping to lure Adolf to the Music Room. He succeeded; Adolf arrived, breathlessly unpacked his fiddle and tuned quickly. We were all wondering how long the orchestral part could be sustained without any music; Donald played the Concerto to the end.' This feat greatly impressed Busch, and on his return to Germany he arrived early one morning at his brother's house, and greeted him with the words, 'Wake up, Fritz; I have found a genius in England'.

The Committee of the Chelsea concerts had meanwhile decided that if these concerts must needs be given during the

[1] The hospitable home of Mr. and Mrs. Deneke was a focus of music in Oxford. Tovey had soon gravitated there and had formed a lasting friendship with all the members of the household.

London season, they must be removed to a hall in the West End
if they were to maintain their importance. Retaining the title
of 'Chelsea concerts' a series of five was given during April and
May 1912 in the Aeolian Hall. Casals took part in two of these
concerts, and an item of particular interest was the Brahms
Clarinet Trio played by Tovey, Charles Draper, and Casals.
Miss Weisse had been instrumental in securing the services of
Strecker as business manager for these concerts, and thereafter
until 1914 he acted, in a limited capacity, as concert agent for
Tovey. In him Miss Weisse made a wise choice—albeit too late
—because, although he was a business man and wished to see
the concerts on a financially sound basis, he was not the ordinary
entrepreneur and he rated music above the box-office. He was
probably the only person with whom Tovey—at this rather
intolerant and disturbed period of his life—could have dealt
as a manager.

It was Miss Weisse's custom to give a musical party every
year at Northlands on Tovey's birthday, but this year the entry
in her diary on 17 July records 'Donald's Housewarming'. 'The
Pantiles', as the new house was called, had been planned with
much care and affection by Miss Weisse. It was a charming
house with a pleasant music room and study on the first floor
from which an outside stone staircase led into the garden, so
that when Tovey felt disposed at any hour of the day or night
to 'take his compositions for a walk' he could escape quietly
without going through the house. It seemed ideal—and yet it
was one more fetter binding him to Northlands—a 'golden
cage', as some of his friends bitterly called it.

Miss Weisse was more than usually tired when she left for her
Kur in the middle of August. Tovey went to Spain to spend a
month with Casals and his wife in Vendrell.

It was during this visit that Tovey's father was taken ill.
'Chère Miss Weisse,' wrote Casals on 16 September 1912, 'Ce
mot pour vous dire que Donald est plus tranquille; les premières
nouvelles de son père l'avaient éprouvé—mais les suivantes de
plus en plus rassurantes lui ont fait du bien.

TOM SPRING-RICE, D. F. TOVEY, F. SPEYER, AND ANOTHER
(1898–9)

SIR WALTER PARRATT, VICTOR HELY-HUTCHINSON, D. F. TOVEY
(*c.* 1912)

MISS WEISSE, JOHN TOVEY, D. F. TOVEY, AND SANDY (SPRING 1925)

'Il a beaucoup travaillé—pour des vacances un peu trop peut-être, mais il se porte bien.' 'In spite of the heat I never felt better in my life', wrote Tovey. 'Exercise consists in disturbing the waters of the Mediterranean. The piano is marvellously out of tune.'

Soon after this a great misfortune—indeed a near tragedy—occurred, when serious personal differences arose suddenly between Casals and Tovey. Guilhermina Suggia was then a young woman at the height of her beauty, if not yet at the height of her powers as an artist. Maybe she played with fire—maybe the hot Mediterranean summer had a disturbing effect on the finely balanced emotional poise of three ultra-sensitive people—and certainly Tovey showed that unhappy lack of *Menschenkenntnis* which Miss Weisse had long deplored. He idealized his friends—the more so when they were musicians of such calibre, and was deeply disturbed when he found that human nature has a distressing way of conflicting with the ideal. Moreover, he lost his sense of proportion more disastrously than a more worldly person might have done: the affair of the Classical Concerts Society had already made this evident. That there was no *real* cause for a quarrel did not make it any the less bitter, and the Englishman had quite as hot a temper as the Spaniard.

Then, on 29 September, the Rev. Duncan Crookes Tovey died at Guildford. As he had apparently been recovering from his illness, Tovey was ill-prepared for the shock of his death, and it came at a moment when he was in any case exceedingly unhappy. His mood came very near to despair, and he was far from fit to appear at the concerts for which he had been engaged during the autumn. There was, of course, no question that the engagements with Casals could be fulfilled, and, except for a recital with Madame Soldat on 1 November, Tovey dropped out of the Classical Concerts Society's programmes.

Driven by a desire to get things clear, and encouraged by well-meant but ill-advised friends, Tovey made further efforts to straighten out his misunderstanding with Casals. He rushed off to Liverpool, where Casals was playing; but, instead of attempting to see him, Tovey spent the evening in his room at the hotel, drafting a long and elaborate letter, in which he endeavoured to explain clearly his point of view. Expressions of anger and grief, and explanations which would have sounded natural and spontaneous in the spoken word, were thus frozen into an unnatural stiffness, and the letter could not possibly have been answered by anything else than the short, formal reply which came from Casals, closing the incident.

It would have been a real loss to the world of music if this unhappy triangular quarrel had permanently estranged three such artists—as everyone then thought it must do. Happily it was not so, and after Tovey became Reid Professor, Casals played many times with him in Edinburgh. The renewed friendship between the two men was warm and lasting, and, indeed, touching in Tovey's last years. On the occasion of Casals' last appearance in Edinburgh—before politics robbed the world of its greatest 'cellist, but after Tovey's death—he visited the flat in Buccleuch Place where his friend had lived. There, sitting at the beautiful old Bösendorfer piano which had come from Northlands, he played, with that wonderfully expressive touch which he has on the keyboard, the opening of the 'cello concerto —Tovey's last work, dedicated to him. 'He was the greatest musician we had,' he said, with tears standing in his eyes. Tovey's portrait still hangs above the famous 'cellist's desk in Prades.

Miss Weisse was inclined at first to minimize the importance of Tovey's quarrel with Casals, and to imply that he had been victimized by friends whose Latin temperament had misconstrued his perfectly innocent behaviour. But when she found that the shock was having most grievous effects on Tovey's work and health she became desperately anxious about him, and—later—extremely angry with him.

'Donald has just called to bring me the final proofs of his works which will now at last be ready for printing', wrote Strecker in November to Miss Weisse; 'he promises to send more to-morrow or the following day. I hope he will, for work is the best cure for his other troubles. . . . We must try to get him quiet now, and create for him as little worry over the thing as possible. This can only be done when one lets him act according to his conscience, and he will only that way be calmed and really relieved.' But Tovey was disturbed and irritable beyond endurance, and Miss Weisse was glad when he went off at the end of November to Vienna to represent Oxford at the Centenary of the *Gesellschaft der Musikfreunde*. This opportunity he owed to Sir Walter Parratt, who, being unable to go himself, suggested Tovey in his place, in a kindly desire to get him away from the trouble that was obsessing him, and the gossip which the ill-disposed were only too ready to spread. Professor Röntgen was one of the Dutch representatives at this ceremony, and the presence of this trusted and kindly friend did much to help Tovey in his distress.

Postcards arrived to Miss Weisse from Vienna: 'Had tea with the Mandyczewskis. They ask eagerly after you. Charming postcard from Busch arranging lots of things. Schalk asks me to lunch on Thursday.'

'Oh dear, what a lot of unnecessary trouble Sonnleithner, the librettist, gave poor guileless Beethoven, who didn't know enough of the stage to protest. But Sonnleithner founded this *Gesellschaft der Musikfreunde*, so there was an expedition yesterday to lay wreaths on his grave! I was elsewhere.'

The apparent high spirits of these staccato postcards concealed his real state of mind, as Miss Weisse was well aware, and she brooded incessantly on the situation, which was disturbing enough without magnifying and distorting it out of all reason. When Tovey returned from Vienna in mid-December Miss Weisse wrote to Mrs. Trevelyan that he was white-faced and strained-looking and completely estranged from her. 'He has been and still is ill, and must be treated like an invalid if he is to recover and have a free mind again.' But Northlands at that moment must have been the worst place in the world for anyone suffering from nervous exhaustion. Fortunately, he spent Christmas in Wales at the home of the delightful aunt who had become a Welsh Bard.

Early in January 1913 Tovey went to Aachen to play his pianoforte concerto under Fritz Busch who had just been appointed Director of Music there. It was the first occasion of a public performance with this new and congenial friend, and he was immediately asked to return for an engagement in April. Fritz Busch also proposed that he should write a symphony to be performed at Aachen as soon as possible, and the idea of a ready-made opportunity for the performance of a full-sized orchestral work was so attractive, that work on the opera—which had in any case been very intermittent since September—stopped forthwith.

Things did not promise well for his London concerts. One of his best friends, Hugh Godley, had resigned from the Chelsea Committee, and although Strecker and Miss Weisse had re-organized the series, Tovey said he thought it would be the last he would give in London. Strecker did all he could to help Tovey's reputation, and he wrote to Robin Legge, the music critic: 'I was glad to see that you mentioned in your last article Busoni's words about treating a genius well while he is alive: here, I think is a chance.' He goes on to say that most of the recognition of Tovey had come from abroad, where he could enjoy 'at least the reputation of a Reger or a César Franck', but that his modesty was almost hopeless nowadays in this country. An extra concert of Tovey's music was arranged at Northlands. 'The occasion of the playing of the string quartets and the Flute Variations is to let the Streckers—Père et Fils—hear them,' wrote Miss Weisse to Mrs. Trevelyan. 'I am more and more sure that Donald's best chance of really becoming known and taking his proper place is through these people.'

In spite of every effort, however, the London concerts were a greater financial loss this year, and Strecker wrote to Miss Weisse at the end of the season: 'I do not know what advice to give you about the continuation of the beautiful Chelsea Concerts, which strike me as being somehow or other in their present form not practical for the modern public. . . . The concerts were as beautiful as they could possibly be, and I do not see why you and Donald should bear unnecessary expense. In a big city like London there ought to be enough supporters of serious art.' But this was the end of the venture.

A month later, however, Miss Weisse received a card from Strecker with a cutting from the *Daily Telegraph* of 1 July 1913 which ran: 'I hear that Mr Donald Tovey is now creating widespread interest in Germany. Casals, the Klengler Quartet, Adolf Busch, Julius Röntgen and many more are playing the Tovey chamber-music all over the Continent. Does any compatriot of the composer ever look at his music?' Strecker's comment is 'Another result!' (i.e. of the publication of these works—arranged for by Miss Weisse.)

The symphony was due for performance at Aachen on 11 December 1913. A card to Mrs. Trevelyan says: 'I'm a miserable sinner but not a liar! I have just discovered my note to the Poet, (which I told you truly I had written last week,) *poche restante* in a coat I had changed. So I send it to Ridgehurst with ajolopies. . . . The Symphony goes well and will be out of the way by September.' But in September Miss Weisse began to be anxious lest it should not be ready. Remarking in a letter to Mrs. Trevelyan that 'Donald is ill to live wi', but oh how much "waur to want"', she then adds: 'The only thing I can do now is to hide every sign of my anxiety about this symphony. It is probably ripening quite well, and it *may* still suddenly go down on paper and be ready in time. On the other hand it may not, and then I dread the overstrain beyond anything, and the horrible consequences it has for my poor Donald and for me.' By mid-November there was still no note of the finale on paper, and there were four copyists furiously busy making the orchestral parts of the other movements. Tovey had been quite serene and equable this autumn, but he was endeavouring at last to follow the advice of the friends who said he really ought to take his concert affairs into his own hands. As he never had a vestige of

business instinct, the immediate result was the loss of a projected
tour in Holland.

He worked night and day in order to finish the symphony by
the end of November, when he was due in Germany to fulfil
various concert engagements. 'Donald has vanished into space,'
wrote Miss Weisse, 'except for a beguilingly optimistic telegram
about the superiority of German copyists. I know not one thing
about the concerts except what I heard him telling Mr Speyer.'
With the ink hardly dry on the orchestral parts, and with heroic
efforts on the part of all concerned, the symphony was produced
on the promised date by Fritz Busch. It was well received, and
Tovey felt released at last from the sense of frustration which the
collapse of the Chelsea concerts and his break with Casals had
induced. Later in December he paid visits to Steinbach in
Cologne and to Strecker in Mainz, going on to play at Vienna
early in January. 'I think all the travelling about is good for
Donald', Miss Weisse wrote. 'He is already better and engaged
on a Concerto Grosso for String Orchestra. Strange to say his
playing is in perfect order.'

During spring and early summer of 1914 plans were in train
for a more extensive German tour for the coming winter. Tovey
had abandoned his unsuccessful attempt to manage the business
arrangements in connexion with his concerts, and Miss Weisse
was in her element again and full of high hopes. The symphony
was to be performed in Berlin, Munich, and Cologne, and recitals, chamber music concerts, and concerto engagements in
Germany and Holland were fixed. The libretto of the opera was
also being translated into German, and Tovey hoped that he
would shortly be able to finish it and to have it produced by
Fritz Busch.

In April he was again in Aachen in order to play the continuo
in the *St. Matthew Passion* for Busch. The problem of filling out
Bach's continuo parts was much less understood then than it is
now, and Tovey was probably the greatest master of his time of
the art of playing from a 'figured bass'. 'Fritz asked me to give
him some particulars as to how we're going to do the continuo,'

he wrote to Miss Weisse, 'and why it is different from the usual *Gebrauch*; these particulars go *as per contract with the town,* into six local papers! He shewed me an article that was written just before he came, prophesying ruin and destruction to Aachen music if the youngster the Town Council thought fit to elect didn't shew powers quite inconceivable at his age. Apparently what Fritz then proceeded to do was to catch hold of the writer, and tell him that whoever wrote such an article shewed a tactlessness inconceivable at any age. However he's got it all his own way now.'

Then the Chair of Music in Edinburgh University fell vacant in June and Tovey applied for it. That he did so at such a juncture surprised many of his friends. Two or three years earlier, when he seemed to be falling between—not two—but many stools, Miss Weisse had suggested that he should consider the possibility of a Professorship, as offering more congenial scope for every side of his musical work; the vicissitudes of these years no doubt made him consider the attractions of such a post. But now the opportunity of building up an international reputation as pianist and composer seemed to offer itself, and, in spite of his long-felt desire for financial independence, the taking of such an eminently practical step to secure it at the risk of restricting his artistic career was very unexpected.

The testimonials which he sent in support of his application were so overwhelming and from so great a variety of distinguished men, that any university would have felt justified in accepting such a candidate on his own terms. The Chancellor of the University, Lord Balfour, was of course precluded from giving a testimonial, but his views were very generally known, and Tovey's appointment in July 1914 was a foregone conclusion. Miss Weisse, who once would have regarded this achievement with satisfaction, was shattered. She wrote to Mrs. Trevelyan: 'Donald says he is going North at once, *but* he says he is keeping to an engagement with Tom Spring-Rice on Friday, and going to the Plymouths on Saturday. I feel pretty sure he will want to go to you on Monday or Tuesday. . . . I do beg you to head him off the Opera this year and to cause him to practise. He acknowledged to Fritz Busch and me yesterday that since his first launching nothing so important has opened before him as these concerts in Germany, and that he urgently needs practice. Yet here he is—insisting on giving an autumn term in Edinburgh, insisting on working at his opera—and he has neither practised nor re-written his symphony, and Methuens are clamouring for the Beethoven book. . . . The doctor was not at all satisfied with Donald yesterday; besides all else he has a "rotten pulse". I am hoping I had been over-anxious—really I have not been nearly anxious enough.'

At the end of July Tovey saw his friend Fritz Busch off from London among crowds of other Germans who had been recalled to their country. Even then, neither he nor Miss Weisse could bring themselves to believe that there really would be war, and they parted for the summer deeply estranged by his insistence on taking up the Edinburgh appointment and imperilling the success of important concert tours. 'It is piteous', she lamented. 'And with such a really wonderful genius, more and more I know it; and so lovable. And here is a fresh flood on which he should ride into real fame and enter on his true sphere, and I can't sleep with misery to think that he will miss it by taking up this grotesque amount of other work.' Three days after Miss Weisse left for her holiday in Germany, war was declared.

This intervention of fate upset all the plans for concert tours. In retrospect the Edinburgh appointment appears as one of the most fortunate accidents in the whole of Tovey's career; it set him free at exactly the right moment, and enlarged his field of activity at a time when the circumstances of war might have diminished it. A return to the confines of Northlands and London at this juncture might easily have been disastrous for him. That Tovey realized this is evident from a letter to Trevelyan: 'My position, both now and for the next few years, is entirely saved by the Edinburgh job. The postponement of my foreign concerts, even if the Dutch ones fall through (which is by no means certain), is a very different affair as a result of a European war, from what it would be as a result of any fault or misfortune whatever. Now that my income will be indisputably the result of my own exertions, my artistic career can only gain by having to wait. . . . My attitude towards people whose policy has been animated by jealousy of Miss Weisse, is, and always will be, implacable. All my friends have known how I longed for real independence.

'There is going to be trouble in Edinburgh about the founding of a conservatoire there. I shall, as a committee-man, from the outset lay stress on the fact that the British problem of musical education is nothing compared with the problem of what to do with the musicians when you've turned them loose.'

A letter on 13 August from Peterborough, where he was staying with the Hely-Hutchinsons, told Mr. Trevelyan that news had come through Holland that Miss Weisse was safe in Hanover and that there was no immediate cause for anxiety. It continued: 'Whatever my prospects for the next three years, and whatever becomes of Fritz Busch, I can do nothing but try to work as if nothing was changed. It is *awful* trying to get on with my revision of the symphony, every note of which is Fritz's private property; but I can't afford to lose it, nor, if he comes safe through the war, could I face him without it in perfect condition. And the same applies to the opera. We must carry that on—German translation and all. . . .

'At the same time I must make a striking and solid success of my first term's work in Edinburgh. So far everything is in good order, and my time-table is in print in the University Calendar. . . . At this moment I think that the best I can do is to stay out my time here. Victor's talent is a thing of immense importance, and the problem of saving him from the appallingly bad musical taste of his people is very serious. . . . I am fairly hopeful of getting things right, for they are good people with the fine goodness one ought to understand by "breeding". But it has been a tough job; and we have in Hal Goodhart-Rendel an example of what bad feeding can do for the finest material in the world.

Both he and Victor had at ten years of age certainly more talent, better health and stronger brains than I had.'

Tovey wrote to his brother about the same time:

'Dear Duncan,

Your news is satisfactory, and it is a relief to think that duty requires the London Scottish at home. It's no use hoping this will be a short business; but I think the end is certain, as far as Prussian Junkerdom is concerned. . . . I have never yet seen a German of any intelligence who was not on the one hand convinced of the benefit of military training, and on the other filled with the utmost disgust and contempt for the military caste of his country.

'I hope we shall come out of this convinced that military arts and crafts are an education that does all that athletics professes to do, with none of the temptations to idleness, vanity and vicariousness (by which I mean the football crowd as distinguished from the players). We have made education compulsory,—and have done so on an antiquated basis that ties it to the writing desk. Why not make military craft an essential part of our education instead of calling it conscription? Military geography is the only kind of geography that can possibly mean anything to the young . . . and if we become a nation of soldiers we should still remain no more militant than the police are now. Militarism is no result of training; it's a question of character.' Then, following some biting observations on 'atrocity' stories which filled the papers, and on the treatment of a naturalized German in Peterborough, Tovey remarks that Miss Weisse will probably contrive to get out of Germany before term time, and concludes an immensely long letter 'In haste, Ever of Thee, D. F. T.' (a letter-ending which he often used when writing to intimate friends).

Tovey was anxious to have news of Busch, and wrote to Trevelyan: 'Would it be fair and right for me to send the enclosed card to the Röntgens? The temptation is so great that I really cannot tackle it myself. I'm tormented with the most childish

hopes of seeing Fritz again, and I can neither sleep nor work.'
But when news did come at the end of the month, it was that
Fritz was just going off to the front, and that some of the members of his Aachen orchestra were with him in the same regi-
ment. Miss Weisse, despite Tovey's increasing anxiety about her
and his endeavours to find a port of exit for her in Denmark
rather than Holland, arrived home in mid-September, 'stricken
with dismay'—as she wrote—'to find Donald so ill'. He was not
ill, but he *was* suffering from the mental anguish which, in times
of war, all must feel who have personal friends in the camp of
the enemy.

'Miss Weisse is in very high spirits and surprisingly good
health,' he wrote to Mrs. Trevelyan. 'She is jingo German in
cork-shooting effervescence and certainly has some extremely
important, if partisan, light on the subject. As she was under
military—not merely *diplomatic*—protection during the whole of
her travels (her little governess whom she was conveying to
Berlin is the daughter of a General), and has a German name,
she was no doubt regarded as a person to be fed carefully and
returned to England properly charged.'

IO

ON 9 October 1914 Professor Tovey delivered his Inaugural Address in the Music Classroom of Edinburgh University, appearing for the first time in his new capacity on the platform from which during the next twenty-five years he delivered such a wealth of musical teaching. At the age of 38 his tall, loosely knit figure had still something boyish about it, but his face possessed already the unmistakable stamp of the maturity of a great mind. Laszlo's portrait represents faithfully if somewhat formally the finely chiselled features, but fails to catch the visionary look in the eyes.[1]

The lecture which he proceeded to deliver—*Stimulus and the Classics of Music*—was exciting to a degree, and gave immediate and striking evidence of vital originality of outlook. Complete absence of self-consciousness and an exceptionally clear and beautiful speaking voice were two of Professor Tovey's great natural assets as a lecturer. Neither his trick of addressing his remarks to the remotest corner of the ceiling of the lofty Music Classroom, nor the occasional pauses, which in the early days proved sometimes disconcerting, were attributable to nervousness. His thoughts ranged far and fast—faster than speech—and he had a scrupulous desire to present them as completely and as accurately as possible. He never used notes, and some of these extempore lectures were even greater *tours de force* than his published writings.

It is impossible to exaggerate the electrifying effect of the Inaugural Address, which began with a generous tribute to his predecessor and friend, Professor Niecks, and continued with an

---

[1] Tovey's eyes were unusually widely set. Dr. Cameron, the Edinburgh eye surgeon, was struck by this when he measured him for his first pair of glasses. It was a feature which the eye specialist had noted in the copy of Beethoven's death-mask in the University. He measured this and found the two to tally within a minute fraction.

exposition of the value to the student of the right approach to the Classics. Quotations alone can give some idea of the fresh current of original thought which that day began to stir the musical life of Edinburgh and which maintained its vitalizing influence for nearly a quarter of a century.

'Some elements of revolt have always been traceable at one or more points in the career of every master who has ever become a classic,' said the new professor. 'What is new in the artistic spirit of revolt at the present day is its bitterness and its universal range. Without entering into controversial questions, I may venture to assert that to-day it has, as it seldom had before, the aspect of a grievance. The mildest, and therefore perhaps the most serious form of the grievance, is that the load of classical tradition has long been so heavy as to repress further creative impulse, and that it is always increasing. And I am unable to see any lack of logic in those who, feeling thus, argue that they must shake off this load even at the cost of a violence that shall destroy, at least for themselves, the very record of what the Classics have been. . . .

'What I do believe to be fundamentally wrong is every attitude towards Classical masterpieces which does not make them a stimulus instead of an oppression. . . . It is wrong to contemplate a masterpiece with the thought in mind that the present can never hope to rival the past. This thought would have extinguished every one of the Classics themselves. It is irrelevant to the contemplation of a masterpiece, and still more irrelevant to the creation of one. The contemplation of a masterpiece demands one's whole attention; and the act of creating so much as a decent piece of school-work demands a kind of athletic mental form in which modesty has the place that it has in rock-climbing. Modesty comes before and after; . . . no man, woman or child ever did a good stroke of original work without feeling, for the time being, that it was the finest stroke that the mind of man could conceive. No sociable person wishes to retain that feeling after its function is accomplished.'

The most brilliant features of Professor Tovey's lectures,

however, were his illustrations. He had a genius for apt musical quotations, and he possessed until the last two or three years of his life a prodigious memory. No printed record of his lectures and addresses can give any idea of the facility with which he produced on the pianoforte a wealth of examples from every branch of musical literature. The reproduction of orchestral scores, string quartets, and *a cappella* vocal music magically took on some of the quality of their original colour under his fingers, and it was a breath-taking experience to turn the leaves of a Wagner score for him. The illustrations to this Inaugural Lecture ranged from Mozart's Twelfth Mass backwards and forwards across the centuries via Handel, Bach, the sixteenth-century Des Prés, Palestrina, and Chopin, to Beethoven's choral style—a stimulating variety, all bearing on the main argument. The penultimate paragraph runs: 'When critics adopt the 18th-century method of saying that such and such a Classic ought to inspire us with noble feelings because its sentiments are edifying and its form perfect, we may legitimately argue that it is useless to tell us that we ought to feel this and that, when as a matter of fact, we feel quite otherwise. On the other hand, we shall do well to beware of the exclusively subjective methods of criticism so much in vogue since the latter part of the 19th century: methods which may be but mildly caricatured as consisting in sitting in front of a work of art, feeling our pulses and noting our symptoms, before we have taken the slightest trouble to find out whether the language of that art means what we think it means.'

These quotations suffice to show how mistaken was Professor Dent's view that Tovey was 'haunted by a horror lest "the enemy blaspheme"', or that, while he—Tovey—permitted himself to criticize, if anyone else should do so, he would be told that he was 'perky'. 'There are two extreme errors possible in our attitude towards the Classics', said Tovey in the Inaugural Address; 'the indolent reverence that admits nothing in common between our minds and the minds of the great masters; and the irreverence that would reduce the mind of a great master, or for that matter, any other mind, to the exact level of our own. Both these errors are forms of inattention and lack of sympathy.' 'Inattention' was what he could not tolerate, producing the attitude of mind which he labelled 'perkiness'. Dent's views probably dated back to undergraduate days when in many ways he found Tovey infuriating. Writing in 1935, however, to congratulate Tovey on his knighthood, Dent said: 'I want you to realize how profoundly grateful I am for all that I have learned from you. I entirely lack, and am inclined to mock at, your "reverence for the great masters" (having that sort of Cambridge mind which prefers to anatomize them): but your principles and methods of analysis have been of infinite value to me for the last thirty years or more, and I am always trying to impress them on my pupils.'

Hard on the heels of the Inaugural Lecture came the Pianoforte Recital with which Professor Tovey opened the series of University Historical concerts for the season 1914–15. Many who were present have spoken in later years of this concert as one of the most memorable of their musical experience. Here was not only a learned professor, but also a pianist with great technical equipment, profound intellectual grasp, and a rare and sensitive poetic imagination—a combination of qualities which made him unique. As one who was associated with him first as a student and then as a member of staff throughout the whole of his period in Edinburgh, I probably heard more of Professor Tovey's playing both in public and in private than did anyone else. Although only a schoolgirl I was able to appreciate that first recital by virtue of the fact that my own playing and knowledge of pianoforte literature were advanced for my years. I shall always remember vividly the Brahms' *Paganini* Variations and Schumann's *Humoresque*. The memorable thing about the Brahms was not merely the brilliance, which must impress in any first-rate performance, but the masterly way in which the successive variations were built up to form an integral whole; this indeed was characteristic of Tovey's playing of all great sets of Variations and I have never heard another player who could impart such impetus to this particular form. Incidentally he would never tolerate any interference with Brahms' own order of the *Paganini* Variations, and the compound of the two sets which is commonly heard from great virtuosi was anathema to him. The Schumann *Humoresque* was a revelation of the fantastic and sometimes sentimental humour that is the essence of Schumann. Tovey was particularly happy playing such works; there was a side of his nature which had much in common with the whimsical genius of Schumann, whose profound qualities he also understood so well. He brought to *Kreisleriana* and the *Davidsbündler-Tänze* such gusto and boyish exuberance, and to the *C Major Fantasia* such sublime poetry, that I can only think of these works in terms of his playing. And he was the only person who was the equal of Fanny Davies in playing *Kinderscenen*. Curiously, however, his playing of the Schumann Pianoforte Concerto was never really satisfactory, and he invariably had a disconcerting slip of memory (never twice in the same place) in the Finale.

It is vain to describe in words the qualities of an artist's playing; one can only put on record the recollections of some of his most memorable performances. Such were the six Beethoven recitals during the winter of 1916–17 which included twenty-two sonatas and five sets of variations. The arrangement of these programmes is very interesting, since Tovey had a special flair for programme-building, and a keen sense of fitting contrast of mood, character, and colour. Each concert was preceded by a public lecture, and many conscientious and tidy-minded concert-goers were exasperated by these. 'The study of Beethoven's Pianoforte Sonatas', wrote Tovey many years later, 'is evidently incomplete unless it is at all points linked with the study of his other works, not omitting the opera *Fidelio* and the Mass in D.' Obviously it was impossible in half-a-dozen lectures to cover such a tremendous field. Those who did not mind digressions—which were always illuminating—who did not care how long the lectures lasted nor whether they dealt with the whole of next day's programme, or only with one movement of one sonata—were thrilled. Others could only see in the wealth of knowledge that was poured out before them a lack of method and orderliness such as might be expected from an eccentric musical genius. That was the beginning of his unpopularity with a certain conservative and snobbish section of the Edinburgh public, which could not tolerate that which it was unable, or unwilling, to understand.

The high lights of these recitals were undoubtedly the *Diabelli* Variations, the *Hammerklavier* Sonata, and the beautiful set of Bagatelles op. 126, all works of Beethoven's last period which few could make so intelligible and so impressive as Tovey. To hear him play *any* Beethoven was always to hear the music afresh, but in particular he could make an over-familiar work, such as the so-called *Moonlight* Sonata, sound magical again— and he often did so in later years when this and other popular sonatas were 'request' items on the programmes of the Sunday Evening concerts. On his first appearance with the Scottish Orchestra in December 1915 he created something of a sensation with the G major Pianoforte Concerto, and roused the normally sober and decorous audience to showing genuine enthusiasm.

Equally revealing was his playing of Bach, and it is probable that he knew, if not by heart, at least familiarly, every note of Bach's klavier-writing, including the organ works. A well-known musician once said, 'If all the works Bach wrote for the keyboard were destroyed, I believe Tovey could reconstruct at least three-quarters of them'. Someone repeated this to Tovey who said half-jokingly, 'Well, you know, there *would* be some misprints!' The spirit of Bach literally lived under his fingers, and the most complex polyphony sounded clear, natural, and transparent. His playing of the *Goldberg* Variations is quite unforgettable, as are also performances of the F sharp minor Toccata, the Partitas, the fugues from the *Kunst der Fuge*, and—not least—his own gorgeous arrangement of the F major Organ Toccata, which was unhappily never committed to paper. Eloquence, simplicity, and clarity were the characteristics of his playing of Bach, and one of the most beautiful pianoforte broadcasts I have ever heard was his playing of the Bach D minor Concerto at one of the Proms in September 1931.

It would be as wrong to give the impression that Tovey as a player was mainly concerned with Bach, Beethoven, and Brahms as to infer from his writings that his attention was mainly concerned with these composers. With Schubert's sonatas he was particularly happy. By reason of his fundamental reverence for all music that bore the imprint of greatness, and of his own naturally spacious and unhurried manner, he was never impatient of the redundancies and stiffnesses, or of the unhandy pianoforte style which present such obstacles to the performance of these works. The great B flat and G major sonatas never sounded lengthy when he played them; the first movement of the B flat was profound, and the last movement of both, which he took at an extremely leisurely but steady pace, had true Viennese brilliance.

In the course of his Edinburgh recitals Tovey must have covered practically the whole of Chopin's works, and on many of these occasions something of the unearthly delicacy of Chopin's pianissimos certainly lived again. I remember chiefly, however, the great beauty of the lesser-known mazurkas, and, curiously, the A flat Ballade; but the F minor, of which he was very fond, never sounded well. Modern music (apart from chamber music) was largely represented by Debussy—in particular by the preludes—and by stray pieces by Brucken-Fock and other little-known composers.

One never talks of 'Tovey's interpretation' of a work, however clearly one may remember how he played it. His personality never intervened between composer and listener, and his playing seemed to illuminate the music so that it reached one with unforgettable vividness. Nowadays, when his fame rests on his writings *about* music, many may not realize that he was, first and foremost, an artist. Those who know *what* an artist he was will always profoundly regret that no recordings exist to preserve the memory of his playing when he was at the height of his powers, during the first fifteen years or so of his Edinburgh life.

Professor Newall of Cambridge, commenting on Tovey's readiness to play anything and everything, once asked him how long he thought it would take him to play by heart everything he knew, playing eight hours a day. Tovey said, 'Oh, about four weeks', and then, after thinking a little, corrected himself and said, 'No, I think it would take eight weeks, or seven at least.'

Although they were shadowed by the clouds of war, Tovey's first years in Edinburgh were happy years. He enjoyed the independence which he had long desired and which he had now achieved by means of a congenial appointment. Miss Weisse's disapproval and her pro-German views were very vexing, even at a distance, but he believed that time would soften her attitude. He was no stranger to Scotland or to Edinburgh, and he was happily one of those Englishmen who never rub even the most prickly or sensitive Scot the wrong way. There were distinguished and agreeable colleagues among the professors of the other faculties in the University[1] and many hospitable doors were open to him. In all, the change of surroundings and circumstances was a heaven-sent antidote to the bitternesses and frustrations of the last years in London and to the closing of prospects which promised a career of international repute.

University duties and 'Historical' concerts did not prevent him from carrying out the projected Dutch tour in December and January 1914–15. He felt indeed that he owed this to Miss Weisse, who had been so indefatigable in making all the arrangements, and who was backing the concerts in Holland. 'The concerts seem to have been very successful,' she wrote to Mrs. Trevelyan, 'and that helps to keep the artist in Donald alive.' Not for the world would she have admitted that his Edinburgh concerts fulfilled the same function.

He had not yet lost touch with the concert world in London, and gave—among many other concerts for charity during the

---

[1] These included Professors Barkla (Nat. Philosophy), Cossar-Ewart (Nat. History), Grierson (English), Kennedy (Hebrew), Lodge (History), Paterson (Dean of the Faculty of Divinity), Sampson (Astronomy), Schäfer (Physiology), Walker (Chemistry—a keen amateur musician), Whittaker (Mathematics), and Sir William McCormick (Secretary to the U.K. Trust).

war years—six Beethoven recitals in the Aeolian Hall in February 1915 in aid of the Red Cross Motor Ambulance Fund and the funds of the Committee for Music in Wartime—an undertaking which involved continual night-journeys between London and Edinburgh. In May his symphony was performed for the first—and, as it proved, the last—time in London by the London Symphony Orchestra under Verbrugghen. There were also various concerts at Northlands during the summer, when he was free from professorial duties, since the Faculty of Music in Edinburgh University had only two terms, autumn and spring.

A second Dutch tour had been arranged for the following winter, but Tovey felt doubtful about getting permission from the University to fulfil this, and indeed wondered whether 'the Court may not prove of opinion that a Faculty of Music is a useless luxury in wartime'. He was, moreover, still of military age and the recruiting authorities were appealing for men. His brother had been wounded, though not badly, and his conscience was very sensitive as to his own duty. He even contemplated a job in munitions, though it would be hard to imagine anyone more totally unsuited to such work. Eventually he wrote to Miss Weisse: 'I went and got myself attested at the recruiting office ten days ago. The medical officer, a nice lively young man with a brilliant moustache, after making me jump and poking me where my necktie used to be, remarked, "You needn't bother about this damn thing"; which statement—or words to that effect—is on my registration card. So I don't suppose there will be any trouble' (about the Dutch tour).

'Arrived in Holland,' he wrote early in January 1916: 'On Sunday it will be rather amusing in its way at the Hague, for there is a troupe of *Follies*, consisting of interned English soldiers and sailors from the early Antwerp contingent, and several friends of my brother will be among them. . . .

'Dordrecht was very quaint; the floods (which are very distressing in some parts) compelled me to go by boat. Only a small pianoforte could be got there; the platform was a stage drawing-room with practicable windows, and into the piano there stared, through one of the windows, a policeman, with a rope and axe. I took him for a waxwork until about the middle of my programme, when he moved! He wasn't an executioner ready to inflict the penalty for bad playing, but was a watchman to guard against fire.'

From Amsterdam he sent news about her brother-in-law to Mrs. Trevelyan: 'Röntgen has been writing some most beautiful unaccompanied choral music: Psalms against war, beginning (with a certain shrewdness which I think characteristic of him) with "Put not your trust in princes".' He was also full of enthusiasm about the début of the Röntgen String Trio (consisting of the father and his two eldest sons)—'as I listened to a rehearsal I felt very much as if something like the Joachim Quartet was still alive and young'. News that Fritz and Adolf Busch were safely out of the fighting line was also very satisfactory. This, however, was the last contact he had with his Dutch friends for some years.

During his first season in Edinburgh, Tovey engaged a number of players from the Scottish Orchestra for the third Historical concert; an interesting programme, illustrating Aria and Concerto forms, included a Bach cantata and the Beethoven G major Pianoforte Concerto. This concert was very successful, and during the following season provision was made for two orchestral programmes, one 'illustrating the use of the small orchestra in large designs' (concluding with the *Eroica* Symphony!) and the other 'illustrating the Groups and Composition of the Full Orchestra'. The latter programme (given in February 1916) was indeed very remarkable:

1. *Tragic* Overture   *Brahms*
2. Symphonia Sacra *Lamentatio Davidi*   *Schütz*
   (for bass voice, four trombones, and organ)
3. Serenade in B flat for thirteen wind instruments *Mozart*
4. Two Symphoniae Sacrae   *Schütz*
      (*a*) *Anima mea* (for two baritones, two Corni di Bassetto, 'Fiffari' and organ).

(*b*) *Freuet euch des Herrn* (for tenor, baritone, and bass;
  with orchestral violins, double basses, and organ).
5. Overture for the Consecration of the House, op. 124
               Beethoven

Before these two orchestral concerts took place, however, Tovey was invited to conduct a very different body of players for the Edinburgh Musicians Annual Benevolent Concert in November 1915, in aid of the funds for British Prisoners of War in Germany. He accepted with alacrity and, with a large and heterogeneous orchestra composed of local theatre, picture-house, and café-players, gave a programme which began with Elgar's *Pomp and Circumstance* no. 1, and concluded with Beethoven's C minor Symphony; other items were a set of Mozart dances and works by Berlioz and Dvořák. It was an extraordinary undertaking. My memory does not register anything remarkably bad about the performance, though it cannot have been very good! It had, however, far-reaching results, for out of this concert sprang the initial idea of the Reid Symphony Orchestra, the project which was so dear to the Professor's heart for the rest of his life. The programme-notes for the concert are the *only* short ones that Tovey ever wrote, and the four concise paragraphs on the C minor Symphony are of great interest.

Tovey's first experiment in taking music outside the precincts of the University was made in the spring of 1916, when he inaugurated a series of New Reid concerts in the Freemasons' Hall. The purpose was to give not only classical but modern chamber music, such as could neither be appropriately included in the Historical series, nor be accessible to the public through concert agents who must consider the box-office. Three concerts were given, the last including a Bach solo cantata with a small string orchestra assembled by Mrs. Alexander Maitland, whose home was now in Edinburgh, where it was the focus of much excellent semi-private music-making. The New Reid concerts were abandoned after one season owing to the wider developments which took place in the following year.

During his first two years in Edinburgh, Tovey found time to range through the very large and valuable Music Library attached to his classroom, and such were his powers of memory that in after years he could always tell the exact spot where anything could be found, despite the fact that the arrangement of the books was far from orderly. Much to the distress of the grim and faithful custodian, Wellby, who looked at first on the new professor and his ways with profound disapproval, but who later became touchingly devoted to him, he disturbed the dust of ages in many forgotten corners. In one he found a bundle of manuscript which caused him to write to Miss Weisse, 'I've made a discovery, viz., The Real Works of General Reid,[1] Six *quite good* sonatas for German flute, or Hautboy or Violin, 2nd Edition. They contain all the tunes that have been so vilely arranged by Bishop and other Illustrious Predecessors who literally weren't half so good as that jolly old boy. . . . He is a very competent 18th-century chamber-musician and would have been excellently qualified to hold the chair he founded, at least according to any standards of his own time. Doesn't it show up the brutal conceit of British early-Victorian musicians!'

At the end of his second session, after a very short engagement, Tovey married Miss Margaret Cameron, daughter of Hugh Cameron, R.S.A., on 22 April 1916. His friends were surprised and delighted; now that he had a wife to see that he did not neglect his health or forget his engagements, surely Miss Weisse would realize that she must finally delegate her care of him. Moreover, as the lady was the daughter of an artist, presumably she would have some idea of the extent to which music filled her husband's life. The prospects seemed good.

Although absorbed in his work Tovey did not forget old friends, and about this time he wrote to the Hon. R. D. Denman, M.P., who had been Chairman of the Chelsea Concerts' Committee:

'Dear Dick,

Can you do anything to get Strecker out of his internment-

---

[1] The founder of the Reid Chair of Music.

camp? He is very philosophical about it and told me, when he knew it was inevitable, that he thought it as well to keep as quiet as possible and, above all, to avoid attracting the attention of the press.

'Still, though it is not a specially bad case, one really can't see one's friends treated so for no fault of their own without trying to do or say something.

'I don't know if Simon would remember me well enough for me to have any weight with him, but perhaps you could assure him of my personal knowledge that Strecker is a completely trustworthy person, and infinitely more useful to the interests of English musical publishing than any native.'

In the autumn of 1916 the first rehearsal of the Reid Symphony Orchestra took place. Thus Tovey's cherished idea of founding a local symphony orchestra materialized one year after the Musicians' Benevolent Concert had shown him its practical possibilities. There were sixty players of varying degrees of proficiency, forty-five of whom were professional members and fifteen non-professional. Even had it been possible financially, it would have been difficult in wartime to raise a purely professional orchestra, and Professor Tovey—though no one ever had the welfare of the professional musician more at heart—had no prejudices against using the good amateur and the good student. The co-operation and goodwill of the Musicians' Union was behind the scheme; indeed Tovey was invited to become an Honorary Member of the Union—'I said, with truth,' he wrote, 'that, no other honorary membership would gratify me more.' The fact, however, that the orchestra was recruited originally in this—the only possible—way, led its opponents in later years to attempt to discredit it as an 'amateur' orchestra, which it never was. Nor was it a University orchestra. Its founder and conductor was the Professor of Music, it rehearsed in the spacious Music Classroom, and its rehearsals constituted a class in orchestration in the curriculum for the degree of Mus.Bac.: it stood, in fact, in the same relation to the

Faculty of Music as the Royal Infirmary to the Faculty of Medicine, and in this respect Edinburgh University Music Faculty was unique in the country. In the early years the orchestra was financed by payment from the University for the weekly rehearsals which constituted the class, and by concert fees paid by Messrs. Paterson (who promoted the early concerts). The money paid by the University was the sum available for Historical concerts, and for two seasons Tovey gave a series of pianoforte recitals without fee in order to free these funds for the use of the orchestra. After three seasons, the Scottish Orchestra, which had been in abeyance since 1916, came to life again, and Messrs. Paterson relinquished their share in the Reid enterprise save as concert agents; a small body of guarantors then assumed sole responsibility for the concerts, under the chairmanship of Robert Finnie McEwen, friend and patron of many musical enterprises, and a fine musician himself.

On 5 May 1917 the orchestra made its first public appearance. In the light of later events, observations by the *Scotsman* critic are of interest: 'The orchestra acquitted itself with a degree of artistic success which even those most favourably disposed towards the new venture could hardly have anticipated. The concert was, indeed, one of the most interesting and agreeable musical experiences of the present season. What was much more important, however, was the proof that there is in Edinburgh the material for an excellent concert orchestra of moderate but sufficient dimensions. These materials Professor Tovey, as the result of a winter's hard work, has already brought into most promising shape. Henceforth, there will be no grounds for regretting the lack of a permanent local orchestra in Edinburgh. There *is* such an orchestra; whether it becomes permanent or not, rests entirely with the public.'

The training of a new orchestra—on the basis of one regular and one voluntary rehearsal per week—to the stage of giving public performances was, as Tovey well knew, fantastic; he also knew that circumstances offered no other possible alternative. Only a man of highest ideals and courage would have risked his reputation on such a venture. The programmes caused some surprise when announced, but Tovey knew what he was doing. On the occasion of the twenty-fifth concert (March 1920) he wrote: 'When the Reid Orchestra held its first practice in the Music Classroom, anybody could have pointed out that it was unfit to execute at its first concert a programme ranging from Beethoven's *Coriolanus* Overture to Brahms' *Variations on a Theme of Haydn*, and Dunhill's *Irish Songs*.[1] Yet, at quite an early stage I was able to write to Sir George Henschel—"we are making good progress. The difficult passages go well, and even the easy ones are beginning to sound quite decent." The plain truth is that if we had taken the advice of the wise people who warned us against being too ambitious, not only would progress have been impossible, but we should have begun at the wrong end of our task. If you are training a child, you have to begin with what suits the childish mind and childish limbs. But there is nothing childish about the infancy of an orchestra; and when you are training grown-up people it is quite as necessary to keep them interested as to keep children interested. And the very first things you can get an organisation of grown-up people to prac- tise seriously are the technically difficult things, provided of course that the difficulty is reasonable and solid. Not until we had some practice in things of which inexperienced players and listeners can see the difficulty, could we expect to have a clear idea of the kind of tone production and rhythmic accuracy that is necessary for playing simple things broadly, naturally, and persuasively. I confess to have been much amused at finding that one of the programmes in which we played Mozart's E flat symphony and Beethoven's 4th symphony was considered in some quarters a marked success on the ground that for once we had selected things well within our power. Mozart is always a very dangerous composer; as for the Beethoven symphony, that serene expression of health and happiness is one of the most nerve-racking things a young orchestra could possibly tackle. . . . Well then, one of the "vicious circles" through which our enter-

[1] Sung by Gervase Elwes.

prise must struggle may be described thus—that an orchestra ought not to be brought before the public until it is worth listening to, and that it will never be worth listening to until it has been brought before the public many times. The only way to get out of this circle is to stretch it. The public must be patient and generous.'

It has often been said of Tovey that he was no conductor. This is profoundly untrue. He had some deplorable, and—because unconscious—quite incurable habits, which distressed his audience in greater or less degree according to the importance they attached to looking as well as listening. The worst habit of all was the trick in slow and quiet passages—of grasping the knob of the rostrum in his left hand, gently crossing his right foot over his left, and allowing the music to flow on under the lightest of beats. This *looked* shockingly bad, but the result was often a surprisingly serene and smooth piece of playing. His beat was, for physical reasons, rather ungainly in appearance, but the characteristic 'shovel' action in climaxes was by no means devoid of effect, and the intention of the beat was clear to the players. What the players did hate, however, was the fact that he was incapable of covering up any mishap! Slips which would in nine cases out of ten have passed unobserved by the average concertgoer were inevitably made evident by his immediate and involuntary reaction, which often made matters worse by drawing attention to the player concerned.

The irregular rhythms of some modern works gave him trouble on occasion, and Mr. Frank Merrick no doubt still remembers with horror a performance of the *Dynamic Triptych*, for pianoforte and orchestra, by John Foulds, during the last movement of which the beat swung in a wild and ever wilder circle, and players and audience alike more or less shut their eyes and prayed for the end. (Tovey's footnote to the composer's own programme note says of this rhythm: 'Pronounce at a brisk uniform pace the words "*one* two *one* two three *one* two three four" again and again without pause, and with an accent on each "one", and you will feel the powerful swing of this rhythm.'

But he could not translate it into lucid action.) This, however, was an exceptional case of failure in conducting technique; despite the unorthodoxy of his methods, there was a quality in his conducting comparable only to that of his own playing, which made the reality of great music more vivid to the listener than it often was under the guidance of famous virtuosi of the baton.

The music seemed to radiate from Tovey during a performance, fusing the sometimes inadequate forces under him into an expressive musical instrument. This force one felt in varying degrees of intensity whenever one played with him. My earliest memorable experience of it was in 1919. As the war was not yet over when I graduated in 1918, I had to wait another year before going to study with Fanny Davies in London, and the Professor suggested that meanwhile I should study his pianoforte concerto and play it at a Reid concert in the spring. It was a typically quixotic gesture to entrust the first Edinburgh performance of his work to a student with no real experience of concert-playing and with an obviously imperfect technique. In those years the University laid an embargo on a professor taking private pupils, so I had no direct lessons to help me, and became increasingly terrified as the date of the concert approached. At the performance my nervousness vanished, and the music somehow—miraculously—came through all the technical difficulties. The unexpected fee and the beautiful bouquet which I received were tokens of the generous encouragement which Tovey was always so ready to give to the young artist. In 1935 I was called upon to play the concerto again at very short notice; I had, of course, played it a number of times in the intervening years, but on this occasion Tovey was to be the soloist and Fritz Busch was to conduct. Tovey's hands were already showing signs of the rheumatism which finally crippled them, but he seemed sure he would be able to play. A fortnight before the concert he told me that he could not possibly play and asked me to take his place. Then he said, 'I always remember your first performance, and I remember you wore a dress of a very pretty, soft blue which seemed exactly to suit the music.' I was taken aback, both because I had chosen the dress with that in view, and because one never imagined that he noticed such details.

In rehearsing and training an orchestra Tovey's most priceless assets were a fine sense of balance of tone, an equally fine sense of rhythm, tempo, and phrasing, and a wonderful imagination for the sounds represented by the printed page. He also had a marvellous insight into the nature and possibilities of orchestral instruments; one of the best horn players the Reid Orchestra ever had used to say 'Professor Tovey taught me more about my instrument than anyone else'. His total lack of a sense of time—other than musical time—was, however, a serious drawback, for he often spent much of the precious three hours of rehearsal on one movement of a symphony, to the detriment of the rest of the programme. He was firmly opposed to the idea—so beloved of orchestras—of 'running through' a work to begin with. Moreover, he was no disciplinarian. His ideal was an orchestra which played not because it was drilled in the music but because it knew and understood what it was playing, and because it was composed of musicians whose aim was the realization of beauty in the terms of an instrument they loved. The unique quality of the Reid Orchestra lay in the fact that Tovey awakened this spirit not only in the leaders, but in so many of the rank and file who played for him; from these he brought out much more than anyone deemed possible.

This method of training an orchestra—plus the fact that students, other than the few who were allowed to play, attended the rehearsals as a class in orchestration—often necessitated long explanations, indeed miniature lectures, which also consumed valuable time. Normally an orchestra would rebel against this; but what Tovey had to say was vitally interesting and frequently amusing, and the orchestra realized that he must say it in his own way.

The course of the rehearsals was not always smooth; Tovey was patient with genuine difficulties but intolerant of musical obtuseness, and the sight—for instance—of a hardened orchestral player packing up his instrument exactly at the end of the stipulated three hours when there were only another fifty bars to play, would arouse one of the terrible explosions of wrath which shook everyone present, and which often hit hardest those at whom it was not directed. But what no one knew during the first four years of the orchestra's existence, was that a loss of temper for a seemingly trivial cause was often due to the nervous strain of living through a desolate period of domestic tragedy. During these years, Donald Tovey fought, devotedly and uncomplainingly, a losing battle for the sanity of his wife, in whom the signs of mental disease, which had shown themselves when she was a young woman, became increasingly and terribly apparent.

The difficulties which had to be overcome in the early days of the orchestra were many and varied. The nerve-wracking uncertainty of not knowing until the week of a concert whether or not a travelling conductor would accept a deputy in the theatre to replace a Reid player, constituted the most vexing problem—never to be entirely overcome. The occasional use of a player from a military band was even more risky, for on more than one occasion a first horn or a first trumpet sent word *on the morning of the concert* that he could not attend, as his band had to play at a regimental football match. In the first season, moreover, it was impossible to secure low-pitched instruments for certain of the wood-wind. 'Perhaps it has done us no ultimate harm,' wrote Tovey, 'that we have had to screw something more than fiddle-strings up to high tension in our first season; and we look forward with confidence to resuming our work in October at a point not lower (in any respect but pitch) than that to which we have so far struggled.'

I I

TOVEY and his wife, after several changes of address within six months, settled in a house of their own with a pleasant garden at 2 St. Margaret's Road in the summer of 1917. Communications with Miss Weisse had been virtually broken off since the previous autumn. Tovey had been greatly distressed by her attitude towards his marriage—though it must be recorded that he gave her some cause for offence by forgetting, until a late date, to send her an invitation to the ceremony. She feared the cessation of his work as a composer; and, as she no doubt reflected that no one could found an orchestra, carry on a pianist's career, adequately fulfil the duties of a professor, and have sufficient leisure to produce new compositions, this was probably the core of her continued hostility to his Edinburgh work. With a characteristic volte-face she wrote to Trevelyan in October begging him to urge Tovey to finish the opera, and she laid plans to interest Beecham and others in the work: 'If it were ready at the beginning of the year, and of practicable—that is of not more than artistically right—length, I believe it would be produced next season under good auspices. . . . It would be an untold benefit to Donald, and the saving of his career as a great artist, to get it out now. His present provincial activities are in reality nugatory.'

Term had already begun, however, and Tovey did not view his work in Edinburgh as nugatory. During that autumn he threw himself with enthusiasm into yet another venture—the resuscitating of the Kirkhope Choir. Mr. John Kirkhope was a well-known business man and a keen amateur, who had gathered round him a choir of about fifty voices which, under his conductorship, had done excellent work over many years. He had just retired and the choir had been disbanded. With Kirkhope's enthusiastic consent, Tovey revived it under its old name, and

arranged that it should make two appearances during the season
at the Reid concerts with groups of sixteenth-century motets
and Bach's *Jesu, meine Freude*.[1] The material for the Palestrina
motets was unobtainable, so Tovey copied the scores, barring
and editing them in a new way, and had his copies photographed
and issued as *The Kirkhope Choir Magazine, An Anthology of Pure
Polyphony*, 'which', says his programme-note, 'is not (as I fear
some disappointed purchasers must have thought) a literary
periodical full of bright local and general news, but a special
attempt to provide ourselves and kindred spirits among choral
societies with such music as demands special methods of editing
and conducting in order to bring out its true rhythmic declamation'.

At this time Mr. Fuller-Maitland, the music critic of *The
Times*, was living in Edinburgh. He had just retired, but it is
evident that a lifetime of criticism had not dulled his musical
enthusiasm. He wrote to Miss Weisse:

'It strikes me that you may like to hear how Donald's position
and work here impresses an outsider, and as I have lately heard
him go through his beautiful opera, and have seen something of
him, I am venturing to write and tell you about him, although
of course he does not know that I am doing so. *Ariadne*[2] seems to
me to be quite masterly in conception and treatment, and the
whole is so spontaneous and emotional in effect that one feels
sure it must succeed eventually.

'His playing is, I think, as fine as ever, though the Beethoven
recitals *last* winter were in some ways better than anything I
have heard from him this year. His training of the very rough
material of his orchestra is really very wonderful, and the results
have shown a steady improvement in every concert they have
given. His choir-training, too, is excellent, but here he had a
more developed article ready to his hand. The Weelkes madri-

[1] In the middle of this season the concerts had to be moved from the admirable
Music Hall, which had been commandeered by the military, to the McEwan Hall,
which belongs to the University and is dignified in appearance but devastating in
its acoustics.
[2] The original title of the opera.

gals at one concert and the Palestrina motets at another made a profound impression, and altogether his position here is now fully established upon a far higher plane than (I should suppose) any of his predecessors have attained. Forgive my troubling you with this letter, but I felt I could not help telling you of his delightful well-being and health in every sense.'

The Kirkhope Choir, unfortunately, did not survive a second season. A choir depends on personal contact with its conductor in a way that an orchestra does not, and Tovey failed to capture the allegiance which had been given to the benign Mr. Kirkhope. Moreover, sixteenth-century music was severe diet for Scottish singers, and although a few rare spirits were fired by its beauties, the majority found the rehearsals very trying. Plans for the following season were made but never materialized, and the choir was finally disbanded in 1919. This was a great disappointment to Tovey, who for many years felt crippled in his work through not having a choral counterpart of the orchestra.

At the time of editing *The Kirkhope Choir Magazine*, which of course also died a premature death, Tovey was occasionally in correspondence with Dr. (afterwards Sir Richard) Terry. In writing to this acknowledged authority on sixteenth-century music Tovey remarks that he is 'no expert at all'. That obviously depends on what is understood by 'expert'. 'What I find I want for reading any music where "scholarship" is wanted is *footnotes*,' he writes. 'Take this question of accidentals: some are absolutely certain, e.g. the Tierce de Picardie and the various forms of undoubted leading-notes. They may just as well go straight in, as part of the ordinary modern notation. But what of cases where the singer judged by his own part only? Did the composer *never* think the singer wrong? Is the score-reader to be left with no guidance as to whether an augmented 6th was an oversight or, as the Irish judge said, "an accidental interposition of Providence"? I am sure that a more accurate classification of the cases is possible than that which Haberl[1] leaves us with. He

[1] The editor of the complete works of Palestrina.

says that he has put more accidentals in Lasso than in Palestrina. Now, why? Is it because Lasso is a livelier and more experimental person and wants more; or is it because Haberl thinks him more difficult and less complete in his notation (which would surprise me); or is it because there aren't enough accidentals in the Palestrina edition? Evidently what Haberl's vagueness conceals is, amongst other things, the growth of Lasso's style from chromatic experiment to diatonic purity. Footnotes on the difficult cases would have taken little more room and done immense good.'

Shortly after the end of the second season of Reid concerts in March 1918 Tovey wired to Trevelyan, 'Successfully resuming operatic scoring during University examinations' (in those days he acted as invigilator himself). Quite apart from the fact that he had been too fully occupied to take up work on the opera any earlier, all the material had remained in the south, and he had at first some difficulty in getting Miss Weisse to send it to him. It was just at this time that he found out about her past arrangements with his publishers, and he was in great anxiety until he got every scrap of manuscript out of her hands.

He found that the part already finished needed little revision. 'I began in the examination room, racing Mus.Bac. candidates in paper-spoiling. . . . When this job is finished I believe we shall both of us feel that I have not been unreasonably long over it. . . . With a work of this size most of what people say *a priori* about one's development of style is bosh. . . . Look at the *Ring*. There are fourteen years in *Siegfried* alone between the middle of the 2nd act and the end (1857–1871): and the scoring of the whole *Ring* (I'm not speaking of the libretto or sketching) lasted from 1853 till 1874. Then clever people go and say clever things about the difference in style between *Götterdämmerung* and the rest. Well, Wagner, if anybody, was a man who had reasons to change his style: yet when he has to quote whole passages in *Götterdämmerung* from *Rheingold* he has nothing to do but to copy as far as the passage goes and to add and alter only what the new situation needs.' A postscript to this letter adds that Mrs.

Tovey had been overdoing it and had been ordered to take a rest.

Mrs. Tovey was, to all appearance, a quiet and sensible woman, who, as a girl, had been pretty in a gentle way. She had little or no appreciation of music, and when she found that she was totally unable to understand anything of her husband's work, the outer layer of conventionality which protected an unstable personality gave way. Jealousy of his work caused her to adopt a censorious attitude towards everything he did, and Tovey was susceptible to this in inverse ratio to the reasonableness of the attacks. When it became clear that his wife had no domestic talents he sought outlets for her on other lines; he was endlessly patient in his efforts to avert disaster. They went to Oxford in April, where presently she had to go into a nursing-home. Later she and her husband went to 'The Shiffolds' with, says Trevelyan, 'rather more than half his opera in its final shape (at least thirty huge sheets of music-paper which he called his "bath-sheets"); they stayed till sometime in June, when he finished the last sheet. He would sit at a table most of the day scoring, and often stayed up working till three in the morning, or even later. One night he wakened us about two o'clock, and made us come out into the field above the house, where he had set up his telescope. We took turns at looking through it at a close conjunction of Saturn and Venus (or some other planet); then we returned to bed while he went back to his scoring.

'At this stage, when he was making his final score, he preferred to work at a table in our drawing-room, with all the life of the house going on around him. He would even enjoy listening to my wife reading aloud to us in the evening. Nothing seemed to interfere with his power of concentration on his work. Sometimes, though not often, he would get up and play a few chords on the piano; but he considerately refrained from doing so after we had gone to bed.'

The improvement in Mrs. Tovey's health was only temporary, and she was seriously ill in a mental home near Oxford during the rest of the summer. Tovey's closest friends were perturbed because of reports from Oxford about his unkempt appearance; and cruel derisive remarks were made about the beard which he grew to humour a whim of his wife. ('I'm wanted by the police,' he told his young nephews, 'and so I've disguised myself as Abraham Lincoln!') He was tireless in his efforts to help his wife, though to begin with these efforts were made in face of the hostility of her family. 'She has suffered for the last twelve years from repression of all her talents,' he wrote to Mrs. Trevelyan; 'We must have a housekeeper, and she must have a studio.' Early in October he wrote that his wife was making a 'splendid recovery', though even *his* optimism was tempered by the persistence of disquieting nervous symptoms, and he had to be granted a fortnight's leave from the University before he was able to take her home to Edinburgh.

During the winter of 1918–19 Tovey effected a *rapprochement* with Miss Weisse. He never forgot what he owed to her and he was more loyal than many sons might have been. She was able only intermittently to check her will to dominate and to interfere, but at no time did he desire the painful solution of a total estrangement.

At the end of a letter from London on 19 April proposing to pay her a visit, he writes once more in the old characteristic vein: 'Taverner's *Western Wynd* Mass on Easter morning was interesting. More I do not feel inclined to say. Our Tudor church music was archaic until it became seriously disorganised by the Reformation. Our really great people, Byrd and Tallis, simply didn't know what church to write for if they were to keep their heads upon their shoulders; and the result is that the Mass is not an English musical art-form. Patriotism will not induce me to inflate Taverner into a Palestrina. Probably the motets are the things to look up for really great music. The most interesting feature was the rhythms, over which old Taverner was evidently piling up all the Flemish devices he and the Devil could agree upon.

Well, well,
Yours affectionately,
Donald Francis Tovey.'

In May 1919 Tovey and his wife decided, after much serious thought, to adopt a baby boy of five weeks old, who was given the name of John Wellcome Tovey. Undoubtedly this brought some happiness to them, even though Mrs. Tovey was little fitted or able to look after a baby. Tovey was always fond of children, and even if he was a little shy with them they were never shy of him. 'We always looked forward to his visits in our school holidays,' wrote his nephew Duncan after his death. 'We used to go long country walks with him and he talked to us about music and astronomy and literature in a way that made us feel he was treating us as equals. And we used to get him to repeat his stories till we knew exactly how they went, and could set the whole dormitory laughing at them when we went back to school. I remember, too, how popular his visits to our prep. school were, and how the boys clamoured to him to play to them (especially his versions of the Edward Lear Nonsense songs); and the Headmaster never forgot his imitation of some Eton character reading the lessons in chapel.' In later years the fine way in which his adopted son developed gave Tovey real satisfaction.

In consequence of the war Miss Weisse had lost that half of her savings which was invested in Germany. She had also retired from teaching and had sold the school at Northlands. She was still very active and longed to do whatever she could to help Tovey's career. His fears of her renewed interference were temporarily allayed, and when he accepted her suggestion that she should find good copyists and supervise the business of having the score of his completed opera copied and band-parts made, she was delighted. Tovey was meanwhile occupied with the tedious business of making a pianoforte score; but his first tentative efforts at a meeting with Beecham had been unsuccessful, for the flimsiest of reasons.

There is only the evidence of one letter of Miss Weisse's that a meeting with Beecham and 'other influential people' ever took place. The music evidently made an immense impression, but the libretto was criticized adversely. Miss Weisse was amongst those who considered the opera too long and demanded that it should be cut. To anyone who reads the poem, which depends so largely for its drama on innumerable fine strokes of characterization, the impossibility of this demand is obvious. It is even more obvious in the case of the music, which is so closely knit to every word of the text. Tovey and Trevelyan were inspired by ideals which took no account of the commercial stage, and there was no possible means whereby the opera could be brought into line with its supposed requirements. Accordingly the hostility which Miss Weisse had shown to the Trevelyans in former years now flared up again in increasing bitterness, as she accused the poet of having provided a perfectly impossible libretto 'and ruining all Donald's work!'

Nevertheless, Tovey remained hopeful, writing in September 1919: 'Beecham is coming to Glasgow soon, and it is dimly possible that by some miracle he may send me, or bring, the first 145 pages of the vocal score with the letter he promised to write for the benefit of the C.U.K.T.' (A year later Fritz Busch, newly appointed as conductor at Stuttgart, was writing to ask 'ob Beecham so wenig bankrott ist dass er noch dein Oper ausfuhren kann?')[1] Whether or not the Carnegie United Kingdom Trust ever saw the manuscript, the fact remains that the full score of *The Bride of Dionysus* still remains unpublished, and that the opera had to wait ten years before it was performed—on an Edinburgh stage. The failure to get his own work published contrasts curiously with Tovey's own generous words in a letter two years earlier to Mr. Speyer: 'The announcement of the Carnegie musical publication scheme is interesting and surely very satisfactory. I heard Bantock's *Hebridean* Symphony a year ago and was really much impressed by it; quite sufficiently so not to mind the presence of much Bantockishness that would, if unrelieved by bigger characteristics, have been a mere bore. Vaughan Williams' Symphony I also heard here; it well deserves such help as this Carnegie Scheme can give. Both of these works would, with any intelligent tribunal, be foregone conclu-

[1] 'Whether Beecham is not so bankrupt that he can still produce your opera?'

sions; the appearance of the others is a matter to rouse curiosity and interest: and Ridgehurstians have private cause of pleasure in the success of Frank Bridge.'

In the season 1919–20 Messrs. Paterson relinquished their responsibility for the Reid orchestral concerts. At a meeting held in Mrs. Maitland's house a small executive committee was appointed with Mr. McEwen (who was already Chairman of the Guarantors) as Chairman, and Messrs. Thomas Barclay and William Taylor as Joint Honorary Secretaries. Mr. Barclay was a wealthy old gentleman, well known in Edinburgh as a patron of the arts and as one of the remaining few who had known Robert Louis Stevenson. Mr. Taylor was the active half of the Secretaryship. As managing director of a small printing business he was already familiar with the ways of 'the Professor', as he always called him. In his first year at Edinburgh, Tovey had failed to send his degree examination papers at the scheduled time to the University printers, and was told they could not possibly be printed by the date of the examination. This was a disaster, and in desperation he betook himself to Taylor, whose firm printed all the concert programmes for Messrs. Paterson. Taylor pointed out that it was indeed too late to deal with the papers that required the reproduction of *music*, but suggested that this should be done by means of photographs. 'Use any means you like,' said the Professor, 'use a camera—use *Mons Meg*[1]—but get them done!' The papers arrived in time. How often in later years would there have been no Reid programme on the night of a concert had it not been for Taylor's unfailing genius for rushing them through at the last moment! From boyhood Taylor had an unbounded enthusiasm for singing, and he had a very pleasant tenor voice and a real feeling for what was genuine. He was devoted to 'the Professor' as the embodiment of all that music meant, and sang in every choral concert that Tovey ever conducted. Taylor had a robust sense of humour and loved the Professor's jokes; a few minutes of talk with Tovey, when he sailed into the printing office with hands crammed

[1] The famous old cannon on the ramparts of Edinburgh Castle.

with overdue proofs, were compensation for all the additional work and worry. He did beautiful printing and there was rarely an error of *his* making in the programmes.

In the following year, at the instance of Mr. McEwen, Taylor became the paid Secretary to the Reid Orchestra, and acted also, to a large extent, as secretary to the Professor. Tovey, by temperament and upbringing, was totally incompetent in dealing with business letters or in keeping count of his engagements, and unhappily his wife was unable to help him. By some miracle he never made a mistake about *concert* engagements, but the social and other engagements which he muddled or forgot were legion, and his correspondence was chaos. Tovey's technique in dealing with letters was to read them hastily, improvise a reply with equal speed, and then imagine that he had dispatched it. 'Je vous en prie, mon cher Donald,' wrote Fleury about this time, 'surmontez votre horreur d'écrire et envoyez-moi *par retour de courrier* la partie de flute de la sonate de Général Reid. Si facile soit elle, j'aimerais la connaître à l'avance, et je ne puis me résigner à la déchiffrer devant le publique.' Röntgen adopted a more vigorous technique of getting a reply from Tovey. In a letter headed with an appropriate quotation from *Meistersinger* he says: 'Lieber Schweigsamer, Wenn ich auch noch keine Antwort auf meine Anfrage dein Kommen nach Amsterdam für das *Prix d'excellence* Examen betreffend, erhalten habe, so will ich dir doch, in der angenehmen Voraussetzung daß dein Schweigen gleich bedeutend mit deiner Zusage ist, schon jetzt das Program des Schlachtopfers schicken!'[1] The volume of Tovey's correspondence still extant disproves the assertion that he *never* wrote letters, but it was quite unpredictable as to when he would think it necessary to do so, or whether he would send them when written.

Writing to Miss Weisse on the occasion of her birthday in October 1919, he was full of enthusiasm for a new activity—the

---

[1] 'Dear Silent One, If I do not receive a reply to my inquiry regarding your coming to Amsterdam for the *Prix d'excellence* examination, then I will, in the pleasant belief that silence means consent, send you the list of the victims!'

Workers Educational Association, for which he had undertaken to lecture in music during the winter—'I had a post-card from the secretary after the first meeting, saying that all records are broken, 150 having already enrolled for my course and more coming next week. *Per contra* the University music-students are still a miserable handful; but even here there is a remarkable sign of life. The leader of my second violins, a very nice boy who has a brother in Beecham's orchestra, came with his sister to play to me. She accompanied him (although she can only stretch about a sixth) through Lalo's *Caprice Espagnol*, which he played with excellent technique and very unparochial bulldogliness. I then suggested that he should play a Beethoven Sonata with me. His sister said that her favourite was Op. 96 which he said he didn't know. You will be surprised to hear that he played the whole sonata in excellent style, far better than the Lalo; catching up every hint from my phrasing, and getting no end of things absolutely right which no pianoforte could tell him. After this he proceeded to ask questions about the University degree, and he is going to tackle the whole thing, Science Preliminary (with Latin) and all. Not bad for the leader of a local theatre-band. But this isn't the end of the story. Last Thursday his sister turned up at the Orchestral Class and played the piccolo!' (This young man, Ernest Stoneley, got his degree and subsequently made an excellent career for himself; his sister became a fine flautist.) The letter concludes, 'Next Friday my Brummagem recitals begin. I wish there were 68 hours in the day'. Miss Mary Weisse, who was then living at Queensferry, wrote to her sister about the W.E.A. lectures. In one letter she says, 'I wish I could give you some idea of Donald's marvellous lecture' (on *The Comparison between Haydn, Mozart, and Beethoven in Emotional Range*). 'It was nothing short of amazing. On the Tuesday before he had been so little *dans son assiette* that there was not much to note. This time it was an indescribably pregnant and dramatic performance; his face *shone* and positively changed outline.'

The Birmingham concerts were a series of six Beethoven

recitals including twenty-two sonatas and all the big sets of variations—duplicating the Historical concerts in Edinburgh that winter. They marked the beginning of a lifelong friendship with Granville Bantock, whose freedom from pedantry and warm championship of the rank and file musician were so congenial to Tovey. The strong bonds of sympathy between the two are evident in Tovey's appreciation of Bantock's music—an appreciation not always unbiased. In June 1920 Birmingham conferred on him the Honorary Degree of Master of Music.

Among the soloists at the Reid concerts in its fourth season (1919–20—the first under the auspices of the new committee) were Fanny Davies, Adila and Jelly d'Aranyi, Fleury, and Suggia. For the first time since the unhappy events of 1912, Tovey had played with Suggia in the autumn of 1919 at Northlands, where the old traditions were still being carried on by Miss Weisse's successor. Six years later, Casals's name appears on the Reid concert programmes and all traces of the old misunderstandings finally disappeared.

A new Professor of Medical Chemistry was appointed to Edinburgh in the session 1919–20. Professor George Barger and his wife had lived near Northlands, and they already knew Tovey and Miss Weisse. Their coming to Edinburgh was a most fortunate event for Tovey, and in times of domestic difficulty these were the friends to whom he most often turned. Professor Barger was partly of Dutch extraction—a brilliant linguist as well as a brilliant scientist; Mrs. Barger, a gentle and clever woman, was incapable of thinking ill of anyone and forever helping lame dogs over stiles. Professor Barger was not musical, but he had a very real interest in Beethoven's music, the greatness of which he seemed to apprehend in some curious way. Tovey spent hours explaining the symphonies and sonatas to his colleague (as he did sometimes for another great but unmusical scientist—Sir Oliver Lodge). This contact between two first-rate minds of so dissimilar outlook was a great source of pleasure to both. The Bargers had an enormous circle of friends of every nationality, and when Röntgen sent one of his sons to study with Tovey in Edinburgh the young man found himself immediately received into congenial surroundings. The presence of Johannes Röntgen in Edinburgh was a very great comfort to Tovey—not only for the satisfaction of having a student of really solid musical worth, but also because he constituted a link with the wider musical world which was a very lifeline to Tovey in the culminating stages of his domestic tragedy. When Johannes had completed his first term of study his father wrote to Tovey: 'Ich beneide ihn um Alles was du ihm gibst, und empfinde tief, was es für ihn deine Entwickelung als Mensch und Musiker zu bedeuten hat. Wie soll ich dir dafür danken!? Vielleicht macht er dir selbst etwas Freude, daß deine Saat in ein gutes Erdreich fällt, und gewiß einmal zu voller Blüthe kommen wird. Sei dafür gesegnet!

'Ich freue mich auf Fortsetzung von Band XXXIII unseres Briefenwechsel, noch mehr aber hoffentlich baldige Mundwechsel!'[1]

On 4 March 1920 a special concert was given to celebrate the twenty-fifth appearance of the Reid Symphony Orchestra. The programme was as follows:

(1)	Marches nos. 4 and 5	*General Reid*
(2)	Symphony in B flat (Salamon no. 12)	*Haydn*
(3)	Scherzo in G minor (arranged from the Octet by the composer)	*Mendelssohn*
(4)	Prelude to *Sappho*	*Granville Bantock*
(5)	*Conte Féerique* op. 29	*Rimsky-Korsakoff*
(6)	Overture *Leonora* no. 3	*Beethoven*

For once Tovey did not write programme-notes; instead, he wrote four of the seven short articles in the Souvenir Programme. The article on 'The needs of an orchestra' pleads for opportunities

[1] 'I envy him all you are giving him, and am deeply aware of all that you mean to him as a man and as a musician. How can I thank you? Perhaps he himself gives you some pleasure in knowing that you are sowing seed in good ground, and that sometime it will certainly bloom. Bless you for that!

'I rejoice at the continuation of volume 33 of our correspondence, still more at the thought that we may talk again together soon!'

for local players to study and develop their talent, and concludes: 'There is in popular musical aesthetics a good deal of humbug, about which the really great conductors are themselves very outspoken. All the great achievements in orchestral performances have been cases where one musician, disposed by nature and circumstances to take an educative view of his task, has trained a local orchestra. The Hallé Orchestra is our British classical example. Another example, foreign, but perhaps not less significant, is that of the Meiningen Orchestra, which, as Weingartner pointed out in his brochure on conducting, was neither large nor in its first stages composed of first-rate material, but which under the direction of its first conductor, Bülow, revealed the possibilities of orchestral ensemble to towns that boasted the possession of the finest and best established orchestras in Europe. Meiningen is a town about the size of Moffat. . . . I confess that when I see the difference between what our orchestral players can do and what they have to do, it is then that I feel most deeply the sense in which we are an unmusical nation: that is to say, a nation in which the best musical talent in Europe is systematically thrown on the scrap-heap and kept there. And I cannot conceive a more appropriate, or indeed, a different function for a University Faculty of Music than that of making this unmusical state of things impossible.'

During the following season 1920–1 the experiment was made of concentrating the Reid concerts in the spring, when a series of six were given at weekly intervals—in the more favourable surroundings of the new and beautiful Usher Hall. At the second of these Tovey heard in performance for the first time a part of his opera—Ariadne's soliloquy from Act III, Scene 2, which, with the ending he contrived, makes an excellent concert-piece, and which, perhaps for that very reason, is the only part which he finally cut out of the opera itself. This was included in the concert-programmes because he had found, locally, a singer admirably fitted to sing it. Mrs. Sklovsky, though she lived with her husband in Edinburgh, was of German origin and had received a thorough continental training; she abandoned her pro-

fessional career when she married, but continued to maintain
the high standard of her singing. If Tovey had induced some
well-known professional concert-artist to sing the piece, however, it would certainly have found its way on to other platforms,
and might have awakened general curiosity about the opera
itself. In such ways his lack of common sense in matters concerning his own interest was the despair of his friends.

A recital of the three Brahms sonatas which Tovey gave with
Huberman is also remembered as one of the outstanding events
of that season in Edinburgh. In May the University of Oxford
conferred on him the honorary degree of Doctor of Music.
Whatever value he attached to the honour, he certainly loved
his beautiful 'strawberry-cream' gown and enjoyed occasions
for appearing in his academic finery.

Tovey met Fritz Busch again in Holland in 1920 for the first
time since the war. He hoped in the following summer to pay
him a visit in Stuttgart and to go to Switzerland to see the new
double-keyboard pianoforte which Mr. Emmanuel Moór had
invented. When summer came, however, he was unsettled in
plans and mind, and desperately anxious about his wife's health,
which was now making his position in Edinburgh difficult. He
took her to London in the hope that she would be persuaded
to try a new treatment, strongly recommended by a colleague.
Thence he wrote in July to Mrs. Trevelyan: 'I am going to try
and contrive some such dash abroad as may not preclude my
coming back at a moment's notice. The doctor is still convinced
that he can cure my wife if only she will come to him; and so
long as there is any chance of that I must keep my grip of all
opportunities of accomplishing it.' He had thoughts of resigning
his chair, a course that would have been disastrous; even Miss
Weisse was a convert to the value and worth of the work he was
doing in Edinburgh. But such treatment as Mrs. Tovey consented to have unhappily failed to have the hoped-for results.
Her illness had now taken the form of turning bitterly against
her husband; she did not wish him to return to London to
see her, and she did not return to Edinburgh with him in the

autumn. Proceedings for divorce were instituted on her behalf shortly afterwards, and the whole unhappy business came to an end with great distress of mind to everybody in July 1922. The poor lady died a few years later.

Until the actual proceedings in court only a few of Tovey's personal friends had any idea of the extent of his domestic tragedy, and of these possibly only the Trevelyans and the Bargers had any idea of what he suffered over the space of three years. His endurance, his gentleness, and his silence were nothing short of heroic. 'It is certain', wrote a colleague, 'that to so highly sensitive a nature these painful experiences were permanently wounding, all the more because he kept on with his Chair, his duties, his concerts, and the Reid Orchestra. A lesser man would have quitted scenes associated with such experiences, would have gone elsewhere to obliterate recollection in a new milieu. When I first knew him—early in 1924—some pathos attached to his loneliness and the chaotic state of his music: "I know where everything is!" he said, searching for some manuscript,—but he failed to find it. People have wondered why the stream of his compositions ceased, and was intermitted for all those years; but in expressing such wonder they show the crassest absence of imagination, for a composer of integrity composes with the whole of his personality. This demands intact nerves; Tovey kept his personality together, but sometimes with perceptible effort, and at all times at a sacrifice in nerves. I even think that more than one half of the loquacity, the semi-eccentricity, the Edward Lear-ishness, were defensive, or were the external manifestation of the struggle by which will dominated nerves.'

Despite the sad circumstances of his personal affairs, or perhaps as a relief from them, Tovey became keenly interested in two new projects during the summer of 1921, the Moór pianoforte, and a new restoration of Weber's *Euryanthe*. Fritz Busch was anxious to produce this opera—impracticable in its original state—and he asked Tovey to collaborate with the dramatist Dr. Rolf Lauckner in making an arrangement which could really be produced on the stage. Curiously enough Tovey had written a programme-note on the overture to *Euryanthe* for a Reid concert in February of that year, in which he discussed the state of the opera: '*Euryanthe* is both a more mature work of art and a more advanced development of Wagnerian music-drama than *Lohengrin*, though it is a generation earlier. No one who knows *Euryanthe* thoroughly will consider this an extravagant statement. . . . Why then is it so seldom heard?

'Ask poor Weber what he thought of Frau von Chezy after he had got "old Chezy" to remodel her libretto for the ninth time. Ask him how he came to call his beautiful and virtuous heroine "Ennuyante". . . . I am not without hope that some day the right story may be found for his music; but many attempts to improve the libretto have failed through lack of appreciation of Weber's sense of form. It is no use improving the play if you think Weber's huge musical design does not matter.'

The insight into operatic problems gained from his own work and his genius for perceiving the intentions of music other than his own made Tovey an ideal person for the task. The reconstructed *Euryanthe* was produced successfully in Dresden in 1923 and there was talk of translating it into English and doing it at the Metropolitan in New York. A postcard to Tovey from Busch in July of this year has a postscript from Lauckner: 'Everybody is here. You only want—nobody knows where you have hided yourself. *Euryanthe* follows in September.' At the beginning of September Busch wrote again: 'Come as soon as you can. Rehearsals are in full swing and I should like to talk over several points with you. You must play on 28th September—we are doing a Beethoven String Trio and a Brahms String Quintet; you shall do the *Goldberg* Variations in the middle.' (This programme was amended to a lecture-recital on the *Goldberg* Variations, and the critics were enthusiastic not only about the playing of the work, but about the fine lecture—in German— which preceded it.) Following on the success of the Weber, Lauckner and Tovey collaborated again in the rehabilitation of two early Schubert operas, *Der Vierjährige Posten* and *Die*

Weiberverschwörung. In the latter Tovey interpolated as incidental music two of Schubert's four-hand marches, brilliantly orchestrated.

The affair of the Moór-Duplex pianoforte was a strange one. Early in 1921 Moór sent Tovey a copy of his leaflet on *The Reformation of the Piano*, in which he described his invention—a piano with a second keyboard above the first, tuned an octave higher: the white keys of the lower keyboard were raised at the back to the level of the black keys so that it was possible to play on both keyboards at once with one hand; a pedal enabled the two keyboards to be coupled together and there was also a 'cembalo stop'. Tovey's imagination was fired by the possibilities which he could foresee for such an instrument, and Moór, delighted that he should believe in the piano without seeing it, promised to let him have one in Edinburgh in the autumn for the purposes of demonstration; meanwhile he invited Tovey to come to Switzerland to see the specimen which had already been built by the Swiss firm of Schmidt-Flohr. Tovey's enthusiasm on seeing the piano was so great that he wrote, for *Music and Letters*, a remarkable article on the new instrument. While most of those who were interested in it regarded the invention as a means of simplifying virtuoso-technique, Tovey regarded it as the extension of the possibilities of the pianoforte. 'There is no saying', he wrote, 'how long it may take pianists to work out the new technique of the instrument. Many players will probably be quite content to do wonders in public without learning anything new at all, nor do I suppose that the general public will be able to guess very clearly what is done by new technique, and what by the mere use of the coupler; but I do know that there is an enormous field of technique in the simultaneous use of the manuals by one or both hands.' He described some of the technical devices which he had discovered, including 'a pleasing crab-like fingering for legato broken octaves descending in the right-hand and ascending in the left, which remains the same for every scale, diatonic, chromatic or whole-toned'; adding: 'All these devices belong, not to the *bravura* difficulties, but to the elements of the new cross-manual technique. Each of them can be mastered in a five-finger exercise, which I find difficult merely because I am not at the age for learning such things for the first time in my life. A child will learn them as easily as the ordinary technique, and will have far more pleasure in the sound of them. . . . Indeed I have not yet found any position in the new compound technique which is not physically comfortable, though the mental difficulties of the new muscular co-ordinations are formidable at first.' The mental difficulties of playing a duet with oneself—which was his favourite demonstration of the instrument's possibilities—are so formidable that few players could attempt them. Yet there is no doubt that—with the aid of an extension of notation which he also envisaged—great things would have been possible on the lines he indicated.

With regard to the cembalo stop he was more guarded, though he described it as 'an excellent generalisation of harpsichord-tone with the addition of all the pianoforte freedom and control of light and shade'. He was also convinced of the possibilities of developing the instrument into a 'triplex-coupler pianoforte, with a third lower manual an octave below the normal; with the possibility of coupling all three or any two; and a variety of cembalo stops. . . . A little calculation shows that much of the complex technique needed for the solo-playing of four-hand music on the present Duplex-Coupler would disappear if there was a lower octave coupler as well as the present (upper) one. I do not foresee that the gigantic instrument of the future will develop into any such chaotic menagerie as the modern organ. . . . I do not, for example, foresee the advent of a pedal-board. . . . It might be conceivable that to the resources of a triplex-coupler there could be added those of the *sostinente* piano—which I have always been given to understand was by no means unsuccessful'. In fact, the only possibility which he did not explore was that of enlarging the brain of the average pianist who was to play the future monster!

Some difficulties arose in regard to the Swiss firm which was making the pianos, and Tovey was instrumental in putting

Moór in touch with an English firm. From that moment every-thing went wrong. It was announced for the Reid concert in February 1922 that the Bach Cembalo Concerto in D minor would be played on Mr. Moór's Duplex pianoforte, but the instrument did not arrive in time. Even at the demonstration recital given shortly afterwards, it was clear that Tovey had not had sufficient time to become fluent in the use of the new tech-nique. At an Oxford concert the same thing happened, and when he was cold-shouldered out of a London demonstration he had reason to be very angry about the whole thing. The in-vention aroused considerable interest when it was introduced, but after a year or two little more was heard of it. Tovey bought a Duplex-Coupler grand himself about 1928 but made little use of it—though he still believed in its possibilities and even started to write a set of special studies for it. But his instrument was too heavy to be moved readily to and from the concert-hall, and it had rather a coarse, thick tone. When it was still new, his favourite joke was to say to a visitor in his upstairs drawing-room—'I say, have you heard my octave technique nowadays?' and rush downstairs to the music room where the new piano stood, and play a rapid—and apparently impossible passage—*with the octave coupler on*. Harold Samuel's reaction to this joke was really worth while!

12

TOVEY took his University work very seriously, although he did not map out a hard and fast course to be followed during the session. It is possible that this absence of a set plan bore hardly on the weaker students, but there was more method behind what he did than appeared on the surface. He often looked like the popular idea of the absent-minded professor—clothes pulled on hastily (and he always had trouble with what he called the 'flippers' of his gown), tie under one ear, and one end of a very soft collar at a wild angle; yet he contrived to look ridiculous with unconscious dignity. The first thing he insisted on teaching was musical handwriting; how to draw the stem out of the head of a note in one movement, instead of using two movements to make head and stem separately, whereby the two frequently failed to join; how to write long series of quavers and semiquavers swiftly; the best angle at which to hold the pen for speed and the best kind of nib to use; the necessity for making all accidentals large and clear, and for being accurate about tempo indications and marks of expression. He would point out that it was necessary to be able to write swiftly, because in composing one always thought faster than one could write and sometimes even faster than one could sketch, and that serious errors in proportion and loss of a sense of tempo often resulted when a composer was slow in writing down his ideas. Tovey's own musical handwriting is not beautiful to look at, but it is amazingly clear and accurate, and he wrote with great fluency. He *could*, on occasion, write manuscript most beautifully. In his set of the first edition in miniature score of Wagner's operas, there are, towards the end of *Götterdämmerung*, fifteen printed pages missing; these are replaced by exquisite manuscript of the exact size of the original pages. He urged on his students the necessity of clear handwriting, because, he said, clear handwriting generally meant clear thinking. 'My own writing does not *look* very well,' he once said to me, 'but at least I make all my letters different!'

Counterpoint classes began by writing rounds—any number of them—to words that ranged from limericks to a verse of Donne, with the emphasis rather on the side of limericks. I do not know what view some external examiners might take of a counterpoint paper, of which one question was—'Set the following as a three-part round for equal voices:

> There was a young lady of Rio
> Who tried to play Hummel's Grand Trio
> But her pace was so scanty
> She took it *Andante*
> Instead of *Allegro con brio*!'

Corrections on a student's exercises were unorthodox and often amusing; a round, with which I had not been particularly successful, was returned to me with the errors duly marked, and the sole comment a comical drawing of a face with tears pouring down it. As the class progressed to the writing of fugues, Tovey made a point of teaching technical devices like *stretto* and double and triple counterpoint—first reducing illustrative passages from Bach to formulae, in the most illuminating way. He maintained that if a student had mastered that amount of *technique* he could then start the business of *composing* a fugue. He often gave the class words for a vocal fugue; I was inspired to my best effort by the following—'Cursed be he that greeteth his neighbour with a loud voice', (counter-subject) 'arising early in the morning!' My grandmother was shocked and said that anyway these were not the words in the Bible. However, they were to me congenial words for a fugue, and I began with my alto in full flight, at the top of her voice. The comment at the end of my fugue was—'Very good. But *I* should have begun with curses "not loud but deep".'

Tovey always stimulated the imagination. He would point out, for instance, that it is the business of two-part writing to sound full, and of five-part writing to sound transparent, which is practical common sense to a composer, but is the kind of advice one never encounters in text-books. He never used text-books in harmony or counterpoint—except for Morris's *Figured Harmony at the Keyboard*, which appeared much later. His teaching of harmony was founded on Bach chorales and figured basses, supplemented by harmonic analysis of later styles, and exercises for which he invented the material. He was most meticulous in his setting of examination papers, and insisted on working them out first of all to make sure there were no snags, going on the theory that what he could not do in twenty minutes students could not be expected to do in three hours. In later years the papers were 'tried out' on me. He had plans for writing a text-book on harmony and suggested that I might collect the material for him. He even started the book in 1934 when I was staying at Hedenham in the summer. His method was to dictate to his secretary, while I sat ready to interpose if I thought there was anything a student might not understand. The first chapter began with some fundamental propositions, and then continued with a long and involved dissertation on Ruskin. I protested, and was immediately and completely crushed with another dissertation on the necessity of the first. I vowed to myself that I would not intervene again. Next morning he came down about eleven o'clock, and after reproaching me for practising out of tune (he never bothered about the piano being out of tune when he played it himself!), he proceeded, 'You were quite right yesterday; that first chapter won't do. Let's begin again.' We began at least three times, and I am sorry that I did not push the plan of the book more energetically. But he was then too tired for the work. I told Dr. Walker of the proposed text-book when he came over from Oxford on a visit, and of my function to make sure that it would be presented in a form that students could easily grasp. 'Hmph,' he said, 'I can imagine a text-book which Tovey could understand and you could understand, but nobody else could!'

During the winter of 1917–18 (I think) I was the only student in the composition class; the Professor never failed to turn up and I had a wonderful series of lessons on the setting of the Mass by Bach and Beethoven. Almost he persuaded me that I could compose—but *not* that I had anything to say. 'Bad composition consists in mishandling cadences', was one of his favourite axioms; and he had a great belief in the value of writing variations as a means of acquiring technique.

His History lectures and classes in Musical Analysis, Acoustics, and Orchestration were thrilling, and although he delivered them, of course, extempore, he never seemed to forget where he had left off the week before. His wealth of accurate illustration was astounding. He was less happy with the practical classes— Score-reading and Figured Bass, and Musical Interpretation; he could be infinitely patient with technical deficiencies when he felt there was genuine musical intelligence behind them, but deficiencies of dullness and musical insensitiveness left him quite helpless, and his patience would give way quickly under the strain. The Interpretation Class was his first addition to the curriculum—'the theory of music', he said, 'must be based on practice or it is nonsense.' The class was intended mainly to encourage the playing and study of chamber music, although solo playing was not debarred. Whenever a promising piece turned up the Professor spared no pains to help the players with illuminating and constructive criticism. As a teacher he always insisted on the necessity of making things sound beautiful.

The examination papers which he set are evidence of what he taught, and of what he expected from, his students. He had the utmost horror of examinations, and though he would talk of 'speeding the plough', he usually gave the 'border-line' candidate the benefit of the doubt. The standard of the degree was frequently attacked—mostly by those who knew little about it— and certain of these critics were on one occasion completely silenced by the production of the current examination question papers. It was obvious that any student who could answer them even moderately well was a very fair musician. In 1914–18 the average standard of students coming up to the University was inevitably low, and Tovey had to take this into account. But he strove continuously to raise the standard. A letter to Professor Grierson in 1922 (when he was a member of the Faculty of Music and a very present aid to Tovey in the Senatus) discusses new entrance requirements and the inclusion of music as a subject in an Arts degree, and concludes: 'At present I state, unhesitatingly though unofficially, that Musical Degrees, all the world over, are Bosh. But I see no inherent reason why they should be. Get us a special Entrance in Music, and we will soon set a decent standard.' In the course of a long letter to Percy Buck, who was external examiner in 1926, Tovey asks: 'Draft me a set of papers which you would regard as a Mus.Bac. Final as good as you want anywhere, i.e. on the assumption that we don't want (except perhaps in composition) to pass anybody here whom you wouldn't pass elsewhere. I except composition, because I hold strongly that wherever the old cantata-cum-symphony idea of a degree exercise survives, there is implied a demand which no university ought to make or dreams of making in any other subject.' He also slyly remarks: 'I notice that members of my staff have an uneasy feeling that my methods of analysis ought not to be revealed to the young.' By the 1930's, when good students were being attracted to Edinburgh from places as far away as California, the standard of Musical Analysis was certainly higher than anywhere else in the country, with History, Orchestration, and Score-reading a good second. Harmony and Counterpoint were below the academic standards at Oxford and Cambridge, but the musical quality of the work was respectable. On the first occasion on which he acted as external examiner at Edinburgh, Bantock wrote to Tovey: '. . . It has given me a lot of pleasure to read the papers, which, on the whole, show a higher degree of efficiency than we can produce here or elsewhere in England I should imagine. In any case, your questions are a model for present and future generations.'

The first letter I ever had from the Professor was in 1917, supplementing the dread official slip on which the examination results are recorded: 'Your Italian and literature were good; but you fell into a trap common to the pronouns of all inflected languages in the Metastasio scene. . . . Remember for instance that "sa majesté" doesn't necessarily mean "her majesty." . . . I recommend that once famous classic *English as She is spoke* as giving valuable insight; e.g. "he has scratched the face with her nails". Your Acoustics annoyed me considerably—they were wrong in just the things a musician ought to know: e.g.

—a piece of arithmetic without which no thirds are in tune and tonality is a mere figment. Dr. Walker and I would certainly have ploughed them if we could.

'In Rhetoric and English Literature your chief crime was in attempting to fob me off with Sarcasm where I wanted Irony. . . . Taking your illustration of the weather—Irony will not say "it's a fine day" when it is pouring with rain, but will say "Ah wudna wunner tae see rain before ta nicht!"'

Ten years later, when there was a great deal of talk of a Municipal Orchestra in Edinburgh, I received the following comic communication: '. . . What the municipal orchestra business indicates to me is that it is now high time for me to screw up the standard of University degree work. Obviously a time must come when the competent orchestral players of Edinburgh (Sc. Reid players) will be living on well-organized rehearsal work. Obviously in that glorious time I can't do all the conducting myself. Obviously then I must be able to make out a strong case for regarding our graduates as *ipso facto* specially eligible for definite orchestral appointments. And at present you are the only one I could trust.

'By the way: Happy Thought; *why not take your Mus.Doc. as a player and conductor*? Beyond sitting our Exam, there's not a stroke of preparation you require for it. . . . I say, do think of this. It would set such a good example. . . . We could do it this year à propos of your conducting at the last concert. . . . If I thought it meant work and worry for you I would not suggest it; but I cannot see anything in the Faculty Programme, p. 7, section *ix*, that isn't in your present routine. . . . *Do* please consent. It will be such fun, and draw attention to the Faculty of Music most opportunely. And think what a good symbol it would be that my first Mus.Doc. (the second in the history of the Chair at all) should be a conductor.' The idea of a Mus.Doc. had never entered my head, and *of course* it meant work and worry. But in a way it was 'fun'! The seven-page letter ends: 'By the way, I'm full of new details in method of practising the pianoforte; so let's try how they suit you.'

In many ways Tovey was not an ideal teacher; he did not suffer fools gladly, and he expected much from the student's own initiative. But he was an ideal professor—providing the right atmosphere, the right material, and a great amount of scope for the young musician—above all, stimulating and inspiring both his staff and his students in a way that was unique.

On the publication of Holst's *Hymn of Jesus* in 1920 Tovey wrote to the composer—'I've been reading your *Hymn of Jesus*. It completely bowls me over. Your presentation of it is the poem, the whole poem and nothing but the poem. I am thoroughly familiar with that kind of enjoyment of a setting of a poem where one feels "ah—that's a clever way to set this verse—not a way that would have occurred to me—perhaps better, perhaps not quite so good as my idea of how to set it:—aha, I *like* this— etc. etc." Well, your *Hymn of Jesus* doesn't occupy me in that way at all. It is there, just as if neither you nor I had any say in the matter. It couldn't have been done before (—I have not a very adequate knowledge of your works—but it makes no difference what steps or approximations you may have made before it)—and it can't be done again (—i.e. the next equally real thing will be entirely different). It is a blessed abiding fact; and not a matter of taste at all. If anybody doesn't like it, he doesn't like life.

'Some day I hope to conduct a performance of it which shall stand in the same relation to the music as the music stands to the poem; i.e. a performance that just is the thing itself.'

In February 1922 Tovey was able to secure the collaboration of the Edinburgh Royal Choral Union for two Reid concerts, and Holst's great work was given twice in successive weeks. At the end of the first performance Tovey was so completely overcome that it was a moment or two before he could turn round to face the audience.

That concert took place the night before I was due to leave for Prague with Miss Fanny Davies. My share in the programme was the pianoforte part of Beethoven's Triple Concerto, which I played with the leader of the first violins and the leader of the 'cellos. The overture which Tovey thought appropriate to my impending departure was Mendelssohn's *A Calm Sea and a Prosperous Voyage*! It sounded very well preceding Parry's *Blest Pair of Sirens*.

At the second choral concert Tovey conducted Beethoven's Ninth Symphony for the first time. His tremendous essay on this work was published as part of the programme-notes, and there was quickly a great demand for it—abroad as at home—as I found even in Prague. In all, Tovey conducted the Ninth Symphony only five times in his life: of these performances I heard all but the first. Many other performances which I have heard were, technically, far better; but his, no matter what their blemishes, fulfilled the ideal which he desired for Holst's *Hymn of Jesus*—they were 'just the thing itself'.

Tovey was very anxious that a German edition of the *Hymn of Jesus* should be published, and he interested Lauckner in the matter, but financial difficulties proved insuperable. Holst conducted some works of his own at a Reid concert in 1926 when Tovey was in America, but he declined the honorary degree which was then offered to him. He also declined an invitation to act as external examiner: he was, as it happened, under doctor's orders at the time, but his letter said, 'I am much too ignorant to examine students in anything except purely practical things such as counterpoint; it would do me a world of good to sit for the exam myself'.

Holst and Tovey met very seldom, but they held each other

in lifelong esteem. Writing to Imogen Holst in 1934 after her father's death, Tovey regrets having seen so little of him, and adds: 'You, who are also a composer, know that we composers are lonely folk who have great difficulty in helping each other; and you will understand that it meant much to me that your father, whose intensely original and, to me, austere style has so little in common with anything I can hope to write, was always cordial and unembarrassed whenever we met. So many composers (if there can be said to be many) make me feel shy, but he made me feel happy.' Another letter four years later expresses admiration for the 'Holstian directness and economy' of the biography she had written. 'I am simply overwhelmed', it continues, 'by the self-less beauty and simplicity of his life. And I am absolutely crushed to find myself well thought of by him; though my experience more and more convinces me that the chief sign of saintliness is that in the presence of a saint one's burden falls off one's back and one's own horrible faults and insufficiences aren't worth a damn.'

From 1920 Tovey's many-sided musical activities were—despite his many engagements in Europe and America—centred on the development of the Reid Orchestra. He regarded his engagements abroad as of vital importance 'because they enable me to bring good things to my own place'. The achievements of the big choral and orchestral concerts in 1922 made him very hopeful for the future; but the losses on the season's work were serious, and the financial crisis which arose in May was as much responsible for Tovey's thoughts of resigning his Chair as were his personal affairs. 'I have no use,' he wrote to Mr. McEwen, 'for the idea that I am doing wonderful things with inferior material. My material is doing wonderful things in circumstances that would smash up the Scottish Orchestra ten times over;—and catch Landon Ronald[1] putting up with it for a moment! . . . Practically the whole wind-band has a theatre matinée every Saturday *between my rehearsal and the concert*. No ordinary orchestral player would stand that. I shall never get

---

[1] At that time conductor of the Scottish Orchestra.

people to understand what we have here unless I'm given a chance to show these men working under decent conditions. . . . It's no use trying to achieve this by making six concerts a year pay. I get an excellent gallery, thanks to your Nelson Hall people and my W.E.A. The wealth and fashion that cares tuppence about music is in the Grand Circle—that is to say the Grand Circle is nearly empty and I know everybody in it. I don't want to know those Grand Circle goers who aren't in it because I'll neither work nor play for snobs who go only by "established reputations", and with whom reputations are established simply and solely by advertisements on the scale of Pears Soap. But I want their money. Meanwhile the Lord Provost is talking bosh about the lack of cheap concerts and —— is writing worse bosh to the papers and altogether I get moments of such discouragement that I should be quite glad to disappear for good. I never get these moments at rehearsals.' With heroic efforts Mr. McEwen and Mrs. Maitland tided over the breach.

Two years later, however, a more acute crisis arose and it became evident that the whole enterprise must be put on a broader basis. Mr. McEwen resigned the chairmanship and Lord Murray, a judge of the Court of Session, succeeded him. The Reid Orchestra was constituted a Friendly Society, and a Committee was elected which represented not only the Guarantors but also the members of the orchestra; I became honorary secretary. As a Friendly Society the orchestra functioned for the rest of its existence, and a real sense of co-operative feeling helped to carry it through many difficulties. Lord Murray was a tactful and successful chairman. He understood Tovey and sympathized with his ideals, but his first step was to abolish the necessity for the conductor to attend committee meetings. This speeded up business; on the other hand I found that my own task of go-between for the conductor and the committee often stretched my powers of invention to the limit.

The existence of the orchestra greatly stimulated local chamber music. When the Edinburgh String Quartet was founded the Professor was generous in encouraging it, and often after a concert he would go off to a rehearsal which started at 11 p.m. and lasted till the early hours of the morning. Subsiding into the largest armchair in the room, he would patiently coach the players, absent-mindedly reaching out from time to time for a sandwich and gradually demolishing the whole plateful if his hostess was not wary. No one thought of fatigue, and the first major engagement of the quartet—to play the last five Beethoven quartets at the Historical concerts in the spring of 1923—was notably successful. The outlook for local chamber music was so promising that this quartet was able on two occasions to give a series of concerts consisting of the whole of the Beethoven string quartets. Other chamber music organizations sprang up, and it was even possible to get a good wind ensemble.

The establishment by Tovey in 1923-4 of weekly Sunday night concerts provided for sixteen years a platform for all local chamber music of good standard and for every promising young performer (as well as those who were already established). The programmes of this series show what an immense range and variety of music one could hear for eightpence (later, one and threepence) from the gallery of the Usher Hall. The galleryites were mostly young—clerks, shop-assistants, and students—and I often meet nowadays with strangers who tell me what they owe to the unforgettable musical experiences of these concerts. The audiences, though often scandalously small in the great Usher Hall, were much warmer in appreciation than normal Edinburgh audiences, and would even burst into cheers after a fine performance of, say, the *Hammerklavier* Sonata or Beethoven's B flat Trio. The finances of the concerts were *most* precarious, indeed it would be difficult to explain now how they worked at all! Tovey kept them going by pianoforte recitals (without fee), and on more than one occasion shouldered the deficit at the end of the season himself. Distinguished soloists who had come for a Reid concert sometimes stayed to play with him at a Sunday concert, and a programme by local players one Sunday might be followed the next week by a recital by Tovey and Suggia. The orchestra played as often as funds would permit (and sometimes when they didn't). Many young players learned most of what they now know of the art of ensemble from playing chamber music with Tovey at these concerts. He was the perfect pianist in an ensemble, and to play two-piano music (or piano duets) with him was a delight and a revelation. The level of performances at the Sunday night concerts varied a good deal, but the best were first-rate and the worst were still of decent standard.

At these concerts—as at Historicals—Tovey very often gave explanatory talks. Many of these were excellent, but there were always certain members of the public who disliked talks with their music, and there *were* occasions when his habit of digressing got out of hand and, worse still, occasions when he attacked the apathy of the general public of Edinburgh and appealed from the platform—often in unguarded terms—for better support and better opportunities for local musicians. He did himself and his cause a good deal of harm in this way and irritated the press critics. Nothing, however, could be done about it; one had to accept Tovey as he was.

At the end of the Reid concert season in March 1924, the Professor gave a supper party in the Music Classroom for the orchestra. The idea originated with Miss Weisse, and the delightful function became an annual event at which Tovey invariably complied with requests to sing one of the inimitable songs which would have made his fortune on any music-hall stage. There was a printed programme on the first occasion:

Pianoforte solo, *Ce qu'un Faune lisait dans
   son Journal*   *César Cui*
Song, *Triolets Ollendorfiens* (by J. K. S.) *D.F.T.*
   (1st setting by Massager 1890)
   (2nd setting by Deomnibussy 1930)
Hungarian Dances, &c.
   (Madame Adila Fachiri)   *Brahms–Joachim*

Song, *Incidents in the Life of my Uncle Arly*   D.F.T.
Symphony, *A Musical Joke; or The Village
  Musicians*   *Mozart*
  (The Wee Reed Orchestra.)

Shortly after this Tovey wrote to Trevelyan: 'I am surrounded by whirlwinds; what with moving house, providing for Victor Hely-Hutchinson *and* his Mamma, etc;—Miss Weisse is assisting most nobly and efficiently. With diplomacy (both secret and Democratically Controlled) she is really doing wonders, and I should be rather up a tree without her.' Miss Weisse and he moved into two adjacent flats in Buccleuch Street,[1] in the premises where the *Edinburgh Review* was founded by Jeffrey in 1805. The street has declined from its original status, but the rooms have graceful proportions, and the flats were made both comfortable and beautiful by Miss Weisse, who was never happier, Tovey used to say, than when she was having walls knocked in and windows knocked out. Neither cared that it was an unfashionable neighbourhood—economy was indeed a consideration just then; moreover, Tovey was within five minutes walk of his classroom, and Miss Weisse felt satisfied to think that he was bound to have at least a little exercise and fresh air, even on his busiest days.

---

[1] The flat in which Tovey lived is now maintained as 'The Tovey Rooms' for the use of University music students.

13

IN spring 1924 Tovey received an invitation from California to lecture and play at the summer session of The School of the Arts in Santa Barbara. This school was a branch of the Community Arts Association, and its Director, who sent the invitation, was Mr. Morley Fletcher. Before taking up the appointment in Santa Barbara, Morley Fletcher had been Principal of the School of Art in Edinburgh, and he was a whole-hearted admirer of Tovey's work. 'Our School', wrote the Secretary to Tovey from Santa Barbara, 'has as yet no library, musical or otherwise. It will take the sort of inspiration your course will bring this summer to make apparent the uses and value of such. . . . Much is to be done in this direction in Santa Barbara. In the meantime, we have no funds at all with which to buy music.' Pioneer work always appealed to Tovey, and he decided to go, having been assured that he would get other engagements on his way back to New York which would make it financially worth while.

'I hope', he wrote to Miss Weisse on arriving in New York, 'that among other luxurious habits of this country I shall not acquire the aboriginal twang. The cumulative effect of it is dangerously narcotic.

'Customs and passport most civilised and perfunctory. Luggage arrangements amazingly convenient.

'A surprising number of pretty old "Georgian" houses visible on a first glance. . . . Approach on the boat intrinsically marvellously fantastic, and effect heightened by sunshine through mist. Yep.'

The work at Santa Barbara proved disappointingly small, although everyone was highly enthusiastic. Moreover, the President and all the important members of the Board of Directors were absent on holiday, and Tovey had no opportunity—far-off in the West—to make contact with anyone of the least musical importance. The promised engagements in other places failed to materialize. Almost at the end of his visit one or two people bestirred themselves to arrange concerts for him, and the President of the Santa Barbara Association, realizing at last that Tovey was a musician of some consequence, arranged to meet him in New York with plans for the next year.

Tovey wrote from Pittsfield to Miss Weisse: 'On the whole a great deal of ground is covered by a question attributed to Holst while he was in the States, after an immensely rich person had sung a song in an otherwise musicianly concert—"Please tell me the American for *Good God*!"'

'Mrs. Coolidge's Festival is now over: very interesting and in conception quite first-rate; the audience consisting entirely of musicians and Maecaenas and Maecaenasses, with two esses. Enesco, Miss Dorothy Moulton (a very fine singer, as you may perhaps remember), Kindler (a 'cellist I met in Aachen) and others performing: present Harold Bauer (full of Fritz Busch), Harold Samuel (performing), Mischa Elman, several conductors, James and Kate Friskin, Percy Such, Miss May Mukle etc. etc. Performance ranged from the very highest down to a strange mediocrity. Meantime I got into touch with real musicians for the first time since I stepped ashore on these here States. . . .

'I must take the most vigorous precautions against getting side-tracked again. It's not Morley Fletcher's fault and it's no use blaming anything "onto" him; the fact is that my coming to Santa Barbara was in the first instance necessary in order to give this Community Arts movement any sort of position at all. . . .

'I have great hopes that Santa Barbara may (by taking my advice)[1] stimulate Arthur Bliss—who has just settled there in not very good health, but abundant vitality—into making it into a Californian Bayreuth. . . . It is practically certain that I shall go again next year.'

Nobody but Tovey would have been so unpractical as to embark on this American visit without having an agent both in

[1] He had been officially asked to make a report on music in Santa Barbara.

London and in New York. Before he left America his friend John Powell, the American pianist, persuaded him of the necessity of having an agent in New York at least, and put him in touch with Miss Friedberg who undertook to arrange concerts for him in the following year. But his distrust of London agents was such that he made no similar arrangements in this country, and poor Miss Friedberg was sorely handicapped by his unreliability in the matter of letter-writing.

When he returned from America in October, it was obvious that he was not in good health, but he carried out his work of lecturing, conducting, and playing for the first half of the season. He was dangerously insensitive to physical pain, and by the middle of December he was very ill indeed. The doctors were baffled, for he did not respond to treatment. Eventually Professor Barger said to a distinguished bacteriologist, Dr. (now Professor) Mackie, 'Look here, Mackie, we have only one genius on the Senate of this University, and he is going to die if you don't find out what is the matter with him'. Fortunately Professor Mackie did find out; the disease was diagnosed as tropical dysentery when Tovey was almost at death's door. He made slow recovery—nursed with devotion by Miss Weisse—and was able to appear again at the last Reid concert of the season. He was received with great warmth on this occasion, orchestra and audience alike rising to their feet when he came on to the platform, and applauding wholeheartedly.

During this terrible illness he entrusted me with the orchestral rehearsals; the three Reid concerts which took place while he was ill were conducted by Dr. (now Sir) Adrian Boult and Professor Granville Bantock. At the first concert the main item on the programme was Brahms's Third Symphony. Ten years later Sir Adrian wrote: 'I remember the shock in the first few minutes of the rehearsal when I discovered that the Reid Orchestra could give their proper values to quavers in a phrase—a capacity that was almost unknown in English Orchestras at that time. This quality of just phrasing in classical movements they have to a remarkable degree.'

The Sunday concerts fell to me to carry on—mostly in chamber-music programmes; but at the last concert of the series, when Tovey played Mozart's C minor Concerto, I had my first experience of conducting in public. It never occurred to Tovey that there was any reason why a woman should not conduct; he believed truly in equality of opportunity for all, and acted on his belief. It was my good fortune to have many opportunities, but, unhappily, in later years these occurred more and more frequently because of Tovey's increasingly uncertain health.

During the autumn of 1924 the Associated Board published Bach's *Wohltemperirtes Klavier* edited by Donald Tovey and Harold Samuel. If one excepts the *Kirkhope Choir Magazine*, this was Tovey's second appearance as an editor of the classics, the first having been in 1917 when, in collaboration with Percy Such, he brought out an edition of Beethoven's pianoforte and violoncello sonatas. The Bach volume, however, contained a general preface and an illuminating foreword to each prelude and fugue, written by Tovey. The publication was an immediate success. The veteran Mandyczewski, just recovering also from a serious illness, wrote to Tovey from Vienna:

'Lieber verehrter Freund!

Eben bin ich vom Lande zurückgekehrt, da begrüßt mich weihevoll Ihre liebe freundliche Sendung, die zwei Bände *Wohltemperirtes Klaviers*! Tausend Dank für Ihre Aufmerksamkeit. . . . In freien Stunden und in solchen in denen ich selbst im Bette ausgestreckt liegen muß, soll mir Ihre *Wohltemperirtes* eine liebe Gesellschaft sein und eine anregende Lektüre.'[1]

The subsequent authoritative editions which he published of the Beethoven pianoforte sonatas (in conjunction with Harold Craxton) and of Bach's *Kunst der Fuge*—both in 1931—are now known throughout the musical world. Tovey's excitement when

---

'Dear and honoured Friend!
    I have just returned from the country, to be greeted wonderfully by your delightful gift, the two volumes of the *Wohltemperirtes Klavier*! A thousand thanks for your kindness. When I have a free hour, or even when I must spend an hour lying in bed, your *Wohltemperirtes* will be pleasant company and stimulating reading.'

he hit upon the solution of the combination of themes in Bach's unfinished fugue in the *Kunst* was that of a boy discovering a hidden treasure, and it is in keeping with the way his mind worked that he solved the problem by believing that Bach meant what he was reported to have said, whereas the learned editor of the *Bachgesellschaft* had dismissed it as a legend. 'I see no reason to suppose', he wrote, 'that Mrs Bach and the boy Johann Christian did not understand Bach's intentions quite as well as he expressed them. Mrs. Bach sang all her husband's soprano music, and wrote a musical hand which is hard to tell from his. Johann Christian was a better musician at 15 than I was, and I should have had no difficulty at his age in understanding.' This edition of the *Kunst* is dedicated to Schweitzer, for whose personality and scholarship Tovey had a profound regard. (A copy, specially bound to resist the tropical climate, was personally taken to Lambarene by Miss Marga Deneke when she went there to work with Schweitzer.) Tovey made no claims himself to be a scholar, but it may be doubted whether anyone else could have produced such a *tour de force* of scholarship as the completion of the last fugue: and he was naïvely proud of it. 'I am amazed at your achievement,' wrote Elgar, 'and congratulate you heartily on the completion of the section left unfinished by J. S. B. I have a feeling of pride and reflected glory that an Englishman should have done what no fellow-countryman of the mighty author has been able to do.'

The companion volumes of analysis to the Bach and Beethoven publications are invaluable, even though Tovey's carelessness in proof-reading allowed many errors to pass in the latter. Objection has been taken to the diversities of style and method in the Beethoven *Companion*; but it was no oversight that he did not reduce each analysis to the same procedure, and the diversities are stimulating to any student who takes the trouble to make sure he understands what Tovey means. To those who do not, the volume may be quite dangerous.

Such editorial tasks interested Tovey greatly. 'I wish', he once wrote to Bantock, 'that I could make a complete Beethoven (not merely the pianoforte works) and an adequate series of other classics on these lines—i.e. exact statement of the problem of performance in modern conditions with a pure text.'

The publishing manager of the Associated Board, Mr. John Reeves, had no easy task to see these books through the press. He recalls that Tovey's manuscripts 'were untidy and often written on any odd scraps of paper handy to him, especially when he was travelling. He wrote with break-neck speed and confessed "If I try to keep my writing legible it becomes so slow that I can't think; even in fair copies I make mistakes unless I go quick!" His notes on the "48" were received at very irregular intervals, sometimes in batches and sometimes on single slips of paper.' This is not surprising in view of the fact that the years 1922 and 1923 were a very unsettled period of Tovey's life. 'Harold Samuel did nothing but the fingering of the "48",' adds Reeves, 'and I have reason to believe that he did not see eye to eye with Tovey about the disposition of the voices on the staves in some of the Fugues; for that matter Tovey did not always see eye to eye with Samuel's interpretation.'

The publication of the Beethoven sonatas and the *Companion* coincided with a period when Tovey was much abroad, and his harassed publisher found great difficulty in keeping in touch with him. 'Once I tracked him down,' he says, 'I gave him no rest, but he took it in good part. Then I remember spending a whole Sunday with Tovey and Craxton clearing up queries on the final proofs. What seemed to me to be a simple question for these experts as to whether a note should be a flat or a natural often led up to a recital of whole movements illustrating "pros" and "cons"—to which I was, I fear, a rather impatient listener.'

The prefaces to each individual sonata gave Tovey a great deal of trouble, because of the insistence of the Associated Board that they should be as short as possible. 'Dear Craxton,' he wrote, 'Here are some more sonatas viz. Op. 7, Op. 10 No. 2, Op. 26 and the Flapper's Waterloo Op. 13. . . . I hope there's going to be no difficulty as to the length of my notes. They're boiled down to the last degree of intelligible concentration. . . .

The analyses will follow apace. They, too, can't be shortened: the method is *exact*, and I've no use for anything vaguer. I don't suppose I'm at present *persona grata* to the Associated Board or to anyone concerned, but do please, like the sensible and sensitive artist I know you to be, uphold my method against any people who want something shorter.' 'I hope', he adds in another letter, 'that in the long run you will think that the result of our collaboration excuses my slowness in maturing my method.'

Tovey was invited by the University of Glasgow to deliver the Cramb Lectures during the winter of 1924–5. Before the foundation of the Chair of Music this series of ten lectures constituted the only musical course in the University. His illness intervened and the lectures were postponed until April and May 1925, when, although he was still in a weak state of health, they made a great impression. Thereafter he went to Germany to recuperate. In June he left for a second visit to America and Lord Murray received a letter from the boat headed:

'At Stuttgart I began a letter to you returning the MS. and stating my willingness to help the Young Composer; the documents, mine and his, may turn up, but in which piece of my luggage (a suite in eight movements, very polyphonic and badly constructed) I know not. So to save time I write this to go to you from Queenstown.'

Tovey had leave of absence from the University of Edinburgh

until 15 November 1925, and his first important appearances in
New York and Boston had therefore to be made very early in
the American musical season. After his first recital in New York
he wrote to Miss Weisse:

'I think I have made quite a good start here, which may very
well be followed up without unduly encroaching upon my work
in Edinburgh. . . . I cannot help being impressed by the instant
appearance of three engagements after my first concert, but you
may be very sure that I have no intention of getting roped in
for anything harmful to Edinburgh or other European interests.
The way I was side-tracked last year was as nearly disastrous as
anything I have ever experienced; and it would have become
a real set-back if I hadn't followed it up this year—with the aid
of Mrs Gould who is not only generous and kind but exceedingly
capable. . . .

'Frankly, I'm out for money—with as much music-making as
possible. This year's start is what ought to have happened last
year. Properly followed up I could make enough to put a great
many things right next year and, having done so, begin to think
of endowing the Reid Orchestra before I am seventy.

'It was very beautiful, and rather touching, at Santa Barbara
this year, and I think I was of some use. But I was, and still am,
miserably depressed by trying to begin quite a dozen promising
compositions every one of which leads me only into a desperate
sense of its utter absence of connection with what the present-day
musician is thinking about. I daresay I've been pulled down by
illness; but I did not expect it was going to be so dismal a failure
to get back to composition as I find it just now. Mechanical
work is about all I can do at present; article-writing knocks me
to bits because every single point occurs to me first at a furiously
controversial angle.

'Pianoforte technique, and all mechanical things, go well. It
is sometimes said that at fifty one is in one's prime for accurate
efficiency in anything not violently athletic; and certainly I
think the Deppe–Weisse stock is just now very well matured,
though the public performance is far short of the results of

practice. The audiences here ask for encores quite early in the programme; and I am making great hits with unwritten "transcriptions"—notably the Bach F major organ toccata. . . .

'Oh dear; there's great truth in saying the time is out of joint: things don't happen when they're wanted! I should have got my professorship in time to give my father a good few years of pipe-talks with Saintsbury and Grierson;—he would have liked Niecks too; and this year's American opening would have been much more useful last year or earlier. If only I could get back to my composition. Perhaps if I get an alarm clock and have a regular time-table for things other than official work, I shall feel better. I always, from childhood, had a terror that I should be too lazy to hold my job; and it was a blessed relief to find when I went to Edinburgh that I hadn't the slightest difficulty with the routine work—except of course, the examinations, where I still always feel sea-sick and exactly like the worst type of candidate. Well, well, well!'

New York critics were enthusiastic about his playing of Bach: 'The performance of the little-played F sharp minor Toccata of Bach was distinguished by musicianship of the finest quality, by a beautiful singing tone and a noble eloquence. A superior mind and an artist of commanding quality were felt at once in this, perhaps the most significant, performance of the afternoon.' The *Boston Transcript* was attracted by other features: 'As revealed in Bach and Beethoven, Professor Tovey is an erudite, a humorous, a capable musician. With Chopin, with Brahms, and above all, with Debussy he stands forth as a pianist who may command a crystal clear tone overlying sensuous depths. . . . Skilled as had been the pianist's performance throughout the afternoon, the exquisiteness of Debussy proved an unexpected revelation.

'Would that the so-called "practical musicians", who hold that creative music and truly appreciative musicians cannot flourish within university walls, might have heard the effective answer Professor Tovey made, not with words, but unanswerably with music.'

Dohnányi, who was then living in New York, wrote to him 'My wife and I are overjoyed at your enormous success.'

A lecture on the Ninth Symphony at Harvard made a tremendous impression; and when Tovey sailed for home he took with him a gift of one thousand dollars from Mrs. Gould to start an Endowment Fund for the Reid Symphony Orchestra. He arrived in Edinburgh in time for the second orchestral concert of the season; with him was Miss Clara Wallace, to whom he announced his engagement. Miss Wallace had been a pupil at Miss Weisse's school and Tovey had known her since boyhood. When his first marriage came to a disastrous end, Miss Clara Wallace and Miss Weisse were appointed joint guardians of little John Tovey. Nevertheless, his engagement, which, among other things, so neatly solved the problem of a home for John, came as a vast surprise to Tovey's friends—not least to Miss Weisse, who at first made a semblance of approval, but remained to the end unreconciled to the marriage.

Tovey returned again to California in the summer of 1926 and spent October in New York and Boston—his concerts confirming the good opinions formed by the critics in the previous year. Writing of a performance of Beethoven's Sonata op. 101 the *New York Telegram* waxed enthusiastic: 'The performance proved to be the most vital, suggestive, and illuminating reading of the work that one listener at least can recall in a concert-going experience of twenty-five years. Other pianists have often played it with greater captivations of color and richer luxuriance of tone. But this utterance had a subduing thrust and stab alien to the ordinary accomplishment. . . . Listening to such an unfoldment, one obtained the strange assurance that so might Beethoven have proclaimed it himself.'

In the following year his New York agent persuaded him to make a visit in January, when the musical season was in full swing. His programmes would have stunned any ordinary entrepreneur, containing as they did the *Goldberg* Variations ('a performance', wrote one critic, 'inviting the adjective *colossal*'), the Fugue on Four Invertible Subjects with his own completion of

it (this in the same programme as the *Hammerklavier* Sonata!),
the *Diabelli* Variations, and other large and unfamiliar works.
'For the edification of serious music-lovers recent seasons have
proffered few things so unusual as the programs devised for the
four piano recitals by that welcome British guest, Donald Francis
Tovey. Tovey ranks with the most commanding musical scholars
of the age. He accomplished much at his first concert to indicate
anew that his standing is among the major pianists of the epoch.'
(*New York Telegram*.)

It was announced that he would return in January 1929, and
it seemed likely that, 'properly followed up', the success of his
first three seasons might result in his making in America the
financial success which he never succeeded in making in this
country. But in the spring of 1928 Tovey returned to the London
concert platform with two recitals which Ernest Newman declared to be 'among the most interesting musical events of the
season', and which the *Observer* said put him in a class with
Busoni. He also returned to wider fields in Europe, playing in
Barcelona with Casals' orchestra, and acting on the panel of
judges assembled in Vienna for the Schubert International
Festival. 'Hast du gehört', wrote Röntgen, 'daß zu Schuberts
100-jährigen Todestag die unvollendete Symphony vollendet
werden soll? Eine echt Amerikanische Idee! Man braucht dann
wenigstens nicht atonal oder pluritonal zu schreiben, was
freilich leichter ist als "Schubertisch" zu schreiben. . . .

'Wie freue ich mich auf Edinburg und auf dein Haus.

Herzlich dein   J. R.'[1]

Although he had protested that he was 'out for money', Tovey
was really 'out for music' all the time, and ties of tradition bound
him to Europe. The course of events decreed that he never paid

---

[1] 'Have you heard', wrote Röntgen, 'that the Unfinished Symphony is to be
finished for the 100th anniversary of Schubert's death? A real American idea!'
(The scheme *did* originate in America.) 'At least it will not be necessary to write in
atonal or pluritonal style, although that to be sure would be easier than writing in
Schubert's style. . . .

'How happy I am when I think of Edinburgh and your home!'

another visit to America, but soon a trickle of American students began to come to him in Edinburgh.

The marriage of Donald Tovey and Clara Wallace took place on 29 December 1925, and they left immediately for Dresden, where Busch was to give a performance of Tovey's symphony in the following week. The second Mrs. Tovey was no musician, but she took a great interest in her husband's work, getting to know the members of his orchestra and loyally attending all his concerts. She was, perhaps, somewhat appalled at the wear and tear which was entailed by a life absorbed by such a multitude of musical activities, for she did not always realize the compensations which an artist receives from his work. She devoted herself to providing comfortable surroundings for her husband, and the many friends and fellow-musicians who enjoyed hospitality either at the house in Royal Terrace, their Edinburgh home, or at Hedenham Lodge, the beautiful little Queen Anne house in Norfolk, remember her as a quiet, gentle, and gracious hostess. The fine Adam double drawing-room in Edinburgh was lined with music-shelves and was nearly always filled with great bowls of flowers from Norfolk; the music room downstairs housed the mammoth Bösendorfer that Tovey used for his concerts, and a great part of his immense library of music. In later years, when she was crippled by arthritis, no one ever heard Mrs. Tovey utter a word of complaint, and in her devotion to her husband she ignored her own sufferings in stoic fashion.

At the end of the spring term of 1926 Tovey undertook his first series of broadcast keyboard talks. As a broadcaster he was incalculable, for his manner of delivery varied enormously. At its best it was natural and fluent, and it almost seemed as if the owner of the pleasant, friendly speaking voice were in the room with the listener. At its worst, when he was irked by time limits, or by the fact that he could not walk up and down as he discoursed, it was hesitant and discursive, and, however interesting, technically bad broadcasting. He was a great trial to B.B.C. officials because of his inability to conform accurately to necessities of timing, which simply infuriated him, and because of his complete inability to stick to his script—even when they persuaded him to write one. In 1926 the Director of Broadcasting in Edinburgh was George Marshall, who had known Tovey as a boy, and therefore understood the difficulties to be encountered in getting him 'on the air'. By allowing him as much freedom as possible he made these early broadcasts much more effective and unique than anything that Tovey did later.

Tovey wrote incomplete notes for this series of broadcasts, which was called *The Meaning of Musical Art-Forms*. After a short introduction his script runs: 'My first example aims at clearness at the risk of shocking you by frivolity. The best-known of all rounds—(please do not ask me for its date; that is the kind of history from which, as Dr Johnson would say, my attention retires)—is probably (I speak subject to correction from the learned) *Three Blind Mice*. Here is unquestionably a work in which form and matter are one. It even has in a crude and spurious form the quality which I believe true works of art have in genuine essence—the quality of infinity. Unfortunately its infinity consists in the fact that only the mortal fatigue of human performers, the intervention of the police, or the carving-knife of the farmer's wife can bring it to an end. The third mouse-tail has been taken by the first into its mouth, but the resulting circle has no inherent capacity either to contract or to break.

'We can put a little more art into it without altering this state of things. *Three Blind Mice* provides an excellent method for teaching singers and string-players the intonation of that system of musical puns known as the whole-tone scale. Let each mouse take the next mouse-tail in his mouth and descend the whole-tone ladder thus—(illustration). Ascend thus—(illustration). You can, if you like, put the whole scheme into canon; nothing can go wrong in the whole-tone scale, unless you mix it with another a semitone apart.

'Simple rounds with a tonic-and-dominant range occur more often as details in great musical structures than is always realized. They admirably express an innocent, child-like or pastoral gaiety. Illustrations—Mozart, Allegretto of F major pianoforte concerto; Beethoven Pastoral Symphony, 7th Symphony (Development), 9th Symphony (Coda).'

Tovey gave another series of sixteen broadcast keyboard talks in the autumn of 1933 on *Beethoven, illustrated by his Pianoforte Works.* It was said to me of these, by someone who was recovering from a severe illness, that they were the high-lights of the week for her and made her feel that life was worth living again. They were followed by two other series in the autumn of 1934[1] and in the spring of 1935, and by a further series in 1937. Partly for reasons of health, and partly because he had by then become very impatient with the B.B.C. and its ways, the last talks were the least effective. When his *Essays in Musical Analysis* were coming out, Hubert Foss had an idea that some of the broadcast talks might also be published, but Tovey thought otherwise: 'On looking over my B.B.C. *Clavierübung* stuff I have come to the conclusion that, even when restored to its original shape, it suffers too much from the limits of space and scope that were imposed upon it to be up to the standard that you and I require. The re-casting of it would be a tiresome business and the result not attractive.'

It is remarkable that, apart from his keyboard talks, Tovey broadcast so little. The bulk of his broadcasting was done with the Reid Orchestra, and the engineers and others who listened to the rehearsal on the morning of a concert to test the 'balance'

---

[1] 'I shall be very glad to make *obiter dicta* that may be appropriate now and then to the Foundations of Music series', he wrote to the B.B.C., 'but I fear that the plan of arranging my course systematically to illustrate them is quite impossible. Handel, in particular, is a most impossible artist for any treatment except an elaborate stylistic inquiry of a kind which I don't believe in to begin with. He is a very great artist, whose works illustrate themselves and are infinitely easier to understand when you don't explain them. . . . Beethoven was obviously right in considering him the master of all masters and unequalled in producing the most colossal effects with the simplest means: but that does not lend itself to keyboard illustration, and Handel's art-forms are practically non-existent when you come to look at them. I shouldn't mind saying this in a keyboard talk, but it obviously does not lend itself to expanding in a long series.

'If you can give me freedom to take the line I propose, I can promise to shed more light upon your actual programme of the Foundations of Music than if I am supposed to be talking up to them.'

were often surprised at what reached them through their ear-phones. At a rehearsal of Mendelssohn's *A Midsummer Night's Dream* music, with spoken dialogue, the words 'Mine ear is much enamoured of thy note' were followed by an unmistakable and resounding bray. 'Good heavens, what was that?' said the startled B.B.C. official to me, and then, realizing that it was Tovey's contribution to the script, he added, 'For goodness sake tell him not to do that to-night!' When Tovey was told, he said regretfully 'What a pity; I thought I did it rather well.' At the concert, however, he could not resist adding a modest little bray, which merely came over as an inexplicable noise; I was sorry that I had not suppressed the official message.

The years from 1926 to 1929 were critical years for the orchestra. Audiences were small and the press was either patronizing or hostile in a carefully veiled way. Hints were thrown out that the orchestra might give its concerts in the summer so that it need not compete with the imported attractions of the winter season, that it should play 'lighter' music, even that it should get another conductor. These called forth vehement letters to the press, including an impassioned one from Dame Ethel Smyth written shortly after the performance of three of her works at a Reid concert in spring 1928. 'The orchestra', she wrote, 'blessedly free from the many second-rate habits of commercially-run, promiscuously-handled bands, bears in its every musical gesture the stamp of its founder—one of the noblest minds in music. Professor Tovey's conducting of Haydn and Beethoven was an exposition of great art by one of the same family. . . . Certainly his methods are not studiously graceful like those of the competent youths our colleges turn out by the score. But, as real musicians, men like Holst, Casals etc. are always pointing out, what matter, since he achieves his effects?'

The *Scotsman* newspaper was approached with a view to securing for the Reid Orchestra in Edinburgh the kind of support from the press which the Scottish Orchestra in Glasgow received from the *Glasgow Herald*. The *Scotsman*, however, made it quite clear that it considered itself a national newspaper, with no special duty to support the enterprises of its own city. It denied that the weekly concerts of the visiting Scottish Orchestra were given more prominence and more favourable review than the fortnightly Reid concerts, although cuttings from the newspaper were ample evidence of this. Eventually a long leader appeared in the *Scotsman* in November 1928 summing up the situation:

'We do not profess to know the reason why the Reid Orchestra, with a distinguished musician like Professor Tovey to conduct it, and its own excellent personnel, has not made for itself a bigger place in the musical life of Edinburgh. We do know that it has not been for lack of publicity. There is no institution, musical or other, in the city which has more ardent advocates; and there is no institution which has obtained a more favoured place in our correspondence columns. At the end of last season we published letters from Dame Ethel Smyth, Mr Adrian C. Boult, and a number of other correspondents, drawing attention to the merits of the orchestra, and the important work it desired to do and was capable of doing, on behalf of the musical culture of Edinburgh. The result of that campaign has apparently been *nil*. We suggest that Professor Tovey may well pray to be saved from his friends. ...

'Twelve years of hard and well-directed work have brought the orchestra to a high pitch of proficiency, at which point it may well challenge comparison with many more famous orchestras, which are not limited by depending on local resources. In Professor Tovey it has a conductor of unique distinction. But merit and a good purpose, as we all know, are not always rewarded according to deserts; and if the Reid Symphony Orchestra has still to receive the wide public appreciation it deserves, it must keep a stout heart and carry on.'

Tovey could hardly have been blamed if he had abandoned the struggle then and there, and sometimes indeed he felt very like it. During this winter, however, he was full of great hopes for the future both of his orchestra and of his own career as a composer. The Edinburgh Opera Company was to produce his opera, *The Bride of Dionysus*, in April 1929, and every moment of his spare time was already engaged in coaching the singers.

14

THE conditions under which Tovey's opera was produced were quite extraordinary, indeed, almost unbelievable. The Edinburgh Opera Company, an amateur body then in a fairly flourishing condition, had already approached him with regard to his reconstructed Schubert operas which had been given with success in Germany. Nothing came of this, and it was suggested that the Company might tackle his own opera (the vocal score of which had just been published by Schott) if means could be found to finance it.

During the previous summer of 1927, when he was on the verge of sailing for America, Tovey had undertaken to produce music for Trevelyan's translation of the *Oresteia* of Aeschylus, which was to be performed at Cambridge in the autumn. He did not succeed in completing this music ('I should never have boasted that I could tackle this stuff in a hurry,' he wrote regretfully); but the desire to see produced the opera over which they had both expended years of work, was again stimulated, and, with characteristic generosity, Trevelyan offered to finance the venture if Tovey thought it was a practicable proposition. Tovey, when he wished, could believe that any great musical enterprise was a practical proposition, and in this belief he did sometimes actually make it become so; certainly he did on this occasion, when by rights the whole thing should have collapsed not once but many times.

The Edinburgh Opera Company presented a *triple* bill at the Empire Theatre in the week of the production of *The Bride of Dionysus*, the other operas being *La Bohème* (on Monday and Saturday evenings), and *Pagliacci* preceded—curiously—by Gluck's *Orfeo* (on Wednesday). For *Bohème* and *Pagliacci* the company had engaged a 'star' singer in the person of Joseph Hislop, then at the height of his career, and appearing for the *first time* in his native city. In addition, for the performances in which Hislop would appear, the well-known young conductor John Barbirolli was engaged. In the knowledge that the house would be sold out, prices were doubled for these evenings. Tovey shared the conducting of the four performances of *his* opera with the company's own conductor, David Stephen, then Director of Music at Dunfermline.

The undertaking of such an ambitious week of opera would have strained the powers of any local company. Amateurs were thrilled at the prospect of appearing with a singer of international repute and of singing under a conductor from the professional operatic world. The wonder is that Tovey's opera got proper attention at all, but in actual fact the company, almost without exception, worked very hard at it, overcoming with surprising success many of its difficulties by sheer force of enthusiasm.

The insistence of the Company that there should be two casts was a great source of difficulty; it was hard enough to find six soloists for parts which, with one exception, are long and difficult, without having to duplicate these! And, as it happened, the Ariadne of the second cast found, shortly before the date of production, that the part was really beyond her powers, and the four performances were carried through in the frightening knowledge that if anything happened to the first Ariadne there was no understudy to replace her. The singer, Miss Naysmith Young, rose to the occasion wonderfully and gave the performances of her life, though the strain was very heavy for an amateur.

Even more serious were the difficulties of production. The Company's producer was C. E. Hedmondt of Irish–German extraction, a veteran of the operatic stage, who had been in his early days a real *Helden-tenor* and as such had enjoyed considerable success both in this country and in Germany. He was steeped in all the time-honoured operatic conventions, and, although thoroughly proficient on traditional lines, was completely unresponsive to any ideas of production which did not conform to these. It became apparent as soon as the floor rehearsals started that his methods of over-emphasis and

attitudinizing were totally unsuited to the new opera. Tovey tried
to persuade him of this, but Hedmondt had the old hand's contempt for a mere composer's wishes in matters of production;
he also thought the opera might well be cut to make it more
effective. 'The question of cuts', wrote Tovey to Trevelyan,
'drives me plumb crazy, and I can't keep my temper with the
idiotic suggestions that will be made. Per contra, Hedmondt is
wonderfully successful in getting people to work for him. . . . I
make little doubt that I shall get the singers to want to do the
whole thing, but you must put your foot down very strongly in
my support: you are not only the author but have the financial
end of the big stick. But please be very firm. If it should prove
a *physical* impossibility to do the whole, I would rather consent
to the *publicly avowed* omission of the first part of Act II. But I'm
not going to put up with local mutilations. And we won't mention the possibility of omitting half an act till we must.'

A crisis was reached in March; Hedmondt agreed to abandon
his methods and asked Tovey to provide him with a score giving
the exact details of every move and gesture, saying that he would
do his best to carry out instructions. Enlisting the help of his
librettist, Tovey started on this task before realizing that Hedmondt was really throwing the whole onus of production on to
him; this he refused to accept, and Hedmondt officially resigned.
Time was short, and unsuccessful efforts were made to find a
new producer in London. Eventually the task was shared by a
member of the company, Loudon Shepherd, who had some
little knowledge in producing, and Miss Mona Benson, who,
although better known as a concert artist, had also trained at the
Royal Academy in operatic work and was resident in Edinburgh.
In a letter to Trevelyan explaining his resignation Hedmondt
remarks: 'Professor Tovey has written music for music's sake
and not for the drama's sake: he has reverted to a futile inhuman
method of requiring emotional expression in an extended range
that is impossible for the present-day vocalist'—a curious criticism from one who made his name in Wagnerian roles!

The designs for the costumes and scenery were in the hands of

Charles Ricketts, and were carried out on the lavish scale of a London production. 'Hedmondt', said Ricketts, 'at first rather disliked my plans, wishing to use old Wagnerian scenery!' At an early stage Tovey wrote to Trevelyan: 'I wonder if you could see Ricketts before things get too rigid? I find him very reasonable but apt to illustrate quite a different plot; and in two matters I foresee serious practical difficulty—(*a*.) the Labyrinth, (*b*.) the concealment of Dionysus and Ariadne before the apotheosis.' Tovey added: 'I can quite give up my visualising ideas to Ricketts'; but his suggestions on these two points were, in fact, adopted by the artist, for they involved the addition of the large entrance stairway, centre back, which made the Labyrinth setting so splendid, and the use in Act III of clouds and veils—less effective at the first production because of awkward handling.

Unfortunately, Ricketts was distracted while he was working on the designs by the terrible accident to his old friend and fellow artist Shannon, who lived with him—an accident which subsequently led to Shannon's death. It is possible, therefore, that Tovey was right when he maintained that Ricketts had never really read the libretto properly; the stage sets were magnificent and all the details were authentic in design; but the panorama back-cloth (which was then a special feature) was quite clearly wrong, for in the middle of it was painted a large immovable rock. Now the first act takes place on board a ship which is slowly and inexorably approaching the shores of Crete; towards the end of Act I trumpets are heard (off-stage) from the land, at first far off, then nearer, and as the curtain falls the captives are being marched off the ship. And that confounded rock still stood there in visible conflict with all the evidence of the dialogue and of the music. It infuriated Tovey beyond belief; but oddly enough, while he admitted that it was a blunder, Trevelyan felt that, in relation to all the other pressing problems of production, it was of minor importance. But it was a bad mistake on the part of so distinguished an artist as Ricketts, and probably he would have been the first to admit it.

The costumes were magnificent—beautiful in design and

gorgeous in colour and material. Unfortunately, however, the costume of Dionysus seemed inexplicably wrong. In the ancient representations of the Greek gods there appear two ideas of Dionysus—the young Dionysus and the old Dionysus. Trevelyan made it clear to Ricketts that for the purpose of the story Dionysus must not be represented as the athletic young god of the Renaissance painters, but rather as an awe-inspiring hieratical figure. Basing his design on representations of the old Dionysus, Ricketts unfortunately produced a costume which, with its voluminous robes, great beard, and flowing locks, had a faintly uncomfortable suggestion of Father Christmas. In general, however, the mounting of the opera provided a splendid spectacle, although necessarily at great cost. The Reid Orchestra had six preliminary rehearsals for the opera. These were indeed few enough, for of course, in addition to learning a long and difficult work from manuscript parts, much precious time had to be spent in weeding-out copyists' errors, of which there seemed to be an unduly large number.

There was a large and distinguished audience—including many visitors from London and elsewhere—at the first night of *The Bride of Dionysus,* and it was unreservedly enthusiastic. Indeed, as the *Glasgow Herald* said, 'Professor Tovey had, both when he first appeared and also at the close of each act, a reception which the greatest prima donna might envy'. The local press was unanimously favourable—impressed not only by a performance on such a scale by purely local talent, but also by the stature of the musician who had become so familiar a figure in Edinburgh musical life that his achievements were taken for granted. 'If the enthusiastic nature of its reception last night may be accepted as any indication of its fortunes in the future,' wrote the *Scotsman,* 'Professor Tovey's opera is assured of a distinguished position in the musical world. It was, it is true, a friendly audience, but there is a difference which is not difficult to perceive, between the cordiality which is inspired by politeness, and that which is the outcome of an interest which has been profoundly stirred. . . .'

The *Observer* wrote: 'Whatever the ultimate fate of the opera produced in Edinburgh this week—and Tovey is too old a hand to trust too much to the plaudits of a first-night audience—there is no doubt about the personal triumph. One may recall a remark in one of Arnold Bennett's novels (was it *The Roll-Call?*) about some musical Philistines—"They did not seem to know that we had a ——, and a ——, and a Donald Tovey." That was a good long-range hit for Mr Bennett!' Other London papers were less enthusiastic. *The Times* criticism was headed 'Opera Thought Out', and concentrated on the analytical programme: 'Professor Tovey is probably the only living composer who would care to accompany the first performance of a new opera with a pamphlet on the principles of opera composition and a reasoned analysis of the applications of these principles in his own work.' At the end of a long article designed to show that Tovey was a theoretical rather than a practical musician, the critic compares *The Bride of Dionysus* with Busoni's *Doktor Faustus* and continues: 'In contrast to Busoni, Tovey is untroubled by that process which is called extending the language of music. Music is to him an old language, well apprehended, in which a man may think his thoughts and live his life. And it is this which has impressed his Edinburgh audience. They know that whatever he has to say to them, whether in words or in notes, is the product of profound conviction. They honour him for that, but a great opera is not made merely by taking thought.' This was remarkably like an echo of old hostility, written designedly to 'take the conceit' out of the composer, to discount enthusiasm as provincial ignorance, and, on one hearing, to dismiss a new work in a medium in which few English composers had excelled.

Mr. Bonavia, of the *Daily Telegraph*, found that 'a good libretto furnished the composer with an attractive theme in the legend of Theseus', and continued: 'this opera often possesses a somewhat unusual interest in being at once scholarly and imaginative. If some strokes do not seem to tell as effectively as they should (the description of the Slaying of the Minotaur is one of them), the cause must be sought in one of these errors of judgment which are inseparable from a first attempt.' [Other critics found this a most effective interlude, and some regretted that the stage directions were not carried out to show the slain Minotaur at the foot of the stairway—'the light falling on his hands, dark but unmistakably human, stretched upwards above the horns of his bull's head.'] 'But', concluded Mr. Bonavia, 'a single hearing of the opera kindles a keen desire to repeat the experience—and thus we acknowledge that the composer has won his battle. A second hearing can only confirm the impression of beauty and tenderness made by certain scenes of the second act, and it may do something to dispel in others the impression of reticence and control proof against even the divine madness of inspiration.'

The critic of *Musical Opinion* was lofty and patronizing: 'Most of the principals were inadequate vocally to the demands of the music. . . . Nevertheless the opera made a definite impression. The book is well planned, and the text flows easily and musically. . . . I admired particularly the simple eloquence with which much of the work for the soloists has been invested, and pictured the effect that might be made with it by artists of first-class vocal quality and wide experience.'

The success which the opera enjoyed was, intrinsically, a *popular* success, and an unsolicited testimonial from 'the man in the street' must be recorded. A stage-hand who was vigorously, if somewhat incorrectly, whistling some of the themes, was overheard to say to one of the firemen, 'I like the thing we're doing this week; it's got grand tunes'. 'Aye,' was the reply, 'it's a pity we canna' do stuff like it more often!'

Writing of Tovey's compositions after his death Dent says: 'Their rigid conservatism often made them sound rather dull, and if Tovey is remembered in future ages, it ought rather to be through his one opera—though that work is on a scale which makes frequent performances unlikely. Tovey herein showed himself an astonishing master of melodious declamation in which every syllable finds exactly its right rhythmic value. But the drama, like Boito's *Nerone*, assumes an audience of classical scholars' [this, of course, is nonsense, as proved by the conversation quoted above,] 'and its conventions are those of Greek tragedy not of the modern operatic stage. Opera for Tovey meant Gluck, Beethoven and Wagner; of all the representative favourites he would have said "*Non ragionam di lor, ma guarda e passa*".'[1] Dent's assumptions are easily refuted by a passage in a letter to me from Evert Barger, Professor Barger's younger son, recalling his schooldays in Edinburgh: 'I shall never forget being taken by D. F. T. to a Carl Rosa performance of *Valkyrie* (the first time I ever heard it). He loved it all. We went back to his house in a taxi: he hummed it all the way. We had supper at 11 p.m., and then he sat down and started to play it on the piano, with his odd vocal accompaniment that seemed to come from the pit of his stomach. I walked home at 2 a.m. In the interval of the performance he had gone to the box office and bought tickets for the next afternoon—*Don Pasquale*. After tea he played all that fine but different opera with equal relish. He had heard them both as they should be played, not as they *were* played. I was sixteen. He set me on fire. After the opera we went back stage; he chatted with members of the orchestra, encouraged the singers and radiated appreciation.'

In the week of the production of Tovey's opera Sir Thomas Beecham was in Edinburgh to address a meeting of supporters of the Imperial League of Opera. During an interval in the second performance he addressed the audience on the subject of the League. He certainly did not 'radiate appreciation' backstage, but he spoke appreciatively of the opera, and said very truly, 'Had we here the same artistic facilities and machinery that are available to Continental composers, within a month or two of the completion of *The Bride of Dionysus* it would have been put in rehearsal and production forthwith.' But it was clear that he was obsessed with the larger problems of opera in this country, and that he was not, at the moment, interested in the fate of any one particular opera.[2]

---

[1] 'Do not let us discuss them; glance at them and pass on.'

[2] At the Edinburgh Festival of 1950 Sir Thomas conducted performances of

It seems odd that, despite the fact that all the initial expense in respect of costumes, scenery, and music had already been met, no attempt was made to take this opera from the provincial stage to some wider sphere. Tovey inquired of Strecker, who had returned to Mainz, what the possibilities were of production in Germany. Strecker replied that Busch might perhaps do it in Dresden, but added that there was such a strong reaction in Germany against what was called 'neo-classicism' that he doubted whether it would be a good thing to bring forward anything that was not avowedly 'modern'.

Two years later in 1931 the Edinburgh Opera Company approached Tovey and Trevelyan with a view to giving the opera again in the following season. The Company was in difficulties, as were so many musical enterprises at this time of financial depression; but, although it was frankly stated that money was needed, this was certainly not the sole motive behind the suggestion, and there was a genuine wish to repeat a work which had made an unforgettable impression. Those, however, who imagined that it would be easier to produce the opera a second time—and in a different theatre—were greatly mistaken. The Company was persuaded to accept Miss Benson as special producer for the work, but insisted this time on *three* casts for six performances—a nightmare for any producer. The strain on Tovey was certainly much greater during the second production, and it contributed to the serious breakdown in his health later in the year. Miss Benson's task as producer became more and more difficult owing to lack of provision for sufficient rehearsal time for three casts, and at the beginning of February such was her discouragement that she resigned. Sir Hugh Allen, to whom she had written for advice, urged her to go on: 'You will in this case be on the side of the angels, and Tovey in music is really an archangel', he wrote; he also came to the rescue by sending a young producer from the Royal College to talk over the prob-

Strauss's *Ariadne*. In the course of a talk on *The Future of Music*, he challenged anyone to name any opera written in the last thirty years which remained in the repertoire of an international company. He did not explain how an opera might remain in a repertoire if it never got there in the first instance.

lems and to give her the kind of support which neither Tovey nor Trevelyan could give. Even had they been in the position to do so, neither man was fitted to deal with the petty jealousies and misunderstandings that the producer for any amateur company must overcome. Miss Benson with much hesitation, withdrew her resignation, and her work of producing, which undeservedly was little noticed by the press, was warmly praised by the composer and the poet. She did not know until years later that Sir Hugh had sent Jack Gordon north with the advice that if she did not feel she could withdraw her resignation, he should take her place. The chance of producing an opera on this scale is one which seldom falls to a young producer, but Gordon came to the help of his colleague in an entirely self-effacing way, with the one thought of doing all he could to ensure that the work should be a success.

The conductor for the company in 1932 was Stewart Deas, an Edinburgh graduate—now Professor of Music at Sheffield; he shared the conducting of the six performances with Tovey. An attempt was made by the Company to get the B.B.C. to broadcast at least part of the opera, but without success. Tovey's only *expressed* regret for this was that the broadcast fee might have lightened the financial burden on Trevelyan.

The performances in 1932 achieved a higher standard than did those of 1929, for some of the singers and many of the orchestral players already familiar with the work. The audiences, if less numerous, were even more enthusiastic, and the press notices were good. *The Times* critic, however, again had reservations: '*The Bride of Dionysus* is a remarkable work from every point of view save one—that of sheer musical invention. It is extraordinary that Tovey's profound insight into the workings of other composers' minds has apparently left him oblivious of the fact that each made for himself a personal idiom, that each showed his distinctive touch in handling the material of melody and harmony. . . . The actual substance of Tovey's music bears on it no distinctive mark of its author or of its time, nor beyond a certain general appropriateness, has it the character of the persons and situations which it is expressing from moment to moment. . . . Yet, as though this were but a small thing, the opera grips and holds the attention through the whole of its course of four hours. . . . There is no one formula for making an opera. The Russians are formless but melodious and brightly coloured. The Italians think only of strong characterisation in vocal line. Tovey shows that still another mixing of the ingredients will make an opera. If only his themes were in themselves as significant as his use of them is psychologically right!'[1]

The most interesting criticism came, not from a music critic, but from the novelist and essayist, E. M. Forster, in an article in the *New Statesman*: 'Here is an opera not so much in the Wagnerian tradition as in a Wagnerian frame. . . . Mr Tovey composes his own music and not someone else's; his temper is intellectual and meditative, and though he can illustrate action, he declines the intense, personal emotions and the heavy epic grandeur which form respectively the columns and the roof of Walhalla. And Mr Trevelyan's paganism is paganism with a difference; it would not accord with Brünnhilde; Ariadne's union with Dionysus comes as the reward of virtue, the nobility of her own character is the clue which leads her out of the Labyrinth of self into the light. No one is wholly bad. Phaedra the seducer is not wicked, but only pleasure-loving, and Minos has comprehensible reasons for his cruelty. There is much modern psychology and enlightened sympathy all through, and perhaps that is why the scene in the Labyrinth was not as terrifying as it should have been: it was difficult to believe that a Minotaur lurked in those shadows.

'The total effect of the opera was most beautiful. It was too long—over four hours—so that the audience could not keep fresh for the closing choruses, which musically required the

---

[1] In actual fact Tovey's own idiom is unmistakable; but he shared the views expressed by Vaughan Williams on originality: 'Why should music be original? The object of art is to stretch out to the ultimate realities through the medium of beauty. The duty of the composer is to find the *mot juste*. It does not matter if this word has been said a thousand times before so long as it is the right thing to say at the moment.'

closest attention. But one came away feeling that an important work had been given, and wishing for the sake of London that it could be performed in London. Both the production and the performance were excellent. . . . But perhaps the best work was done by the Reid orchestra, which Mr Tovey has trained. A final judgement on his creative achievement has yet to be passed, but it is most certainly not the dull academic stuff which certain critics have been pleased to find it. With the collaboration of Mr Trevelyan he has given us something that is delightful to listen to, interesting to think about, and impressive emotionally.'

The sixth, and last, performance of the opera took place on Saturday afternoon; on Saturday evening the Company, in order to 'round off' the week and give Hedmondt (still their official producer) some opportunity, played *Il Trovatore*. Rather to the dismay of his guests, Tovey insisted that they should all go to this performance, saying that no one should ever miss the opportunity of hearing a Verdi opera. And, in spite of the fact that there was less than an hour and a half between the time when he laid down his baton and the rise of the curtain on *Il Trovatore*, he was back in the theatre ready to enjoy early Verdi as if he had never heard it before.

The only definite proposal for a performance of *The Bride of Dionysus* in London came from Sir Hugh Allen, Principal of the Royal College of Music. He suggested that Tovey should bring from Edinburgh his best singers and his orchestra, and offered the use of the College theatre, £100 towards expenses from the opera fund, and promised to 'make all arrangements for a great occasion'. Unfortunately there were too many practical difficulties, quite apart from finance, to make the scheme possible.

Fuller-Maitland, who was then in failing health, came to Edinburgh to hear the opera on the second occasion, and wrote: 'My dear Tovey, I have let an unconscionable time go by without writing to tell you how very much I enjoyed your great work. But since coming home I have been more or less on the sick list.—It is a most delightful creation, and you seem to have been loyally served by everybody concerned, including those who "produced", or whatever it is called. . . . It is rare, in my experience, to find an opera that goes on getting better, and your third act is really masterly. People are so silly about length, as if that really mattered in a work of great art. There are many short things that are extremely tedious. . . . I do congratulate you with all my heart.' Tovey sent this letter to Miss Benson, saying how much touched he was that Fuller-Maitland—who had just been temporarily cured of the frightful affliction of distorted hearing—should have come to see the opera, and then written so warmly of it.

In his letter of thanks written to Miss Benson a few days after the last performance Tovey told her that she had 'gained, with the friends-and-relations of the three casts, several hundreds of enthusiastic personal friends.

'*But*, they are going to be troublesome; and most troublesome will be one whom you didn't have to gain, being already in possession; the *fons et origo* of the whole bother.

'In other words, I want your help for another Ambitious Project; and I want to begin adumbrating it at once. . . .

'I want you to help me, or rather, to do in your own way, with Interference from me, a minimum possible reduction of a play by Shakespeare, to be set as an opera of the same degree of continuity and composition as the *Bride of Dionysus*. The play is *Twelfth Night*; and on reading it through I am struck by the perfect musical contrasts of the scenes pretty much as they stand, and also by the fact that neither the text nor the plot seems to be in much disorder. With flat scenes such as Harry Lauder uses for his turns we could easily cope with the Elizabethan technique without being either artificially ascetic or Drurylanically panto-mimic.

'The main difficulty will be the cutting. At a rough guess there seem to be twice as many lines as the *Bride*; and I don't want the whole to be nearly as long as the *Bride*. Nor can we rely on my getting the words spoken much faster: I know the statistics of these things very well and can prove that the *Bride* is considerably faster than most of Wagner in the pace of word-handling; and in spite of the apparently huge size of the first orchestral interlude in Act II, very much shorter in all its spacings between the singing. On the other hand, *Meistersinger* gets through its words very nearly as fast as non-musical drama, and faster, I believe, than any other opera.

'Well then, the project is

> *Twelfth Night*
> by William Shakespeare S.A. (Swan of Avon)
> adapted by Mona Benson (M.B.)
> and composed by *ME* (Master of Ell-for-Inch)

The part of Viola will be an alto of the compass of the *Agnus Dei* of Bach's B minor Mass+Phaedra; and will be sung by Miss M. B. as Actress-Manageress. Sebastian will be a Tenor who will, on his first appearance, sing in Viola's thematic vocabulary at the same pitch (glorious Leit-motif transference of "she never told her love" on his marriage to Olivia!). . . .

'It is very unlikely that I shall begin the music until most of the libretto-carving has been done. One reading aloud of the play (preferably by you and me in dialogue) will tell us a good deal about the timing. We will then begin by assuming that we aim at straight Shakespeare drama and will not consider the temptations of vocal ensemble until they are forced on us. If they prove irresistible I would suggest that we look for extant Elizabethan poetry for their purpose.

'But, *nota bene*, nothing will induce me to drift into Elizabethan music: there will be no madrigal style whatever, there will be far less trace of "modal" harmony than in the *Bride*, and folk-song may go Elsewhere. I may not be able to maintain these pious aspirations; a *coranto* must be a *coranto* even though Sir Andrew Aguecheek's scholarship be little better than Bottom's, but I intend to set straight Shakespeare and straight music.'

A later letter said: 'About *What You Will* I suggest as an initial practical measure to find out what are the 1,000 most essential lines for (*a*) plot and (*b*) poetry (I mean essential for both concurrently). . . . It would be disappointing to find ourselves driven to colourless simplifications, e.g. omitting the Malvolio plot—which of course is quite unnecessary to *the* story, but the omission of which would, for that very reason, elevate the whole to romantic insignificance.

'Details begin to get better and better fun; the dear good Duke doesn't know when his madrigalists (singing in Hypo-Phrygian) are really finished and says, 'If music be the food of love, play on,' just when they are pausing rhetorically on a half-close;—and they are just going on again when their leader, a trifle put out, has the gumption to make the best of it.

Yours twelfthly   D. F. T.'

A further letter gave as his proposal for the opening madrigal the words of 'Thule, the period of cosmography': 'I don't think we shall ever find a more quintessentially fitting madrigal-text. It's not so beautiful as to make its comic use blasphemous, and Weelkes' music, though glorious, is too remote to block my way to setting the thing in my own style.' The last line of the madrigal 'Whose heart with fear doth freeze'—[Tovey's rhetorical pause] 'with love doth fry,' offered various amusing possibilities when the Duke broke in.

The text of this libretto was completed, but no note of the music was ever set down.

In 1936 Fritz Busch wrote from Glyndebourne asking for a pianoforte score of *The Bride of Dionysus*, with which, of course, he was already familiar. Tovey had high hopes of seeing his work done by his friend in beautiful surroundings and in ideal circumstances. It was decided, however, that the opera was too large—both as to stage requirements and as to duration, although as Tovey pointed out 'under the heavenly conditions of Glyndebourne the length of an opera cannot constitute any more difficulty than it does at Bayreuth'. Three years later, after some reconstruction of the stage at Glyndebourne the matter was considered again, and it was decided that the opera should be given in 1940. But the war swept away all such plans, and a great opportunity for English music was lost.

15

THE years between the first and second productions of his opera (1929–32) were probably the most active of Tovey's career. He was 54 when the opera was first performed, and was in many ways at the height of his powers, though the flow of composition, dammed up during and since the tragic days of his first marriage, was still checked. Public interest in the Reid Orchestra had been to some extent reawakened as a result of the first opera week, and the committee succeeded during 1929–30 in getting five out of the series of eight Thursday concerts broadcast, whole or in part, with encouraging results to all concerned.

Tovey went to Stuttgart after the production of the opera to have his annual treatment for the nervous eczema which still troubled him, and he wrote to me in July giving suggestions for the programmes for next season. He had great hopes from the interest of the B.B.C. in the work of the orchestra: 'C— tells me that for broadcasting we could get extra players for nothing. This would be convenient with the Respighi violin concerto, if there's no mistake about it. I ran through the concerto with Adila while I was in London. It is a very distinguished work.' The letter ends 'Yours tarrily, D. F. T.

'P.S. Why doesn't Veiel put his Klinik on the seaside so that the patients can make money as minstrels?'

The B.B.C. stipulated that Scottish composers should be represented in the programmes, and works by Mackenzie, J. B. McEwen, and Guy Warrack were given. Writing to Tovey after the broadcast of his tone-poem, *Grey Galloway*, McEwen said: 'I had—for the first time in my life—the experience on Thursday last of hearing my own work through the medium of wireless, and I must say I enjoyed it very much. Apart from the excellent and sympathetic performance—your tempi and interpretation were exactly what I wanted—the transmission was wonderfully good. And to sit in one's own study and hear one's own work ideally performed seems to me, even now, little short of miraculous!'

Among the visiting artists at the Sunday concerts in March 1930 was Röntgen, then in his 75th year, but still exceedingly active both as a pianist and as a prolific composer. His visit was made the occasion of conferring on him the honorary degree of Mus.Doc. This gave him real joy, which he showed in naïve and delightful fashion. At the luncheon following the ceremony (at which a similar degree was conferred on Professor Whittaker, newly appointed to the Glasgow Chair of Music), Röntgen presented with a few humorous words what he called his 'degree exercise'—a bulky manuscript upon which he had been uncomfortably perched for more than an hour. It was dedicated to the Reid Orchestra and entitled *Edinburgh Symphony*; this symphony was performed in the next season.[1] In the years that followed, Tovey derived great pleasure from being able to present for laureation many of his friends, and the roll of the Honorary Graduands of the University was enriched by the names of Casals, Schweitzer, Fritz, and Adolf Busch, Sir Adrian Boult, and, on the occasion of the coming of age of the orchestra, Miss Weisse and Mrs. Maitland.

The roll of music-students also continued to add to its numbers occasional students from abroad. Writing to Tovey on behalf of a young composer who wished to complete his training in Edinburgh, Fritz Busch said, 'You are the only person in the world from whom he could learn what he needs to know for mastery; the only one also who would not impose his own ideas on the lad'. Indeed, Tovey did handle this gifted but narrowly opiniated young man with infinite kindness and tact. Nor did he confine himself to his own department. A letter to Miss Weisse of February 1930 remarks: 'The Greek Class (under Pickard Cambridge) is doing the *Frogs* with Parry's music, and I'm

---

[1] Röntgen's laureation aroused much interest in Holland, where such events are rare, and Mengelberg gave several performances of his new *Concertstücke*, with the composer as soloist.

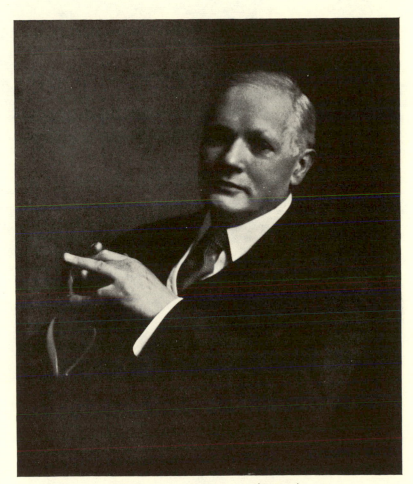

SIR DONALD TOVEY (1935)

(Photograph by Messrs. Drummond Young, Edinburgh)

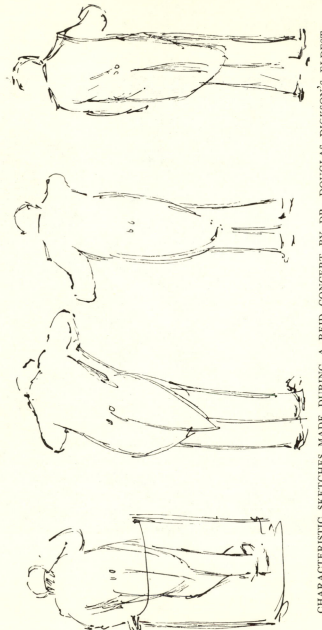

CHARACTERISTIC SKETCHES MADE DURING A REID CONCERT BY DR. DOUGLAS DICKSON'S ELDEST DAUGHTER (NOW MRS. SIDNEY NEWMAN) WHEN LITTLE MORE THAN A SCHOOLGIRL

coaching their chorus. Of course this is one of the most delightful *rapprochements* between our departments that ever happened:— but—Oh My! they must be *awfully* good Greek scholars. Parry's music disappoints me; it isn't nearly pretty enough. I have a notion he did better with the *Birds*. In spite of the awful tow-path noises these students make, I have hopes that in a year or two I may be able to produce Aeschylus choruses in Greek here.'

In a letter to me headed 'Weeks ago 1930' Tovey sketches his plans for the orchestra next season (a season during which matters were much eased by a generous gift of £250 from Mrs. Maitland for the purpose of increasing the number of rehearsals): 'I want to persuade Fanny Davies to give us the Brahms D minor concerto. I *think* she would like to do it; I doubt if she has often had a chance of playing it and she would do it perfectly. Her memory of Brahms' own playing often gets, I think, in her way: her reading of the B minor Rhapsody is to me entirely unintelligible except on the lines of her magnificent powers of mimicry! But I verily believe the D minor will bring out all the beauty of her playing.' Fanny Davies was then almost 70 and, although her physical strength had declined, the beauty and intense vitality of her playing was unimpaired. After a brilliant career, during which she was probably even more famous abroad than at home, she now found herself superseded by younger and more fashionable virtuosi. Tovey's gesture was a timely one to a great artist. He had the piano placed *in front* of the orchestra and the conductor's desk in order to minimize the strain on the soloist, without for a moment suggesting that he doubted her ability to penetrate the powerful orchestration. This was the last time Fanny Davies played a concerto in public and it was a memorable performance. On her death three years later Tovey was persuaded to write an article for the *Daily Telegraph*; it was headed 'Our Miss Fanny', the affectionate term by which she was known at the St. James's Hall 'Saturday Pops' in the eighties and nineties. He quoted a remark made to him as a very young man by Miss Weisse's father, 'who, being blind, had his share of Milton's privilege to see things invisible to mortal sight, and who could listen to music as music. Fanny Davies was playing a Beethoven concerto, and I was carping at details. To which my venerable friend simply said, "Sie hat Weihe"—an expression untranslatable into any English that is not encumbered with irrelevant associations.' (*Vocation* is an approximate equivalent.)

Of the many great artists that I have heard the three that will always remain in my mind as immeasurably the greatest are Fanny Davies, Casals, and Tovey. The two pianists did not always achieve the constant perfection of the great 'cellist, but all three shared the same spacious *quality* of playing, unmistakable because so very rare. As colleagues their instinctive mutual understanding and sympathy was a lovely and inspiring thing, reaching the heights of artistic expression.

Another artist of an older generation to whom Tovey showed practical proofs of his appreciation was Dame Ethel Smyth. During three different seasons he produced some of her most important works, viz. the violin and horn concerto, the Mass in D, and (in 1931) the first performance of *The Prison*, inviting the composer to conduct in each case. (This she did arrayed in her heavy Mus.Doc. robes, which must have been an exceedingly uncomfortable garment for the purpose.) He was not much in sympathy with *The Prison*, but his own feelings did not interfere with his conviction that a major work by Dame Ethel ought to be given a hearing, and that her achievements had not received their due.

The concerts arranged for the spring of 1931 also included a performance of Bach's B minor Mass in conjunction with the Edinburgh Royal Choral Union. Tovey had long wanted to do this work and had spent much time preparing it and writing the programme-notes. His disappointment was very great when an attack of bronchitis resulting from a night journey from London prevented his conducting the concert. Just a year before he had remarked in a letter to Miss Weisse apropos of a performance of the *Magnificat*, 'Just imagine, this is the first time I have had a chance of conducting a choral work of Bach!' Disappointment about the Mass was so general that a special guarantee fund was raised for a second performance, which he conducted two months later.

During this spring, also, the Duke of York (now His Majesty the King) was the Lord High Commissioner at the Church of Scotland's General Assembly in May. Tovey was delighted when, in response to representations he had made in the south, it was arranged that a Command Performance should be given at Holyrood Palace while the Duke and Duchess were in residence. The orchestra, reduced for reasons of space to forty, played in the inner drawing-room, while the audience listened in the outer one, with extremely satisfactory results. The Duchess of York (the present Queen) genuinely enjoyed the music, and the Duke, who is not musical, said that nevertheless he had found it a pleasant evening.

During the years 1929–32, besides the three series of concerts running in Edinburgh, Tovey gave a good many concerts in London again. In 1928 he had made what *The Times* called 'a return' to the London platform with three recitals in April and May. Writing of these this paper said: 'His is not a stereotyped performance; one may be surprised by blemishes; by a piece of muddled pedalling, by ill-considered tempi, by phrasing that is anything but uniform in the corresponding passages of a sonata. One may even be perplexed by the discovery that he plays Debussy and Scriabin better than he plays Bach's *O Mensch, bewein'* or Beethoven's op. 10, no. 3. Students of "pianism" may decide that there is something amateurish about it all as compared with the interpretations of artists who have concentrated on executive finish. But to dwell on this side of it would be to miss the significance of his playing. Every time he sits down to the piano he tells his hearers something that he is thinking now about the music, and he has thought more than most men. . . . Nevertheless no one could hear the vivid and spontaneous interpretation of Scriabin and go away with the impression that Mr Tovey's musical outlook is purely intellectual.'

His reputation as a great musical authority, which was increasing in consequence of his Edinburgh programme-notes, continually got between him and the music critics, though never between him and the public. Not only that; modern developments of technique had produced a slick new style of playing, which concentrated on 'pianism', to the loss of a singing touch and breadth of phrasing. Tovey's breadth of phrasing was notable, and so unaccustomed were the professional London ears to such a style, that several well-known critics remarked on the liberties which he took with the time, a criticism which annoyed him greatly. There are a good many musicians, let alone critics, who could not be trusted to say with certainty what liberties a player is taking with time, particularly in the case of well-known works in which they have become accustomed to certain conventions in performance. What misled the critics in Tovey's case was the fact that, in spite of the immense breadth of his playing, it was astonishingly near to metronomic tempo; to this they were totally unaccustomed and consequently imagined it to be *out* of time! This is certainly true; I have proved it on many occasions. It was Tovey's custom now and again to put any work he was playing 'through the mangle' as he called it— i.e. to play it through with the metronome, in order to make quite sure how much he was deviating from a strict beat, and no one understood better than he how to manage tone and accentuation in order to maintain a steady pace with no suggestion of rigidity. In Beethoven works he believed that a true basic tempo had two aspects, the flowing aspect and the broad aspect—to each of which it was possible to relate the same metronomic beat. Neither the freedom of his Chopin rubatos, nor the 'grand gestures' of his Brahms playing ever disturbed the basic rhythm.

Nevertheless, when I heard two of the six recitals which he gave in the Wigmore Hall in May and June 1931, it *did* seem that his playing in London was inclined occasionally to be wayward, and, in a sense, almost a little aggressive—as if he felt that he was on the defensive, as I think he did. His life was now far too full for regular practice—the Associated Board edition of the Beethoven sonatas, and the edition of the *Kunst der Fuge* both appeared in this year—and even Tovey's terrific technical equipment could not stand the strain indefinitely.[1] Yet after a recital in January 1932 an American visitor, a critic of books and music, wrote to him: 'Last Saturday I took a busman's holiday and went to listen to you. I cannot remember for many years having been so uplifted and carried away; it was hours afterwards before I even began to come back to normal. It was a noble performance; two hours which I cannot ever forget.' After his serious illness in the summer of 1932 Tovey never gave another pianoforte recital in London.

Among other events in London in the summer of 1931 was the Joachim Centenary concert, with the New Symphony Orchestra and the soloists Jelly d'Aranyi, Adila Fachiri, and the singer Gabriele Joachim (all relatives of the great violinist). The conductors were Sir Henry Wood and Donald Tovey, the latter conducting the three Joachim items. In the audience were many old friends of Classical and Chelsea concert days, and for them Tovey's programme-notes revived many old memories.

In my capacity as Honorary Secretary to the Reid Symphony Orchestra I wrote in June 1930 to the University authorities with regard to a proposal to establish a permanent Endowment Fund (a proposal which originated with the gift in 1925 of a thousand dollars from Mrs. Gould of California): 'Lord Murray, the Chairman of the Reid Orchestra, has received from pro-

---

[1] He was dissatisfied with the pianoforte edition of the *Kunst*: 'It is surprising', he wrote to the Oxford University Press, 'that the copies of single numbers for pianoforte have any sale at all. I cannot think that my editing, or anybody's editing, could induce any well-informed person to spend 1/6*d.* on a single fugue when for 2/- he can buy the whole *Kunst* quite competently fingered by Czerny in *Edition Peters*. I beg for the issue of my pianoforte edition in a single volume, at a price slightly higher than that of the unbound score.

'Also the word "arranged" is highly objectionable and should be deleted. The pianoforte score is not arranged at all, and the use of the word imputes to me the same appalling humbug as that of the orchestral arrangers and editors whom I have had to handle with the caution of one who knows better than to slap the porcupine.'

posed donors[1] generous offers which would provide a sum of
£10,000 as a nucleus of an Endowment Fund. This sum, however, can be obtained only on condition (1) that a public trust
be formed, and (2) that a reasonable assurance be obtained that
a minimum of, say, £30,000 can be first secured for the Endowment.'

It was suggested that the University might provide either a
capital sum of £10,000 or an equivalent 'revenue' contribution of £500 a year (which merely meant increasing its usual
grant in respect of the orchestral class by £150). This it was
willing to do, and the Municipality, when approached, agreed
to do likewise. The strongest ground of appeal to the Town was
that of the provision of first-class concerts on Sunday nights at
cheap ticket-rates, for this service to the community conformed
to the desires expressed in the Deed of Gift whereby the bequest
of the money which built the Usher Hall was originally conveyed.

The certainty of an income of £1,500 a year exclusive of
concert-takings, broadcasting fees, &c., was in 1931 a tolerable
basis on which to work, and Tovey felt that at last his orchestra
was a step farther forward to the permanent establishment of
which he dreamed. Soon after the Reid Endowment Trust was
formed, however, the question of a National Orchestra for Scotland was raised; in this the Choral and Orchestral Union of
Glasgow (i.e. the Scottish Orchestra), the Edinburgh Choral
Union, a small newly formed body of players (called the Scottish
Philharmonic Orchestra), and others were interested. The
Scottish Philharmonic Orchestra played outwith the Reid season
and used a number of Reid players around the nucleus of the
B.B.C. octet—there being no Scottish B.B.C. Orchestra at that
date. The question assumed such proportions that the B.B.C.
arranged to hold an inquiry into the matter in January 1932,
and sent a distinguished chairman to preside over a large body
representative of all interests.

In a letter to me dated 1 January 1932, Tovey wrote: 'It is

[1] Mrs. Alexander Maitland and Mr. Thomas Barclay.

extremely important that I should not allow myself to be manœuvred into the position of obstructing the formation of a national orchestra. Therefore it behoves or behooves (as well as behorns and be-long-spiked tails) that such an orchestra should not be allowed to be projected only, or mainly, by people who wish to ignore or undermine the Reid. My letter to Lord Murray simply contains what I can say in private before things go too far. By the time I return to Edinburgh, it will be quite impossible for me to say anything at all. But it will be vitally important that somebody, the more people the better, should damn the impudence of any suggestion, or implication by omission, that the Reid is not *de facto* the nucleus of a national orchestra. . . . The opposition to us is by no means united; and its various sections would all fight shy of an open quarrel with me. The danger is that they might manœuvre *us* into opposition: this would unite them in the "national" interest. Hence my anxiety. But I, personally, must be as silent and adhesive as the Tar-Baby.' He then proceeded to outline a new and more brilliant orchestral programme for the reopening of the Sunday concerts after the Christmas vacation, and concluded: 'Do you know anything about Poulenc's harpsichord concerto? And here 's another composer frae Pairth (letter enclosed). Auf Wiedersehen, D. F. T.'

The National Orchestra question even cropped up in a letter from Tovey to John, who was at school at Rugby:

'Dear John, Many thanks for your interesting letters. Yes, Horace was a Sad Dog; a term which, however, is usually applied to dogs whose behaviour is a sad subject; not dogs whose temper is sad.

'Friday arrived on Tuesday. She is very talkative, and lies about in her most Anglo-Saxon attitudes, chiefly with her paws coiling about in the air.[1]

'There is great excitement here and in Glasgow about a project for joining all the musicians in Scotland in a National

---

[1] Friday was a handsome golden labrador—a lady, despite her name. When she had five beautiful puppies, Tovey immediately invented a name for the family, which he referred to as 'Friday and all the other Squeak-days'.

Orchestra. As that is what I have been aiming at with my Reid Orchestra since 1916 "you'll could immedgin" (as *Nize Baby* says) that it interests me very much. But I have to sit tight and say nuffin!'

The long and tedious meetings of the B.B.C. inquiry came to no definite conclusion on the subject of the establishment of a national orchestra. Tovey was immeasurably the greatest musical influence in Scotland at the time, and it is a thousand pities that he was, as he himself said, so helpless in the matter of musical politics, and that he could never adapt himself to the business of committee-procedure. He was in a strong position; he had created, by his own efforts and with a slender backing, an orchestra of local musicians which was a serviceable instrument, capable of tremendous development if given sufficient work. If he had been more self-seeking—in other words, if he had not been Tovey—he could have dominated events. As it was, he merely became, once more, a storm centre. Opposition to his influence, and hence to the development of his orchestra, though it was not openly avowed, came from the Glasgow Choral and Orchestral Union, which feared competition with the Edinburgh concerts of the Scottish Orchestra, and from a variety of smaller bodies and individuals who were both jealous of Tovey and afraid of him. The most damaging opposition took the line that he was no conductor. Tovey was the most generous person in giving opportunities to others, but he definitely was not willing to be jockeyed out of the position of controlling and conducting his own orchestra. In the years that followed much valuable time and effort was wasted over various schemes which merely dissipated musical energies in Scotland, instead of co-ordinating them on clear lines which took no account of the ambitions of this person and the other, and gave adequate scope to the one great musician whose vision was impersonal.

After the inconclusive inquiry had come to an end, the B.B.C. made an offer in February 1932 to broadcast *all* the Reid concerts, and to use large numbers of Reid players in another orchestra, which would be used by them in outside concerts and broadcasts, and be conducted by someone appointed by them. (This orchestra became the B.B.C. Scottish Orchestra.) The condition attached to the offer was that all members of the Reid Orchestra should individually undergo the test of a B.B.C. audition. This was a somewhat delicate matter; the Reid Orchestra was a Friendly Society and many members felt that the B.B.C. was interfering unwarrantably with domestic affairs and that what was good enough for Professor Tovey was good enough for the B.B.C. The difficulty was surmounted by putting it to the orchestra that anyone who could not pass such an audition was certainly *not* good enough for Professor Tovey. The auditions were fixed for May, and the kindness and tact of Dr. Boult was responsible for carrying them through in a pleasant and friendly atmosphere. Dr. Boult was indeed at all times the most staunch and powerful friend the orchestra ever had.

The national orchestra controversy commenced a few months before the second production of the opera, and undoubtedly added to the burden of Tovey's anxieties. Another controversy, which caused him much greater distress because it touched fundamental rights, arose in that same spring of 1932; it concerned the Incorporated Society of Musicians and the ban which was imposed (at this time of economic crisis) on foreign artists, other than those of international reputation, appearing in this country. A case, involving apparent injustice, arose in connexion with one of Tovey's students, and he immediately wrote to the *Scotsman* intimating his resignation from the I.S.M. as a protest against the Society's attitude to foreign musicians in this country. The reply of the Secretary, Mr. Eames, alleged that in this instance it was the student's fault as she had applied for permission to sing at the concert in question (*a*) too late, and (*b*) to the Ministry of Labour instead of to the Home Office. Professor Grierson,[1] at that time a member of the Faculty of Music, clarified the position in a letter to the *Scotsman*:

'Sir, Referring to Mr Eames' letter to-day may I point out some facts as known to myself?

---

[1] No relation to the writer of this book.

'The singer who has been refused permission to sing at Glasgow is a pupil of Lierhammer, in Vienna, and has also assisted him in teaching at Salzburg. She spent last winter and this as a pupil of Professor Tovey at her own expense. She did apply for permission to take a few pupils. This was refused, and she acquiesced, but she was not forbidden to take engagements to sing, and, as your columns will show, she sang at some of Professor Tovey's concerts and some others, including lately the B.B.C.

'So long a stay in this country was a drain on her means, and some of us, believing that she had exceptional talent as a teacher of voice production, made application to the Home Office for permission for her to take a strictly limited number of pupils, undertaking that we should be responsible for her obedience to whatever rules were laid down. The answer conveyed to me was that the Home Office was quite sympathetic, but that, on being applied to, the I.S.M. had requested the Home Office to refuse permission.

'This was immediately followed by a domiciliary visit and a demand that she should not only not take any pupils, but should not accept any engagements to sing, *paid or unpaid*. Surely the last requirement was harsh. Is even our charity to be controlled?

'In these circumstances it was natural to suppose that the I.S.M. was responsible for this sudden tightening of the restrictions and the forbidding of what had not been forbidden.'

'Professor Grierson's timely letter', wrote Tovey two days later, 'discloses enough to make me more precise as to my reasons for resigning my membership of the I.S.M., and, incidentally, to rectify any injustice my action might do to the excellent work that Society achieves in the interests of music and of musicians, particularly of the class that suffers most in times of distress.

'I was one of the signatories of the petition to the Home Office referred to by Professor Grierson. When the I.S.M. objected to the granting of that petition, either it had been told that I had signed it, or it had not. I am Dean of the Faculty of Music in Edinburgh University. Even if the I.S.M. did not know that I was interested in this case, it omitted a necessary courtesy in neglecting to ask my opinion. If it knew that I had signed the petition, I should be justified in treating its action as a personal insult.' The Secretary's reply to this was—firstly—that if Tovey had signed the petition he should have been aware that he was acting against the declared policy of the Society; secondly, that *per contra* as it was not the policy of the Society 'to object to such a performance as was contemplated—namely, the singing, without fee, of Hungarian songs in Hungarian, which is an addition to the musical life of this country of something we cannot ourselves contribute.' The letter continues: 'I personally telephoned to the Home Office, asking if it were possible to expedite a permit. As a result, the permit was granted in half-an-hour.' (As the singer in question was of Greek nationality, the argument was, to say the least, flimsy.) 'These two facts are entirely separate and distinct. If Professor Tovey feels it his duty to quit the Society over the first, will he not rejoin us over the second, and agree that the old-fashioned British liking for fair-play and reasonable compromise has not deserted even the I.S.M.?'

Sir Hamilton Harty was the President of the I.S.M., and Tovey wrote to him explaining fully the reasons of his resignation. 'Nearly all the mistakes made by England', wrote Sir Hamilton in the course of a long reply, 'are due in the first place to lack of tact, and I do not think that, considering her present musical position, England is fairly represented abroad. I do wish that this unfortunate agitation (against foreign musicians) could be transmuted into a sincere attempt to institute a fairer give-and-take between other nations and ourselves, a sort of artistic Free Trade, which is of course the ideal and only defensible position as far as music is concerned. But I don't think the I.S.M. will do this.'

Tovey viewed the affair from a different angle, and the matter of 'domiciliary visits' was certainly linked in his mind with the disturbing accounts from the Busches, Casals, and others of the state of things in Germany and in Spain. Miss Weisse, it is true, gave him glowing accounts of the regeneration of German youth; but he—concealing, as he so often did, depth of feeling

beneath a bad joke—merely insisted on calling them 'Nazties'.
The wretched business brought him very near to a nervous
breakdown in March. When the performances of the opera in
April and the orchestral auditions in May were over, it was
clear that he was completely exhausted.

He became very ill at Hedenham in June and it was thought
that his heart was seriously affected. I went to see him at the
end of July, when he was allowed to discuss business for a
little while each day. When I arrived he was lying on a camp-
bed in the garden under a magnificent Spanish chestnut tree.
'How arr' ye?' he said; 'Come and look at the wonderful
effects of perspective the patterns of these leaves make against
the sky!'

Schweitzer went to visit Tovey at Hedenham—reversing a
procedure of three years earlier. On that occasion Schweitzer's
health had broken down through overwork; he was unable to
come to Edinburgh to receive his honorary degree, and Tovey
went to visit him at Königsfeld. 'Ich denke oft,' wrote Schweitzer
shortly afterwards, 'an die schönen Stunden, die Sie mit Ihrer so
lieben Frau mir in Königsfeld geschenkt haben! Sie haben dem
müden Menschen wohlgethan.—Und seien Sie versichert, daß
ich immer mit Stolz und Freude daran denke, daß ich jetzt als
Dokt. Mus. von Edinburgh zu Ihnen gehöre! Dies ist ein schöner
Gedanke.'[1] Schweitzer's visit in 1932 almost coincided with
news of Röntgen's death; Tovey, gravely ill though he was,
wrote a touching tribute to his old friend for the columns of *The
Times*. Schweitzer, who never forgets anniversaries, wrote from
Lambarene exactly one year after his visit to Hedenham: 'Ein
Jahr seitdem ich Sie sah! Und jetzt geht es Ihnen so gut! Ich
freue mich darüber.'[2]

After the initial improvement in Tovey's health in July, Miss

---

[1] 'I often think of the delightful hours when you and your dear wife came to see
me at Königsfeld! Your visit did much good to a tired man.—And I assure you
that it is with pride and joy that I reflect that now, as Mus.Doc. of Edinburgh, I
have a definite link with you! That is a pleasant thought.'

[2] 'It is just a year since I saw you! And now you are really well again! I am very
happy about that.'

Weisse, who was just leaving for Nauheim, begged him to go abroad for treatment to one of the great spas that specialize in heart cases—in Czechoslovakia, if he would not go to Germany. But his doctor would not advise this, and he lay in the garden at Hedenham Lodge for the whole of the summer, getting no better. The quiet and peace of that Norfolk garden were what he most needed in the early stages of his illness, but it is a remote spot, and though old friends like the Denekes and Dr. Walker from Oxford, Mr. and Mrs. Trevelyan, and others went to see him, his convalescence might have been of much shorter duration in more stimulating surroundings. Miss Weisse knew this, and feared inertia and depression for him much more than heart attacks; she did not believe in the doctors' talk of heart disease, for she knew of old what curious and abnormal effects nervous exhaustion produced in Tovey. Above all—and here she was certainly right—she feared the damp at Hedenham, situated so near the fen country. She did everything in her power during the remaining years of his life to persuade Tovey and his wife to leave Norfolk for some drier part of the country, but in vain. Her suggestions might have had more success had it not been for the constant friction she caused in these years over John's education, which she would fain have dominated. This kept Tovey constantly on his guard against new possibilities of interference with his life.

It became evident that Tovey would not be able to return to his work in Edinburgh in October. I acted for him as best I could, and received during the autumn a mass of interesting, helpful, and encouraging letters. He was well enough to be consulted on important matters and able to write programme-notes. Miss Weisse's advice to me was to keep him in touch with events, and not to be afraid of tiring him. 'I've just sent off notes on the Bach D major Suite to Taylor' said his letter of 23 October. 'Into the miniature score I've stuck some notes which you won't need, but others may. Still, if I may take a fussy invalid's privilege of teaching my grand-daughter to suck eggs, I will make the following suggestions.

'1. In the overture (Grave) concentrate on ♫. ♪ ♫. ♫♫ :
and (Vivace) insist on *louré* repeated quavers for the trumpets
throughout. Let them say *dadadada* instead of *takataka*. The repeated quavers on the other instruments should be hammered.

'2. Concentrate on the *Air*.[1] We must do something notable
here: merely to play as Bach wrote, though a complete novelty,
is not enough.

'3. *Gavotte* II   (with hardly any consonant to
                                             the 2nd note).

'4. *Gigue*. Get the biggest possible tone in the strings and oboes
in the first four bars.

'About Vaughan Williams *Wasps* suite: I haven't got an
Aristophanes here and can't tell what the incidental music is
about. I should be rather in favour of doing the Overture though
we did do it last year; the suite is so very slight without it. Could
you decide on that with A.B.,[2] and just consult a wasp or two and
add a note yourself as to what kitchen utensils are represented
by what orchestral ones and why.

'*Ruy Blas*. Here's an amusing opportunity of showing what
programme-music can and can't do. This Overture is one of
Mendelssohn's most popular works; and I don't know who or
what *Ruy Blas* is (he's not in the index to the *Enc. Brit.*), nor have
I ever seen any explanation in any programme. Yet Mendelssohn was an exceedingly accurate illustrator. I propose to go
ahead with my analysis of this overture as plain music. Will you
meantime kindly find out for me who or what *Ruy Blas* was—a
Calderón or Lope da Vega, or (for all I know) a Schiller play,
or a character in Dumas (—but I *don't* think Walter Scott):—
what, if aught, he did, and why Mendelssohn mentioned him?
You can add this information to my notes after I've seen it and
got the fun out of the situation.' ('Alas!' said the programme-

---

[1] This is the so-called 'Air on the G string' in its original form.
[2] Adrian Boult.

note written later, 'Victor Hugo's play, which I have just read with great edification, has not more than enough in common with Mendelssohn to show that, though the composer was undoubtedly writing *a propos* of it, his attention to it was perfunctory.')

This same programme—for the third Reid concert in 1932—contains Tovey's notes on Elgar's *Falstaff*, written in ignorance of the fact that the composer had already issued his own notes on the work. In *Essays in Musical Analysis* Tovey reprinted his own notes and corrected them, in footnotes, from the composer's analysis—a most amusing and illuminating procedure. 'I'm green with jealousy', wrote Tovey to Stewart Deas, who conducted this programme, 'at your getting our first performance of the Elgar. I have a boundless admiration for his *Falstaff*, which contains none of the vulgarisms I dislike, and which moreover I really believe to achieve honestly what *Heldenleben* hacks its way through to grab. Few Germans have mastered irony. . . .

'You doubtless realize that Elgar's *tenuto* is an agogic accent and takes *time*; hence its frequent presence in the middle of a legato. We are rather good at that sort of thing in the R.S.O., but of course the beat must allow for it. . . .

'Elgar's scoring balances itself with unsurpassed perfection. But you may find that the first bassoon has to be looked at to prevent him foozling his share of Prince Hal in things like

After the performance, which was broadcast, he wrote: 'Your Elgar was very good and brilliant; but you were, I think, misled by his much too fast metronome marks, and so it lacked Falstaff's essential weight! It seems to be a psychological impossibility for composers to get their metronome marks less than a third too fast.'

The special feature of the first Reid concert of the season

(which I conducted), was the première of Somervell's Violin
Concerto with Adila Fachiri as soloist. Sir Arthur's distress was
considerable when he heard that Tovey was ill and that his new
work (which he refused to conduct himself) was to be entrusted
to an unknown woman. Soloist and orchestra rose splendidly to
the occasion, however, and Sir Arthur not only wrote the most
charming letters to me, but also sent a glowing account of the
success of the concert to Tovey, who had been greatly disappointed because the B.B.C. cancelled the contract to broadcast
this concert. I had conducted concertos which were broadcast
on previous occasions, but in this case either the B.B.C. was
afraid of the risk, or thought that someone more important
should conduct. Amends were fortunately made to Sir Arthur
in a London broadcast.

Sir Adrian Boult conducted the second concert, at which I
played the Mozart A major Concerto. I wrote to Tovey, asking
him to make cadenzas for me, and he replied: 'How about
making your own cadenzas? . . . I won't send you any until you
are really sure the risk is too great.' (I *did* write my own, but I
am sorry now that an opportunity was lost of getting cadenzas
written by Tovey to a Mozart concerto.) 'Practical advice', he
continued, 'for cadenza making—(*a*) compose at the pianoforte (! ! ! how shocking)—(*b*) write down your first thoughts
(sketchily, but enough to record them) before writing anything better—(*c*) don't worry about points of scholarship apart
from the decencies of grammar—you'll find your own idea
of Mozart's language quite adequate.' He also gave examples
of how to fill out the bare outlines at the end of the slow
movement.

When this concert was broadcast Tovey was staying at 'The
Shiffolds', his doctor having at last consented to let him travel.
He wrote immediately: 'You've no idea what a relief it was to
hear so much yesterday. We got, with some fade-outs and inequalities, from the crescendo in the Parry introduction down
to the end of the Dvořák, including *every note* of the pianoforte.
(The applause was also very impressive.) Your cadenza is excel-

lent. . . . The finale was a bit too fast; the fault, however, is on the right side, and your cantabile came through without pin-pricks and in beautiful style.[1]

'The orchestra sounded obviously of first-rate quality through-out. I can't help thinking that these broadcasts will do a great deal for our reputation.'

In this long letter he also discussed University work: 'I don't wonder you find difficulty with the Composition Class. It often leaves me at my wits' end. . . . You will find the point about *tonal* sequence [a point in his discussion of my cadenza—omitted above] very important in teaching composition. Real or modu-lating sequence for squareness; tonal sequence for rhetoric. (See Waldstein and E minor Sonatas.)'

Shortly after this, Miss Weisse—who was very unhappy about the prolonged illness and her own helpless role—wrote to Tovey from Edinburgh to ask when he was coming back to take up his work and to relieve the intolerable burden on others. My next letter was from Hedenham again on 22 November, and enclosed a manifesto to be read to the orchestra, congratulating them on their work up to date, and expressing the hope that the doctors would allow him to resume work after Christmas. The Walton Viola Concerto was to be given for the first time in Edinburgh at the next concert and Tovey's letter continued: 'The Walton will be very difficult—but I am completely convinced by it. The technical difficulties for the orchestra, however, are not such that we can't from the outset concentrate on getting down to *ppppp* as the normal accompanying tone. Wrong notes will be, if anything, clearer the softer you can get them. . . .'

At the concert the concerto was so well received that we per-suaded soloist and conductor to *repeat* it in the second half of the programme, a proceeding which met with enormous success. Tertis wrote afterwards to me: 'This is just to say how enchanted I was with the musical sincerity which I felt all round me. The orchestra did wonders with the extremely difficult orchestral parts, and I enjoyed playing with them very much. I am still

---

[1] I include this because I am proud of such praise.

amazed at the courage of Dr Boult in suggesting to the audience a second performance. I SHALL NEVER FORGET IT!'

Tovey's letter concluded: 'I'm still feeling the effects of Miss Weisse's last letter: such shocks are physical, and reason can do little to deaden them. . . . My own belief is that I ought to be able to get back in February for the fifth concert. Any delay in fixing that programme will be due to my efforts to make sure of being on the spot myself. At present I'm not sure. I know that my progress has been much faster than was expected. Lord Dawson [of Penn] spoke of a whole year—but this I was not told at the time: and my questions since then have not been answered at all clearly.

'It is not for me to say don't worry or don't overwork—especially as it is I who have laid all this burden on you. Never-the-less, *don't.*

Yours *not* hypochondriacally   D. F. T.'

Three weeks later he wrote that he hoped the doctors would allow him to come to some quiet place within reach of Edinburgh in February and continued: 'As to programme I have the following suggestions to make. The ideal come-back for me would be a Brahms programme which I could do by heart and with one rehearsal (apart from your training). The one that needs no extras would be (1) *Tragic* Overture, (2) B flat concerto (conducted by you—so as to let me sit down), (3) Second symphony. (The First would be a better contrast, but the Second is the only one that doesn't need a contrafagotto.)' The idea of letting a man who had been lying on his back for six months play the Brahms B flat Concerto in such a programme was preposterous. He was persuaded instead to conduct only the first half of the concert, Brahms' *Tragic* Overture and Third Symphony—both works with which he was particularly successful—and to leave me to complete it with some fairly riotous Dvořák.

The concert was, as usual, on a Thursday. The anxiety of everyone concerned was very great when Tovey said he would not come for the Tuesday rehearsal, but would take the second half of the rehearsal on Thursday morning. Every member of the orchestra tried to make sure that there would be no possible hitch, for it was clearly understood that what was at stake was the permanence of his recovery. His Edinburgh doctor, Dr. Thin, a very fine and distinguished old man, was present at the Usher Hall throughout Tovey's rehearsal. He was also my family doctor, and he told me, without mincing matters, that he thought this might almost be a question of life or death. As the rehearsal went on Tovey became absorbed in his work, his voice became stronger, and at the end he was not very noticeably fatigued. Tears stood in the good old doctor's eyes as he said to me, 'I would never have believed it. It is almost a miracle.' Tovey had a terrific welcome at the concert that night, and he stayed to the end to hear the Brahms–Dvořák Hungarian Dances which he thought I had rashly put on the programme. He looked almost well again when he came round to say to me, 'You were quite right to insist on doing the Hungarian dances. I wish they had been broadcast to the whole of Europe!' And, indeed, I think that the relief we all felt at the success of Tovey's reappearance was so great, that there was a joy and wildness about the Dances which we might never have succeeded in reproducing again.

Tovey, however, was not yet able to take up his University work again, and although he conducted at the remaining three Reid concerts, he was not able to appear at the Sunday concerts until the closing concert—the twenty-third of the season. That it was possible to keep the Sunday concerts going for a whole season without him was in part due to the fact that there were at that time six good chamber-music ensembles in Edinburgh (including a wind ensemble and a quartet of singers), and in part to the generosity of the strings of the Reid Orchestra, who, in return for much that had been done for them, gave their services on several occasions. Two other conductors appeared besides myself—Stewart Deas and Henry Havergal, also an Edinburgh graduate and at that date music master at Fettes College.

Professor and Mrs. Tovey lived during the spring of 1933 at Black Barony Hotel, Eddleston, some sixteen miles from Edinburgh, among pleasant moors and hills, 'upon which', he wrote to me, 'I am walking as a he-goat upon the mountains, as the minister at Crathie said of Queen Victoria!' Tovey was happy during that time. Weekly visits to Edinburgh put him in touch with his University work again, and he had the satisfaction of knowing that the foundations had been sufficiently well laid for the music department to run on its own for two terms. Furthermore, he had regained his powers of composition and was hard at work on his 'cello concerto. The idea of writing this had been in his mind since the second production of the opera, and he had even mentioned it to Casals, and to Röntgen before his death. He thought of it as he lay under the great chestnut tree at Hedenham and looked up into its depths; but nothing was written down until after the Reid concert at which he recovered so much of his old self. In a letter written to me in March apropos mainly of examination papers, he remarked 'With the return of my power of composition, I'm just beginning to realize how ill I've really been, not only for these last nine months, but for many years back.' A postscript adds: 'Did I tell you that the first movement of my 'cello concerto is now finished and fully scored? It's the biggest single movement I've ever written (or ever want to write) and very much the juiciest. The 'cello dominates a trombone-orchestra quite easily, and the whole thing is as dramatic as I can manage to be.'

With the 'cello concerto still incomplete, he had plans for including 'my forthcoming Overture to *Zuleika Dobson*' in next season's programmes. This overture, of which he often talked, never reached pen and paper; nor did the 'rather goluptious *concerto grosso*' which he had in mind for several years.

Each movement of the solo part of the 'cello concerto was sent to Casals as soon as the ink was dry. On receiving the first movement on 12 March 1933 he wrote:

'Cher Donald, Le jour de l'arrivée de ton concerto marquera dans le calendrier de ma vie—j'en ai une grande joie et j'appré-

cie les sentiments qui se dégagent de tes mots de dédicace aux-
quels j'espère pouvoir faire honneur.

'Tes bowings resteront—si après le travail je vois la nécessité
d'une altération je te la soumettrai pour ton approbation.

'J'attends la suite et aussitôt que possible la partition au piano
qui m'aidera à l'étude.'

The concerto was sketched in full at Eddleston. 'The slow
movement', wrote Tovey to Miss Weisse, 'turns out to be a very
gloomy affair in F minor, which has been in my head for about
six years without my being able to find out what it was to be:—
I had a quite impracticable idea of it as variations for orchestra.
A recklessly sentimental Intermezzo acts as buffer between the
solemn slow movement and a big grotesque finale. . . . I'm
putting down all the bad jokes in my sketches for the finale;
there's such a lot of material that the good ones are sure to
crowd the bad ones out—and I'm quite certain that economy
of material arises in ART, as in NACHAW, from crowding out and
never from eking out. Bow-wow and All That.'

16

THE first moment of real convalescence for Tovey had been the orchestral concert in February. The remarkable recovery which he made in the late spring of 1933 coincided with the completion of his 'cello concerto. He was able, quite against any doctor's expectation, to go to Budapest to act, on Dohnányi's invitation, as one of the adjudicators for the Liszt International Festival Prize for pianists. (When he returned to Hedenham he spent quite a lot of time doing what he called 'tub-practice' of Liszt *études*; though he was not in sympathy with Liszt the composer, he had an enormous admiration for Liszt the player who had such wonderful imagination for sheer pianoforte tone.) He was also in Vienna for the Brahms Festival. On that occasion the chamber music of Brahms was played by some of the most celebrated soloists in the world, whose appearance in ensemble music nevertheless seemed unlikely to produce well-balanced unity of performance. I asked Tovey about these concerts. 'Well,' he said, 'they were very beautiful. Of course, I would not have played Brahms like that, but I think there is a great deal to be said for letting great artists approach great music completely unhampered by tradition. The music has nothing to fear from a fresh approach, and the rediscovery of a tradition might have thrilling results.'

At the beginning of the autumn term Tovey returned to all his usual activities. Among the visiting artists at the Reid concerts were Fritz and Adolf Busch and Rudolph Serkin, who had all now been forced to leave Germany because of Nazi oppression. During this season also Tovey conducted a memorable performance of *The Creation*. The Choral Union had now definitely thrown in its lot with the more fashionable Scottish Orchestra, and a heterogeneous choir was assembled from a number of church choirs for this concert. Although Tovey felt that he did not have sufficient rehearsals personally with the choir to polish its style, the spirit of Haydn's work was realized as I have never again heard it—it was 'just the work itself'. In his later years Tovey became increasingly sensitive to the sublime simplicities of both Haydn and Handel.

In January 1934 his old friend Edward Speyer died at the age of 95. He had retained his mental activity to the last, and his widow, writing in reply to Tovey's letter of sympathy, said: 'You were always in his thoughts, and I wish you could have seen the expression on his face when he listened in to your Beethoven Sonatas last autumn. He hoped that he would some day hear your opera; he felt sure a performance of it would be relayed from Edinburgh!'

Casals expressed the desire that he should give the first performance of the 'cello concerto in Edinburgh with Tovey in the following season. He was increasingly enthusiastic about the work: 'Je reçois ta lettre à laquelle il me faut répondre tout de suite. D'abord, il n'y a rien d'impossible techniquement dans ton concerto — tu le sais aussi bien que moi. Seulement il s'agit d'assimiler ta technique de violoncelle qui est, à Dieu merci, bien à toi, comme celles de Beethoven et de Brahms avaient la leur. Corrige de ton œuvre ce qui pourrait l'améliorer, mais tu ne dois changer quoi que ce soit pour faciliter ma tâche — c'est à moi de me débrouiller et je le fais, crois-le, avec le plus grand plaisir et intérêt.' 'Je voudrais te faire honneur', says a later letter, 'avec l'exécution de cette œuvre magnifique à laquelle ma pensée s'occupe presque exclusivement.'

'Donald has got through the winter much better than I had dared to hope', wrote Mrs. Tovey to Mrs. Trevelyan in March 1934, and the record of his activities for the next fourteen months is astonishing proof of his resilience. In April, at Casals' request, he played his pianoforte concerto in Barcelona, and was made an Honorary Member of the Orquestra Pau Casals, an honour of which he was very proud.[1] A broadcast with the B.B.C.

[1] In a long letter to Miss Weisse about this visit, Tovey says he is somewhat disconcerted to find how little development there has been in his style of composition.

Orchestra in Belfast early in May was followed next day by a recital at Winchester. Then he went to Glyndebourne, where Fritz Busch was conducting at the newly opened Opera House.

'Dear Donald,' wrote Busch on 3 May, 'ich habe wieder eine grosse Bitte. Die "Festivals" müssen beginnen und enden mit "God save the King". Die mir bekannten englischen Bearbeitungen (B.B.C. and so on) sind (*a*) für grosses Orchester und (*b*) schlecht. Ich habe nur das Mozart-Orchester. . . . Kannst du mir schnell eine Partitur schreiben und herschicken. Das machst du (*a*) sehr schön und (*b*) sehr schnell.'[1] The reply to this was 'The Glyndebourne Kynge in G'!

A recital in Oxford on 3 June was followed next day by the Deneke lecture on *Musical Form and Matter*. The Philip Maurice Deneke Lecture perpetuates the name of the household which had been to Tovey since his undergraduate days like a musical home in Oxford; his lecture was a *tour de force*, and adumbrated his prime musical faith in the closing sentence: '. . . let me end, with an appeal to philosophers better qualified than I am to work out the theory that the wholeness of a work of art is a type of infinity.' Later in June he went to Czechoslovakia for a 'cure' at Carlsbad, as one of the noticeable results of his illness was a very undesirable increase in weight. He returned to Hedenham in August to give a short series of lectures to a Musicians' Holiday School at Felixstowe.

During this summer Tovey was full of new projects for future compositions, and he was in correspondence with John Buchan on the subject of a possible opera libretto based on *The Rose and the Ring*. Ever since the second performance of *The Bride of Dionysus* he had been considering off and on the possibilities of

'Moreover,' he adds, 'here are three works dated 1903 (pianoforte concerto), 1913 (symphony), and 1933 ('cello concerto), which could never be put into the same programme because several of the main themes have marked features in common to all three works! This is no more than an accident, though a very tiresome one.'

[1] 'Dear Donald, I have another request to make. The Festival must begin and end with "God save the King". The only English arrangements I know are (*a*) for large orchestra, and (*b*) bad. I have only a Mozart orchestra. . . . Can you quickly make an arrangement for me and send it here? Only make it (*a*) very beautiful, and (*b*) very soon.'

another opera on entirely new lines. *Twelfth Night* was for some
reason still in abeyance, and he had sounded both A. P. Herbert
and Austin Freeman about libretti. In July 1934 he also returned
to the idea of setting a Biblical text (a project undertaken and
abandoned after the death of Watts in 1904). He wrote to Sir
Frederick Pollock about this in July, and received a reply:
'First, and for me the most important question: by what time
do you want the text? Outside my standing duties as editor of
the *Law Reports* my hands are pretty full for this year. So it
would be for the Christmas vacation at the earliest. Then as to
length: is about 200 lines a fair guess? And is a mixture of verse
and prose admissible? There are gems in the Vulgate, though
as a rule our A.V. reads better to an Englishman. And do you
contemplate solos as well as chorus? If so how many solo voices?
I have a pet text in Proverbs *Sapientia aedificavit sibi domum, excidit
columnas septem* (nothing to choose between the Latin and the
English). Those seven pillars I suspect fixed the number of the
Liberal Arts. I fancy it standing at the opening and setting
the general tone (in a literary sense). . . .

'Your quotation from "For my Grandson" is all but verbally
correct.'

In September Tovey appeared at one of the Promenade concerts, playing Bach's D minor Concerto—a performance to
which reference has already been made. Dr. Knud Jeppesen,
the famous Danish musicologist, wrote to him after the broadcast: 'I send you my very best greetings and thanks for your
wonderful interpretation of Bach's concerto. It was a splendid
performance; what a great musician you are! Also the broadcasting was very fine and all sounds escaped happily the waves
of the wild North Sea.'

The honorary degree of Mus.Doc. had been conferred on
Casals, *in absentia*, at the summer graduation in Edinburgh. 'Es-
tu bien sûr,' he wrote to Tovey, 'que le bonnet Universitaire
fera bien sur ma tête?—Rassure-moi, car j'ai bien de doutes!
Je te remercie, aussi que l'Université, d'avoir prévu à mon égard
le *conferment* de mon degré *in absentia*. Il y aura au moins deux

bonnes raisons pour qu'il soit ainsi — éviter l'état de tension que m'occasionnerait l'idée de cette cérémonie ainsi que l'émotion du moment de la même, ceci pour cause de santé, et, raison très nécessaire et importante pour moi, le besoin de tranquillité pour mon travail, surtout de ton concerto auquel je dédie tout mon amour et mes forces.

'En suivant par ordre les sujets de ta lettre, je te remercie de la part des futurs habitants de la rue Pau Casals[1] (rue en construction) pour tes bons souhaits. J'espère aussi que ces habitants aimeront la musique et que mon nom doucement prononcé aura quelque suggestion bienfaisante. Le monument à Granados, qui va être placé tout à côté de ma rue, agira efficacement à cette musicalisation!'

'Next term in Edinburgh', said a letter from Tovey to Miss Weisse in September 1934, 'ought to be the most interesting I've yet had, what with the Busches, Casals, and Schweitzer, who will be giving the Gifford lectures in theology—I hope in my classroom.' At the instance of Sir Hugh Allen, the Worshipful Company of Musicians invited Tovey, in October, to accept the Honorary Freedom of the Company 'in recognition of your invaluable services to the art of music'. This Company is not often in public evidence, but is a very ancient one—'Incorporated by Royal Charter of King Edward IV as *The King's Marshall and Minstrels* 1469, and by Royal Charter of King James I as *The Master, Wardens and Commonalty of the Art or Science of the Musicians of London* 1604.' Some months later Tovey received further public recognition; Sir Edward Elgar, who was then Master of the King's Musick, was the prime mover in connexion with the honour of knighthood which was conferred on him in January 1935.

When the dates of the Reid concerts were fixed, Casals wrote: 'Le 22 novembre sera la plus importante date de ma vie de musicien. Joachim a dû ressentir la même joie et honneur le jour qu'il a remis sur pied le concerto pour violon de Beethoven et celui de la première audition du concerto de Brahms.' It was

---

[1] In Barcelona.

hoped that the 'cello concerto would be broadcast; Casals, however, was to play during the week before with the B.B.C.
Orchestra in London, and was also to conduct one of its programmes. The *première* of Tovey's concerto with the Reid
Orchestra was therefore refused a broadcast, just as the Somervell had been (though for different reasons) two years earlier.

Owing to overwork and to anxieties in connexion with the
situation in Spain, Casals was far from well at the time of his
visit to Edinburgh. He had also a slight infection in the thumb
of his left hand, which subsequently developed so that he was
unable to play for two months. No one could possibly have
guessed that he was in pain during the superb performance
which he gave on 22 November, and the audience was carried
away alike by the beauty of his playing and the splendour of
the work. *The Times* critic wrote: 'Señor Pau Casals wished to
give London the chance of hearing the fine violoncello concerto
by Professor D. F. Tovey, which he produced in Edinburgh
on Thursday evening with the Reid Symphony Orchestra, the
composer conducting. His plan fell through, as such plans are
apt to do, so probably Barcelona and other Continental places
may hear the work before London does. London is unlikely to
disturb itself on that account. Professor Tovey is honoured as a
musician of profound learning, but not as a composer to whom
Queen's Hall need listen. The loss in the case of this violoncello
concerto is to the Queen's Hall audiences. In the B.B.C. Symphony Orchestra we have one of the most richly endowed orchestral institutions in the world. In the Royal Philharmonic we
have a society which for over a hundred years has claimed to
represent, among other things, the best product of native composition. If both decide to ignore a work which is clearly one of
considerable power and intimate beauty and which, moreover,
is sponsored by the greatest exponent of violoncello playing in
the world, they will be very foolish. . . . The whole concerto
grows out of the genius of the violoncello, and it takes all Casals'
genius to display its qualities. That in itself is worth going to
Edinburgh to hear. It should surely make the concerto worth

the expenditure of one hour of Queen's Hall's most valuable time.'

A note from Tovey brought to me at the University on the morning after the concert said: 'Did I understand that you knew of someone who could photograph Casals, Schweitzer and me in our spangles and tights tomorrow morning in the Classroom?' As both great men had received their degrees *in absentia*, neither of them had ever been arrayed in the academic finery, and this occasion pleased them both greatly. The unflattering photographs are unique records of three of the most distinguished personalities of their day, both as musicians and as men.

Dr. and Mrs. Schweitzer stayed with the Toveys during the weeks in which Schweitzer delivered the Gifford Lectures, and the friendship between the two musicians matured. After his visit Schweitzer wrote warmly from Paris in December: 'Lieber Freund, zuerst ein Geständnis: ich kann dich nicht mit Sie anreden und anschreiben! Sei lieb und erlaube mir dir *Du* zu sagen; und wenn du mich für würdig hältst, sage mir auch *Du*. Ich finde es so unnatürlich, wo wir uns so herzlich als Musikanten und Menschen verstehen, dass wir auf Sie miteinander stehen bleiben.

'Widor hat eine grosse Freude an der *Kunst der Fuge* erhabt. Heute nachmittag schreibt er dir durch meine Feder. Sein rechter Arm geht gar nicht gut. Ich musste ihm lange von dir erzählen.

'Und nun lass mich noch meinen tiefen Dank für alles Gute, dass ich in deinem Hause erfahren durfte, ansprechen. Ich bin in der Geographie ganz irre geworden. Capria liegt nun für mich nicht in Italien sondern in Schottland. Und wie schön war es, dich noch besser kennen zu lernen und in den "Tischgesprächen" so viel von dir zu lernen.

'Mit lieben Gedanken und auf Wiedersehn,
Dein treu ergebener Albert Schweitzer.'[1]

[1] This letter hinges on the use of the word 'Du' as a term of address (equivalent to the use of the Christian name).

'Dear Friend, First of all a confession: I cannot speak and write to you as "Sie"! Please let me address you as "Du", and, if you think me worthy of it, please address

One month later, in a long and illegible letter written in the train between Paris (where he had been studying the latest treatment of yellow fever) and Strasbourg, Schweitzer congratulated Tovey on his knighthood and continued: 'Als wir zusammen an Tisch sassen und uns Geschichte erzählten, musste ich immer aufpassen, dass ich nicht aus Versehen in die *Du-Tonart* verfiel. Und wenn ich Ihnen als ansah, dass Sie in der Nacht wenig guten Schlaf gehabt hatten, da wäre ich aus Traurigkeit auch einigemale fast in die *Du-Tonart* gefallen. Aber nun bist Du *Sir* und einem *Sir* wage ich nicht anzutragen, dass wir uns Du sagen!'[1]

Fritz, Adolf, and Hermann Busch with Rudolf Serkin were the guest artists at the fourth Reid concert, and during their visit honorary degrees were conferred on Fritz and Adolf.[2] In honour of this, the programme began with Brahms' *Academic Festival* Overture, and a short ceremony took place in the foyer after the concert, when the Lord Provost and Magistrates received the guests on behalf of the city. It was a happy occasion for all concerned, as well as a memorable concert.

The fourth Sunday concert that season was given in aid of Schweitzer's Hospital Fund for Lambarene. It was, of course, a Bach programme, in which the combined choirs of St. Giles Cathedral and the Edinburgh Bach Society took part along

me also as "Du". It seems to me so unnatural, when we understand each other so well about music and other matters, to continue to use the formal style.

'Widor was delighted with the *Kunst der Fuge*. This afternoon he is going to write to you by means of my pen. His right arm is very painful. I had to talk to him for a long time about you.

'And now may I express my deepest thanks for all the kindness I received in your home. My geography has gone mad. Capri for me is now not in Italy but in Scotland. And it was delightful to get to know you better, and to learn so much from your "table-talk".

'With kindest remembrances and *auf wiedersehen*,
　　　　　　　　　　　Yours very sincerely Albert Schweitzer.

[1] 'As we sat together at table and told each other stories, I had always to be on my guard in case I lapsed into the familiar form of address. And when I saw you, after a bad night, I was always so grieved that I almost found myself using it. But now you are *Sir* and I would not dare to suggest to a *Sir* that we address each other by our Christian names!'

[2] All four artists insisted on coming for travelling expenses alone.

with the Reid Orchestra. Tovey asked Miss Benson to sing one
of the solo alto cantatas on this occasion. She was very nervous
about singing a Bach cantata before Schweitzer, but Tovey said
'Schweitzer is a saint; and one can never seem foolish in the
presence of a saint!' I conducted the concerto which Tovey
played. Afterwards I took Schweitzer back to Royal Terrace,
and the feat of getting him *into* my little Morris coupé was
nothing to the feat of getting him *out* of it! He talked of the
concert and said suddenly to me, 'You are a born conductor.' I
was much taken aback at such a remark from such a man, but
he put it for ever in true perspective for me by adding, 'Of
course, it is just like having blue eyes or brown eyes!'

The fifth concert was a recital by Tovey and Casals. Casals—
like Röntgen—said he would like to offer a 'degree exercise' to
the University, and suggested that it should take the form of a
recital—to which his special contribution would be the Bach
solo suite for 'cello in D major, which is seldom heard. The
programme began with Röntgen's sonata for pianoforte and
'cello, in which the two players re-kindled to great beauty the
music of the old friend, whose memory was evergreen. 'Cher
Donald', wrote Casals from Spain in December, 'Bonne année
nouvelle pour toi et Mrs Tovey. J'entends encore ton concerto
et j'en suis encore ému. Ce fut une grande journée pour la
musique que celle de la naissance de ton œuvre à notre monde.'
The letter goes on to say that his brother had been imprisoned
on political grounds for six weeks, but had fortunately been
released just before Christmas.

A Sunday programme later in the season contained the following amusing item—'Sonata in F sharp minor ——? (*Note*—
The name of the composer will be announced after the sonata
has been played)'—'for', said Tovey, 'nobody is going to listen
to a Clementi sonata if you tell them first it *is* Clementi!'

Tovey had been anxious to keep in touch with the United
Churches Choir which had sung *The Creation* for him the season
before: 'The most economical thing for them to do would be the
Ninth Symphony and the *Hymn of Jesus*', he wrote to me. These

were 'economical', because we possessed the material and he had been asked to cut down on music expenses! The choirs were, not unnaturally, afraid to undertake two such works, and the ambitious programme, with which he had hoped to stimulate the new Churches Choir, offered instead to his opponents evidence in support of allegations that he was unpractical. There was no choral concert this season, but the defection of the Churches Choir gave rise to a new scheme in the following year.

The first two volumes of the *Essays in Musical Analysis* appeared in January 1935. In a long article in the *Daily Telegraph* nearly a year before, Richard Capell had remarked: 'when Tovey takes off his coat to an analysis the result is one of the most impressive phenomena to be observed in the whole academic world. We think, for instance, of his Beethoven Centenary Essay on the C sharp minor Quartet. No one with a musical interest ever found a detective story half so engrossing as those pages.' The *Essays* received lengthy and laudatory notices throughout the press: 'Here is the finest writing on music achieved in our time,' said Neville Cardus in the *Manchester Guardian*; 'Sir Donald's culture is as broad as it is humane; he carries it lightly. He writes with a growing excitement—and with delicious humour. He manages to avoid telling the great composers how to compose (a duty that may safely be left to musical critics who operate further south). . . . All "musical appreciation" is here—and none of the blarney.'

The success of the *Essays* presently overshadowed Tovey's reputation in this country as a pianist and composer, a fact which he found somewhat vexing. It was, however, during this spring that the first threat of serious trouble with his hands began to be manifest, though it did not as yet affect his playing. Curiously, also, the nervous eczema which had been such a cause of distress all his life, was now replaced by troublesome susceptibility to bronchitis.

The Busch Quartet played Tovey's *Variations for String Quartet* op. 11 both in Oxford and in London in March 1935. 'Deine herrlichen Variationen,' said a telegram to the composer, 'haben das Londoner Publikum begeistert. Herzlichen Glückwunsch zu aussergewöhnlichem Erfolg. Dein Adolf.'[1] And *The Times* critic concluded his notice by saying: 'At the end of this fascinating work we were left wondering at the neglect of our English masters and grateful to these German artists for recalling one of them to the attention of an English audience.'

Tovey went to Barcelona in April 1935 to conduct his 'cello concerto. In addition to Lady Tovey, Miss Weisse and John also went for the occasion on Casals' invitation. 'When we arrived in Barcelona', says a description written by Miss Weisse on a scrap of paper, 'the great 'cellist was at the station to receive his fellow artist. It was announced that there was to be a rehearsal of the concerto for orchestra alone at 9.30 or 10 o'clock the same evening. And here it may be said that it seems that this is the natural hour for the practice of music in Spain, though the very remarkable concert on Sunday was in the afternoon, at 5.30. Urged by his sympathy with the workman musician of theatres and cinemas, Casals has created an orchestra of the finest quality, very similar to the Reid Orchestra, which had a like origin. The hall in Barcelona, the *Orfeo Catalan*, like the very fine Usher Hall in Edinburgh, holds a large audience, considerably larger than the Queen's Hall in London. And at both concerts it was full—filled by a breathlessly attentive audience, which, the moment a movement was over, instead of coughing and fidgeting, broke into warm delighted applause such as draws both artist and audience together, and speeds the whole work as a warm breeze fills the sail. A very old concert-goer— I can never sufficiently deplore the recent custom of refraining from the natural expression of enjoyment when a movement comes to an end.'

The concerto had great success; one notice remarked, 'it contains passages of great beauty and luminous inspiration which some would regard as incompatible with the British temperament'. Tovey, who was, of course, no stranger to the Barcelona

[1] 'Your masterly variations have been received by the London public with enthusiasm. Heartiest congratulations on this splendid success.'

SEÑOR PAU CASALS AND SIR DONALD TOVEY
at the *Orfeo Catalan*, Barcelona (April 1935)

THREE GREAT MUSICIANS, 23 NOVEMBER 1934
(Schweitzer and Casals, whose autographs appear, are seated on the organ-stool:
the photograph was taken in the Music Classroom of Edinburgh University—see
p. 284)

A PAGE FROM THE FACSIMILE REPRODUCTION OF THE
FULL SCORE OF THE CELLO CONCERTO

audiences, had a great reception both as composer-conductor, and as pianist at the second concert in Beethoven's G major Concerto.

An invitation came from Arbos asking Tovey to come to Madrid to conduct the 'cello concerto there at a Festival which was shortly to be held in honour of Casals. This he was unable to do, for immediately after the concerts in Barcelona he had to make a hurried journey to Belfast to play with the B.B.C. Orchestra there. Any sensible person, barely twelve months recovered from a serious illness, would have arranged concert-dates more conveniently, but Tovey was never sensible about this. He was always quite clear about the length of time which it took to get from one geographical locality to another, but he made no allowance for any time to recruit his energy between one engagement and the next.

It was hardly surprising that his health broke down again in June, despite a previous visit to Carlsbad in May. He made a reasonably good recovery in a few weeks, but his hands were still so painful and stiff that playing was an effort and practice not to be thought of. A summer spent at Hedenham was no help to any rheumatic condition, although Lady Tovey, who now also suffered severely from arthritis, maintained that the climate was not at all harmful. She was alarmed, however, because her husband was often very depressed. Writing to Miss Weisse at the end of August, Tovey said he was 'in the dismallest stages of convalescence, no longer being an Object of Sympathy for whom Allowance must be made'. 'But', he concluded, 'I'm slowly restoring my pianoforte playing by means of the clavichord. My! How it shows things up. But it doesn't blister one's fingers.' A letter to me written about the same time avowed 'I'm in the lowest depths of *Neue Kraft fühlend*, and it feels merely like bad temper. The brain is atonal (all empty except for green scum).'

He returned to Edinburgh in October 1935, reasonably restored in health and spirits, and incurably optimistic about the recovery of his playing. His hands were still in a worse state than he would admit, and Schweitzer—who delivered a second set of lectures in Edinburgh during that winter and, of course, stayed again at Royal Terrace—was shocked at their condition. After his visit he wrote to Lady Tovey: 'Je suis toujours en soucie pour les mains de votre mari. Je crois qu'il fait bien de continuer les bains, même si l'effet n'est que passager. Car cela ne peut pas se passer d'un jour à l'autre.'

Tovey had plans just then for editing Bach's *Musikalische Opfer*: 'It is much shorter', he wrote to Hubert Foss of the Oxford University Press, 'than the *Kunst*, but a more complicated task; and I think the commentary should not be separated from the text. My project would include Bach's text as in the B.G.,[1] but I think it will be enough to give my own realisation of the figured bass without reprinting the one ascribed partly to Bach and partly to Kirnberger.' A letter to Foss a few days later said: 'Please tell Mr Walton that the reason why I cannot come to hear his symphony is that I am producing his viola concerto here with a local viola player[2] (he had to be born somewhere and why not here?). Incidentally, he is following the printed text, as he shares my feeling that Tertis is a little too anxious to turn the viola into a violin. . . . I am very glad that Walton likes my notes on the concerto.'

Arrangements had been made for Tovey's 'cello concerto to be produced in London under the auspices of the Courtauld–Sargent Concert Club on 11 and 12 November 1935, with Casals, of course, as soloist and Tovey as conductor. This proved to be an altogether unhappy event. Too little time was allotted to the work at rehearsal, and the entirely competent but routine-hardened London instrumentalists not only failed to understand Tovey's ways at rehearsal but were frankly irritated by his explanations and impatient with him. It was all extremely uncomfortable and, although the audience was appreciative, the press was not. Fox-Strangways in the *Observer* went so far as to say 'the composer conducted, and proved himself the enemy of Casals and of his own music'. Tovey was considerably hurt and enraged. 'What I chiefly resent,' he wrote to a friend, 'are the

---

[1] Bach-Gesellschaft edition.   [2] John Fairbairn.

sporadic attempts to discredit me as a conductor. I don't claim
that conducting, as distinguished from training an orchestra, is
one of my strong suits: but I resent the imputation that I am
professionally incompetent, and the evident determination of a
good many wire-pullers that I shall not be given the chance of
conducting. . . . Somehow or other I failed to secure a Courtauld
programme, in which Edwin Evans availed himself of my score
and my Edinburgh notes. He boiled them down not unfairly or
unskilfully into his own language, but Ernest Newman seems to
have got hold of them and used them in evidence against me
with the object of discrediting me as a self-deluded self-laudator.
Next time I produce any notes of my own I shall point out that
experience shows that no composer must use any epithet whatever in describing his own work.'

The bitterness of his mood was not merely due to his lifelong
sensitivity to criticism. The Courtauld concerts coincided with
Tovey's realization that he could not possibly play his own
pianoforte concerto with Busch at the Reid concert on 5 December, as he was totally unable, owing to the state of his hands, to
deliver the opening bars with the requisite force. And he was
facing, for the first time, the possibility that the scope of his
playing might become increasingly restricted.[1] There was no
reason, however, to suppose that anything would affect his conducting, and he hoped to rely more and more on this as a means
of expression. In this situation the reaction in London on his
appearance there as a conductor was truly discouraging, despite
Casals' letter: 'Quel énorme plaisir pour moi ce fût l'exécution
de ton concerte à Londres. Si tu as eu de la satisfaction c'est cela
qui compte—le reste est bien peu de choses.' Casals spoke from
experience, for he had also found, when he appeared as a conductor in London, that some orchestral players and some critics
took the view that his own lack of what Tovey—somewhat
bitterly—called 'trade-finish' implied inferiority as a conductor.

The Reid Choir was founded this winter as an outcome of the

---

[1] Nevertheless, while he was in London he gave a morning recital with Casals,
in memory of Fanny Davies, at the Francis Holland School in Chelsea.

Churches Choir fiasco, and Tovey looked forward with keen delight to having, for the first time since the collapse of the Kirkhope Choir, a body of singers working under his direction with no obligation to any other organization. The Choirmaster was Dr. Robert Head, organist of St. Mary's Cathedral, who was a most experienced choir trainer. Tovey, though in many ways an exceedingly patient person, would never have had the patience to teach a choir words and notes, unless every member of it had been a highly trained professional musician who would understand straight away matters of phrasing and dynamics. When the spade-work had been done by Dr. Head, however, he was able to develop the higher qualities of the choir to a remarkable degree. 'My latest exploit, of which I am inordinately proud,' wrote Tovey to Dame Ethel Smyth in February 1936, 'has been Haydn's *Seasons*, with a small choir of a little over a hundred. The press, which I feared might snuff us out, was quite obviously overawed.' This performance called forth as a programme-note one of his liveliest essays, and it is a pity that the reprint in the collected Essays omits the two beautiful facsimile pages from the original score which appeared in the Reid programme.

The occasion of this correspondence with Dame Ethel was the appearance in the *Daily Telegraph* of a long account of an interview which she had with Casals on the subject of Tovey's 'cello concerto. Although the distortion of hearing from which she now suffered prevented her from going to the concert, and even from reading the score, her interest in the work was very real. 'I am told', she wrote to Tovey, 'that your concerto is *magnificent*. Maurice [Baring] said that tears poured down his cheeks.' She had been stirred to anger by the tone of many of the press notices and thought of this way of intervening in support of the composer. 'Rather more than three months ago', her article began, 'a particularly sad result of my being cut off from music was that I had to forgo hearing Pau Casals play Donald Tovey's Violoncello Concerto. My personal acquaintance with Señor Casals was slight, but I felt a strong desire to hear him at least talk about the concerto.' Casals talked to Dame Ethel not only of the concerto, but of Tovey's playing and conducting, and her article continues: 'And of Tovey's qualifications as a conductor, of the influence he exercises, Casals said: "For any of us, whether solo artists, members of the chorus, or the last violinist at the last desk of second violins, it is an honour to stand on the same platform with him. So ennobling is the spirit that emanates from such as he, that to criticise his technique as conductor is childish." He added, "Being what he is, he gets results that lesser men, however highly trained, can never hope to achieve". And he cited the *Leonora* Overture, conducted in Barcelona by Tovey "as he had never heard it".' 'He really meant *Fidelio*', wrote Tovey in a letter of thanks to Dame Ethel, 'but it doesn't matter. . . . I am sorry that the D. T. has omitted some of your article, because the omissions are just those which would give verisimilitude to an otherwise coruscating and incredible hagiology.'[1]

Tovey's letter concludes, 'pity me for being now in the middle of examinations, the most miserable time of the year. I enclose a forlorn attempt to inspire my poor contrapuntists.

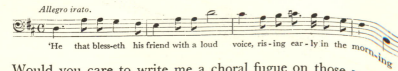

Allegro irato.

'He that bless-eth his friend with a loud voice, ris-ing ear-ly in the morn-ing

Would you care to write me a choral fugue on those words? Show it to Lady Betty [Balfour]. It was one of my father's favourite texts.' (It is—in the correct Biblical words—the text that had once inspired my student efforts.) He also refers rue-fully to the state of his hands—'I can just manage my Bach concerto tomorrow, as it has no stretches. Later on, at a Sunday concert, I am going to manage the Schumann quintet with the enormous improvement of leaving out most of the useless doubling. So gout may be of some use to a player after all. But a little of it goes a damnably long way'.

The invitation to write a chorale fugue was not so casual as it seemed. A letter written a few days later shows how concerned

[1] 'Casals did say *Fidelio*; it was my mistake,' replied Dame Ethel, adding, 'It did give me joy quoting Casals on you as a pianist!'

Tovey was that a composer should be cut off from music: 'Now please don't be angry with me if I touch on a personal matter in which I am not wholly inexperienced in my own way. I see no reason to doubt that you may yet do some of your greatest work. At present the shock of the physical disorganisation of your ear is doubtless too painful for you to think of encouraging your memory and imagination. And no doubt the torment of a distorted hearing must be far worse than the mere deafness which cut off Beethoven so early from the control of his performances. Probably at present the sight of music conveys to you painful impressions of the distorted form in which it would reach your physical ear. . . . But I am quite certain that you will soon find that a score which you have not heard too recently can give you vivid recollections of its proper sounds. Moreover, this withdrawal into your private imagination would soon enable you to hear things as you have never hoped to hear them in real life. It was not by accident that Beethoven after his deafness did more to revolutionise orchestration than any other composer before or since. . . . I am sure that the imaginary conducting of music is a thing which would soon not only supersede the actual hearing of it, but would stimulate you to your greatest work.

'Forgive this well-meant intrusion where angels fear to tread, but I am so sure of the truth of my advice that I think it infinitely less harmful to risk the annoyance, or even pain, it may give you than to miss the opportunity of the good it may do.' It is a touching letter from one crippled musician to another.

At the second last Sunday concert of this season, in March 1936, a very charming and unique programme was given by the strings of the Reid Orchestra and Miss Waddell's Junior Orchestras, in which the first item was Mozart's Serenade for four orchestras. Tovey always referred to Miss Waddell's Junior Orchestras as the 'nursery of the Reid', and their *personnel* ranged from babes of four and a half, swinging their heels high off the ground, to 17- and 18-year-olds, boys and girls alike. Miss Maimie Waddell and her sister Ruth (a pupil of Suggia and a 'cellist of real distinction) were two of the original members of the Reid Orchestra.[1] Their father had been a prominent Edinburgh musician, and had known the Weisse family in the days when old Mr. and Mrs. Weisse lived in Edinburgh. At the very first meeting of the Reid Orchestra, Tovey, recognizing the Waddell sisters, immediately recalled in a delightful fashion how he remembered hearing their father's orchestra on the occasion of one of his early visits with Miss Weisse. Their Junior Orchestras, which are still in a lively state of existence, consist of their own pupils and those of their assistants, and the standard of playing and ensemble which they attain is probably the highest in the country. The natural and spontaneous manner and the extremely fine sense of style shown by the children moved Fritz Busch almost to tears when Tovey took him to a rehearsal. The public association between part of the Reid and its 'nursery' was an occasion of the greatest delight to Tovey; he shared the conducting with Miss Maimie Waddell, and got at least as great a thrill and as much fun out of the performance—which was a huge success—as did the children.

In the midst of this busy season, though he neglected much correspondence, Tovey found time to write a long letter to Elizabeth Maconchy about the pianoforte concerto which she had just sent him: 'Like any work of yours, it must command my interest, and I should be very glad of an opportunity of doing it here. If I can get rid of the gout which at present prevents me stretching more than a sixth, I would like to play it myself, and my students (who have the sense to admire you immensely) and the general public would consider the occasion more interesting if you cared to conduct it. If you preferred to listen from a distance, Dr Mary Grierson will be a most capable conductor, and the days are not yet passed when it is still useful for women to be seen working together in public. . . . You will see from this that I am not calling the intrinsic value of the work in question. The following criticisms have relation merely to what I think you could do.

'As compared with the orchestral work' (her suite *The Land*)

---

[1] Both sisters have since received the honorary degree of Mus.Doc.

'which we did last year, I have the impression that your notions of the pianoforte are inhibiting your imagination.' He proceeds to demonstrate this in various lively ways and then reaches the subject of Rachmaninoff's concertos: 'Rachmaninoff starts his C minor concerto with beautiful rolling arpeggios for the pianoforte while all his strings in unison do a fine Roman-nosed melody supported on well-scored sustained chords for low wind and brass. All very fine. Then, seated at the pianoforte himself, he gives out the same melody in chords which sound quite well to him, but are little better than a mildly melodious click of billiard balls against the still magnificent orchestral background. . . .[1] You don't catch Beethoven delivering a piano-forte theme in terms which the orchestra has stated much better.' His indications of specific passages show that he had given serious attention to the score—but, although the work was per-formed in the next season, he was not able to play it.

'Send me something you like—but wickedly beautiful, for the sake of my orchestra and audience,' Tovey had said in an earlier letter to Miss Maconchy. Some time after the performance of her pianoforte concerto she sent him the score of her viola concerto. 'The score shows your usual mastery and also your understanding of the psychology of a concerto', he wrote, 'but I don't think that gout and old age is the whole explanation of my growing distaste for the physical jerks which you moderns inflict upon conductors by your rhythmic anfractuosities (Dr. Johnson's finest word). The conviction grows, among younger musicians than myself, that many of these tuggings at the horse's mouth have arisen from actual misconception of 16th-century rhythm and of speech rhythm.' But the letter ends: 'Go on: more power to your elbow.

Your sincere old fogey

Donald Francis Tovey.'

Fritz Busch, who was now conducting at Copenhagen during

---

[1] This is not what happens in Rachmaninoff's C minor Concerto; it seems as if Tovey, writing—as he so often did—from memory, had confused the opening of this work with that of Tschaikovsky's B flat Concerto.

the winter months, was anxious to produce Tovey's 'cello concerto there. But Casals was still in poor health, and the situation in Catalonia was uncertain, and so negotiations fell through. 'Cher Pablo,' wrote Tovey from Bath in April 1936, 'Comme tu comprends et parles l'anglais beaucoup mieux que je parle français, je t'écrirai en Macaronique, selon les règles de la Duchesse en *Alice in Wonderland*: "Speak in French when you can't think of the English for a thing."

'J'espère que tu te portes bien. Moi, je me porte sur mes deux jambes, et grace aux bains et à la traitement de Bath, je commence à croire that some day I shall be able to play octaves again.

'Je comprends bien que le voyage à Copenhagen serait trop fatiguant à présent. En telles circonstances tu comprendras bien que Busch veut faire exécuter notre concert par un de tes élèves déjà connu en Copenhagen, et que je n'ai su faire objection que nous prêtons à Cassado une exemplaire pour qu'il étude l'œuvre avec toi.

'C'est dommage aussi que je ne peux pas venir à Barcelone pour la S.I.M.[1] En vérité, c'est plus important de faire guérir mes mains que de partager en des discours musicalogues dans les langues étrangères. Tu sais que les musicalogues en général me font toujours peur. . . .

'On dit qu'une gramophone company quelconque veut faire une disque de notre concert, et qu'elle attend l'occasion qui sera convenable pour toi. Pour moi, ce qui arrivera à Copenhagen ne fait rien. La première disque de notre concert sera jouée seulement par toi dans les conditions que tu préfères. L'idéal sera avec ton orchestre à Barcelone, soit dans un studio, soit en publique, et dirigée par moi; au moins que tu ne partages l'opinion de the *Observer*.' Tovey made the suggestion of recording in Spain because he feared that Casals was in much worse health than *he* was, and he was anxious to spare his friend any avoidable strain.

Tovey added that the Oxford University Press had under-

[1] La Société Internationale de Musique.

taken to publish the concerto, and asked Casals to edit the 'cello part with such bowings, fingerings, and revisions as he thought fit, and to allow his name to appear in the publication as the reviser. The full score, published in 1937, was reproduced in facsimile of a beautifully clear manuscript by the composer, and bears the inscription, 'written in honour of Casals by his friend Donald Francis Tovey'.

Immediately following on his 'cure' at Bath, Tovey played the Schumann concerto with the B.B.C. Orchestra in Belfast, carrying off the performance with great success, despite the fact that many of the passages tried his hands severely. Astra Desmond sang several of Bantock's songs at this concert, and Tovey wrote to tell him how well they had gone, concluding his letter with the remark, 'I've got a new string quartet in A minor started,' and giving—in the neatest manuscript—the first twenty bars of it.

On 20 May he delivered the Romanes Lecture on *Normality and Freedom in Music* in the Sheldonian Theatre at Oxford. 'It has come out very dull and far too suitable for these times,' he wrote to me. 'It merely distinguishes the normal from the usual. The usual has more soda and goes forrader.' During this month, also, the last of several attempts to meet Sibelius was frustrated, this time through Sibelius's illness. 'I shall ask Bantock to *vermitteln* a meeting with Sibelius,' said a letter to Miss Weisse; adding 'I hope S. is *not* conducting much; his works want doing with a sense of tempo and climax, and I hear that he gets slower and slower and explores every bit of lichen on the bark of the first tree he has planted.' But, in spite of this admirable description of the Finnish composer's conducting, Tovey had a very real appreciation of his genius, which he amply demonstrated at different times by giving the first performances in Scotland of Sibelius' Fifth, Sixth, and Seventh symphonies and of the Violin Concerto.

Tovey was in good spirits when he visited Glyndebourne this summer, and also when I went to see him at Hedenham. Apart from interminable proof-correcting and a little desultory practice, he was, as he said himself, 'disinclined to work between meals!' He generally proposed a run in the car during the afternoons; and, in a county which excels itself in confusing indications at small cross-roads, it was surprising how often he would say—in a diffident fashion—'Er—er, I think, Miss Morrah, if you took the right-hand fork' . . . and go on to describe where it would lead. On Bank Holiday, for some ridiculous reason, the afternoon expedition reached Yarmouth. He insisted that I should go into the Fun Fair; at one point I lost him, but presently he emerged from 'Noah's Ark' bearing an ice-cream cone in one hand and his hat in the other. In the evenings after dinner he sometimes read aloud—he was one of the few who could make this enjoyable; occasionally he played—little-known Haydn quartets, Handel's choral works, even a bit of Meyerbeer's *Le Prophète* in which he had found some fine effect of 'theatre' or of scoring. At other times he would join in a game of Mah Jong, which Lady Tovey liked, but which he seemed to enjoy mainly because the counters were so pretty—no one had a high standard of play. Corinthian bagatelle also had a great fascination for him.

Although ostensibly he did not do any composition that summer, I am fairly sure that a good deal of the String Quartet he wrote of to Bantock matured in his mind, and possibly much of the *Zuleika* overture, of which I heard the themes.

In the autumn of 1936 the question arose of a broadcast of the 'cello concerto, including a simultaneous recording. Tovey waited for weeks for any confirmation of this either from the B.B.C. or from Casals. The 'cellist was still in Barcelona, and Spain was on the brink of civil war. On 19 October Tovey wrote to Miss Weisse: 'I have just, to my great relief, got a postcard from Casals saying that he is playing my concerto for the B.B.C. on November 20th. He wants to know if I consent to Adrian Boult conducting it—"tu sais ce que je pense." Of course I consent and have replied that A. B. knows the conditions of *gramophone* reproduction (which is also in question) much better than I do. But of course the main thing is the (temporary) evidence

that P. C. is safe so far.' One week later he received a note from
Casals enclosing a letter from the agents which informed him
that the B.B.C. had decided not to perform the concerto 'for
various reasons, the chief of which is lack of time for adequate
rehearsal'. 'J'ai fait un très long travail,' wrote Casals indig-
nantly, 'en vue de cette audition, et dans des circonstances bien
pénibles. Cette lettre est venue après une insistance de ma part.'
Deep though the disappointment was to himself, Tovey felt the
discourtesy to his friend even more. In the midst of political
turmoil which was finally to drive him out of Spain, and in face
of ill health, Casals had been arduously practising in order to
assure the success of the broadcast and recording which should
establish the reputation of this concerto once for all, and he had
received a casual note from an agent to say that after all the
work would not be given! The most elaborate explanations
which the B.B.C. was able to offer concerning a change of
policy in their Sunday symphony concerts—even the fact that
Dr. Boult had been ill and had been unable to write himself—
seemed an inadequate excuse for such treatment of a great
artist.

17

THE Reid Symphony Orchestra reached its twenty-first season in 1936–7. Despite the setting up of the Endowment Trust in 1932, the prospects of the orchestra's being securely established were as remote as ever, for more *work* as well as more money was required if anything approaching conditions of security was to be ensured. Tovey envisaged the problems very clearly, but in the matter of practical planning to attain the ends desired he had no executive ability, nor had he time to tackle the problems. What was really needed was some body which could have fulfilled the function which the Council for the Encouragement of Music and the Arts (C.E.M.A.) admirably fulfilled during the 1939–45 War—that of both supplying and creating a demand for good music in Edinburgh and elsewhere; and, further, some body which could undertake the drastic education of municipal and educational authorities in Scotland with regard to the place of art in civilized life. All Tovey could do was to continue his heroic efforts to educate the Edinburgh public, and to give his blessing to his best players when they were offered positions in other orchestras which provided a better means of livelihood. From 1932 there had been a steady trickle of such losses, and an agreement with the B.B.C. Scottish Orchestra, whereby former Reid players (and a few others) were permitted to play with the Reid Orchestra, became increasingly difficult to handle each year.

Finances derived little material benefit from a Special Appeal, in pamphlet form, which was issued in the autumn of 1934 over the names of an influential Publicity Committee.[1] In the criticism of the first performance of Tovey's 'cello concerto, in November 1934, *The Times* had referred to this: 'The Reid Orchestra's

---

[1] The Chairman of this Committee was my father, Sir Andrew Grierson, who had just retired after a lifetime spent in the service of the city of Edinburgh.

permanence, after nineteen years of persistent work under the Reid Professor, seems to be in doubt. An appeal has lately been issued for fresh financial support, and there is good hope of its success. Failure would be more than a local disaster. For to hear this orchestra rehearse is to realize that it studies to give practical expression to its conductor's experience and fine taste in the interpretation of the classics. . . . Further, the Reid Orchestra has the courage of its conductor's convictions. It can give music that is real without asking first whether it is in fashion at the moment.'

Tovey chafed under conditions which showed so little prospect of improvement. 'The pressure of six hours a week rehearsal in competition with an orchestra that gets thirty is the most serious strain I have,' he had written to Schweitzer in 1933, when he resumed work after his serious illness. The Scottish Orchestra, and the B.B.C. Scottish Orchestra, not only got far more rehearsal time than did the Reid, but also had far more concert work and frequent opportunities for playing an item more than once. But Tovey also remarked in a long letter to me in response to a request from the Reid Committee for more popular programmes during the season in which the appeal was issued— 'the brutal truth is that *I'm* not popular. . . . What we have to contend with is *not* indifference but *opposition*.'

A furious correspondence broke out in the local press in April 1935 as a result of a singularly tactless remark by the chairman of the Edinburgh Concert Society 'that for Edinburgh there is only one orchestra, and that is the "Scottish"'. Tovey was in Barcelona at the time, but there were many who took up the cudgels on his behalf. 'It is well known to friends of Sir Donald Tovey', said one letter, 'that he deplores such jealousies as exist between supporters of the Scottish and Reid Orchestras, and would like to see the Scottish flourishing as well as his own. What a contrast to this attitude is that of the chairman of the Edinburgh Concert Society in ignoring by implication the very existence of the Reid Orchestra!'

Such were conditions at the beginning of the twenty-first

season, and although Tovey never thought of giving up the struggle he began more often to feel discouraged. The opening of the season was further clouded by the death of Lord Murray, who, as chairman of the Society, had piloted the orchestra through many difficult times and had been regarded by every player as a trusted friend. In memory of Lord Murray, who was an ardent lover of Mozart, the Sunday concert which opened the season on 11 October began with Mozart's *Masonic Dirge* (a wonderful piece which is never heard[1]), this being followed by the grave beauty of the same composer's C minor Concerto. The C minor and C major Concertos of Mozart were special favourites with Tovey.

The first Reid programme of this season included Mahler's Fourth Symphony: 'I shall be boiled in oil', wrote Tovey to Bantock, 'for my irreverent programme-notes.' These are written in a more flippant and discursive style than usual, and have, on that account, never been reprinted. The description of the last movement is irresistible. 'The words are a poem from the famous anthology of folk poetry, *Des Knaben Wunderhorn*. . . . I forbear to transcribe or translate the poem word by word. No reasonable person will be shocked at its innocent profanity; but, until we have all learned to accept Mahler as a classic, we had better not expose him to the blasphemy of the enemy who would cast doubts upon the composer's reverence for sacred subjects. . . .

'I have already remarked on Mahler's emphatic forbidding of any touch of parody in the performance of this finale. The poem describes the pleasures of a simple soul in Heaven, far from the strife of the world, which exists only in order that *Weltgetümmel* may rhyme with Himmel, as it does in Bach's most solemn cantatas. We live an angelic life and dance and skip while St. Peter in Heaven looks on.

'The next stanza brings back and develops the farmyard sounds of the first movement. A certain savagery in the tone is accounted for by the fact that Herod is the accepted family

---

[1] Presumably because it requires a *corno di bassetto*; the Reid Orchestra was able to muster also two *oboi d'amore*.

butcher in this unorthodox heaven, and that St. John and St. Luke allow him a free hand. St. Luke kills his ox, the wine of the heavenly cellars costs nothing, and the angels bake the bread.

'The third stanza describes the heavenly vegetable gardens, with gardeners who, contrary to the severe Scottish baronial tradition, will let you have everything. Game of all sorts runs towards you, and all manner of fish swim into St. Peter's net.

'. . . The last stanza describes the music of Heaven with St. Ursula smiling upon her eleven thousand virgin dancers, and St. Cecilia and all her relations as the most excellent of court musicians.

'After all, we have the authority of Dante in more than one of the sublimest passages of the *Paradiso* for supposing that, though Heaven is not confined to what any mortal can understand, it includes all that we can understand. Bruckner understood considerably less of most things than Mahler. He would probably have been horrified at the notion of setting this poem. I, for my part, would be horrified at the idea of Meyerbeer setting it. Mahler I suspect of having wept as copiously over it as Dickens over *Little Nell*, or Macaulay over the end of the *Iliad*. Such a temper has its dangers for judges and administrators; but it is much more useful in the present state of music than tastes that are too refined for Beethoven, and it is positively antiseptic against many types of morbid art.'

The letter to Bantock was written on the reverse of a copy of Tovey's cadenzas to Beethoven's G major Pianoforte Concerto, which had just been published in sheet-form and which he liked to use as 'special notepaper'.

The third volume of the *Essays in Musical Analysis* also appeared this month. Of this Tovey wrote to me: 'I find Vol. 3 very stiff: but, perhaps for that reason, it's much the most important of the whole set. I have also', he added, 'a disagreeably outspoken article in *Music and Letters* on the Musical Imagination.' It would hardly be true to say that Tovey 'prided' himself on his astounding memory, but he sometimes relied on it to a dangerous extent. The worst example of this which I know occurs in Volume 3 of the *Essays*. In the analysis of Mozart's Pianoforte Concerto in A major (K. 414), the description of the last movement is totally and madly wrong. He was obviously writing it from memory, and he not only confuses two themes, but refers to a theme which he did not quote by giving the reference number of one which he did! This is probably the only serious error of the kind in the whole of his writing (which is a tribute in itself) but it must baffle anyone who tries to make sense of the analysis. He was a very bad proof-reader, and a good many printer's errors escaped his notice, but this error is in quite a different category.

To commemorate the coming of age of the Reid Orchestra the University conferred two honorary degrees. In a speech much longer than that which is usually delivered in presenting the honorary graduands, Tovey paid generous and sincere tribute to the debt which he and the orchestra owed to Mrs. Alexander Maitland and to Miss Weisse. It was a graceful and a timely gesture. Mrs. Maitland, as one of the pioneers of the Petersfield Festival, as a distinguished amateur pianist, and as the conductor of a small band of players—part amateur and part professional—which was absorbed into the Reid Orchestra when the latter was founded, was clearly of sufficient eminence and influence to be accorded the honour; especially since, as Tovey put it, in every stage of development of the Reid Orchestra, her advice had been invaluable and her material help substantial. The case for Miss Weisse was more difficult to represent. 'The Reid Orchestra', said Tovey, 'must have come into existence sooner or later if the Reid Chair of Music were to fulfil its function, whoever its occupant might be. But whatever character that orchestra might be said to owe to its present founder and conductor, it owes primarily and ultimately to Miss Sophie Weisse.' Thus, at the age of 84, Miss Weisse received, at the instance of her greatest pupil, recognition of her undoubted genius as a teacher. The third name put forward by Tovey had been that of Lord Murray.[1]

---

[1] Lord Murray was succeeded as Chairman of the Orchestra by another Edin-

Tovey's symphony was successfully broadcast in the seventh concert of the season, on the national wave-length. Trevelyan wrote to Miss Weisse as well as to the composer after this broadcast. 'Dear Mr. Trevelyan,' she replied, 'a Codetta to your kind letter about the symphony. Yesterday morning I was beginning a late breakfast in my flat in Buccleuch Street, when Donald came charging up the stair like a majestic King Elephant, and said I must come at once, *at once*, as he and the orchestra were rushing down to Broadcasting House to hear a London replay of the symphony to Edinburgh. So we bundled down and found ourselves amidst clouds of witnesses, each grasping an instrument in an unwieldy case, hurrying up to a room very politely prepared to seat us all, with a vast loud-speaker all ready to testify. You should have seen how greatly pleased and interested all these devoted people were, how they listened with beaming faces as what they had played 'came through', especially the softer and lower wood-winds whom Donald encouraged to listen for themselves; and my dear Donald sitting rapt with his head thrown back, and Mollie Grierson with every note of the score in her head. Such pleasure never was, and at the end Donald got up and looked as affectionately as if they were, regardless of chronology, his own children, and made a speech of thanks to the B.B.C. That is the Codetta, and a very pretty one I think.—The reason they all carried instruments was that they had just started a rehearsal when the message from the B.B.C. came.'

'The B.B.C. Blattnerphone reproduction is not nearly so good as the MSS. records,' wrote Tovey to Bantock, who had urged him to get the MSS. Recording Co. to take a record from the air. 'The result is, of course, not good enough to put into permanent shape; there was obviously no means of making plausible divisions into sixteen disks. But it is good enough to vindicate my orchestration and also my conducting, and I now have objective evidence that the Reid Orchestra has a big rhythmic

burgh lawyer and distinguished amateur musician, Douglas Dickson, a lifelong friend of the orchestra and successor to Mr. Finnie McEwen in running the remarkable 'Nelson Hall' concerts.

style and that its balance gets over hundreds of inequalities in the opportunities and technique of its personnel. There was one wrong entry in the first *crescendo*, some fairly hefty brass note, *which I don't remember in the performance*!

'But, gosh! you should hear the difference between rehearsing my symphony and rehearsing Elgar's *Alassio*! There 's no flattering unction I can lay to my soul in the matter; I can only say that my orchestration is all right, demonstrably economical, and effective when adequately rehearsed. But dear old Elgar has me beaten to a frazzle; it's as if nothing could go wrong, and, Heaven knows, it's not simple! Why my symphony should be so difficult I cannot think.'

This letter to Bantock which was dated 'Ages ago, 1937' was completed after the last Reid concert, at which the Reid Choir sang *Israel in Egypt* (authentic portions only). 'I have seldom been more shattered by the power of a classic. The enclosed programme will show you that I dealt pretty drastically with the diddle-diddle. . . . Well as I once knew my Handel, I can truthfully say that the total effect was a revelation to me. Of course we couldn't afford anything like a quarter of Handel's reed tone—though four oboes and two clarinets were not noticably different from six oboes, and another three flutes in unison help remarkably. For the *Darkness* chorus I had three bassoons, two cors anglais, a clarinet and a corno di bassetto, and four muted horns = eleven reedy, snuffly sounds quite as like Handel's twenty bassoons as we are likely to get. Mendelssohn's organ-part, though in many respects wrong, proved much more useful than I expected.

'The most amusing thing was the discovery that Handel's genuine trombone parts (discovered by Chrysander and obviously dead right on the head of every possible nail) are incomparably noisier than poor old Macfarren's.'

This was a most impressive performance. From where I sat at the harpsichord,[1] Tovey—now rather stout in figure—towered

---

[1] Tovey's harpsichord, built by Dolmetsch, but disappointingly weak in tone, so that I had to use it full strength all the time.

up like all the Hebrew prophets rolled into one, and slow tears slid down his cheeks at the climax of *The people shall hear*.

Persistent treatment throughout the summer of 1936 had helped Tovey's hands to such an extent that in a letter to me from London in June he wrote: 'A great event happened to me on Sunday night at the Fachiris'. I suddenly found I could play the beginning of the Beethoven B flat trio *correctly*; so we celebrated the occasion in the obvious way. Tomorrow we are going to try the Brahms' C major.' Later in August, after a further 'cure' at Aix, he hopefully promised 'as soon as I get the Cramb lectures out of the way, I shall be free to practise enough to get into condition to pull my weight with recitals on Sundays'. And indeed he did, for during the season of 1936–7 Tovey appeared at every Sunday concert. In the three recitals before Christmas he included in each programme two large-scale works for four hands, so that, with the aid of another pair of hands (my own and those of Grace Johnston, Mus.Bac.) he was able to begin and end with a good volume of pianoforte sound, which was really a foil to his own reduced tone. He admitted regretfully in a letter to Miss Weisse that his tone *was* much reduced, adding: 'I can't strike big stretches with any confidence. This also impairs my memory as even scale-intervals seem a different size.' Schweitzer, writing from Lambarene in November—as he did each year—recalling the two Novembers he had spent at Royal Terrace ('beautiful memories are a wonderful possession'), said how happy he was to hear from Miss Deneke of the improvement in Tovey's hands, and in his health generally. After Christmas Tovey gave (alone) a Bach programme and a Beethoven programme, and a recital in which I assisted him with two two-pianoforte works. His hands *did* show some improvement—in spite of the fact that writing was becoming difficult, and in the amazing Beethoven programme that concluded the Sunday series he not only conducted the Second Symphony and *Coriolanus* Overture, but also played the Fourth and Fifth Concertos, which anyone with hands in perfect condition would consider a fairly big undertaking.

A note on the last page of this programme said: 'On the completion of the concerts for the season 1936–7—the twenty-first in its history—the Reid Symphony Orchestra may be said to have come of age.

'In view of arrangements for Coronation Festivities, it is proposed to celebrate this anniversary in an appropriate manner at the first concert of the ensuing season.'

For the last three years of his life Tovey's activities were practically confined to his work in Edinburgh, although his reputation was steadily increasing throughout the musical world. 'The great event in musical history at this moment', he wrote to Miss Weisse in July 1937, 'is the appearance of Hindemith's harmony book. Strecker is sending the translator to consult me tomorrow.' Tovey had been asked by Strecker to give his opinion of the translation, and had agreed willingly, suggesting also that if the author would care for him to do so, he would like to write the preface to the English edition himself. Owing to the unsettled international conditions, however, this translation never appeared.

Strecker was then also interested in another matter which caused Tovey considerable concern—the so-called discovery of the lost Schumann Violin Concerto, based on 'spirit messages'. The concerto was Schumann's last work, written for Joachim, but never played by him, because it was believed that the work showed 'morbid features' associated with the composer's last illness. When Joachim died the manuscript was deposited in the Berlin Library with a proviso that it should on no account be published or performed until a hundred years after Schumann's death. It could not be said to have been lost, but few people knew of its existence, and, of these few, most had forgotten about it. Following an article in the *Listener* of 22 September 1937 giving the story of the 'spirit messages' and announcing the forthcoming first performance in England by Jelly d'Aranyi, Tovey immediately wrote to *The Times* a long and fine letter dealing with the whole matter most skilfully: 'I would rather be thought officious than neglect the duty of doing what I can to protect both the work and its performance from misunderstanding.' He advanced the view that the production of the concerto would be 'much more serviceable to the cause of beautiful music in this year 1937 than it would be if deferred to 1956, when its production could only be a centenary affair with no effect as reparation of an injustice'. He also pointed out that Joachim's criticism 'with all its severity would, with the aid of a few musical quotations, make an ideal programme-analysis for concert audiences'. (This course he followed when he came to write the programme-notes.) With regard to the 'spirit messages' the letter was tactfully non-committal. The first performance was postponed for some months because of a hitch in getting the material. Eugenie Schumann, the composer's last living daughter, then wrote to *The Times* making a 'plain statement' of all the facts, but showing that she was deeply hurt that the condition that the work should not be produced for a hundred years should be set aside. Tovey intervened again with another letter, over which he took great pains. There is no doubt that by these letters he prevented the affair of the Schumann Concerto from causing a great deal of distress to his friends who were concerned in it—the Joachim family, Adila Fachiri and Jelly d'Aranyi, Strecker, and Eugenie Schumann herself; and the music itself was freed from associations which could have done nothing but harm to its reputation. Tovey produced it himself in Edinburgh with Jelly d'Aranyi at a charity concert in March 1938.

Sir Herbert Grierson had retired from the Chair of Rhetoric and English Literature at Edinburgh University in 1935. His colleagues desired to make some appropriate testimony 'to the services rendered by one of the greatest scholars of the age to learning, to letters, and to the cause of university education', and two years later a handsome presentation volume, entitled *Seventeenth-Century Studies*, was produced. Tovey's share in this tribute to one of the best of his Edinburgh friends was an essay called 'Words and Music: Some Obiter Dicta'. 'I owe you thanks', he wrote to the joint editors, 'for the skill and tact with which you have compressed into shape a piece of work about which I had felt very much depressed. . . . I am sorry that I was not able to write on Purcell, as you suggested. He is exactly the right subject for a study of English music in the 17th century; I could have tackled him long ago if anything like his complete works were accessible, and if the 17th century in music were not for me the Slough of Despond. But my main trouble over this contribution arises from the fact that as a musicologist I am nothing but a populariser—not, I hope, an unscholarly one, but a person whom even the *Encyclopædia Britannica* had to select for that reason rather than for special knowledge. Of course, my special knowledge is music. But scholars can be readable about the most difficult questions in literature, because the difficulties are themselves explained in terms of literature, even if the subject be Chinese metaphysics; whereas no prose-writing about music can possibly be music. So far my only contribution to real musical scholarship is my edition and completion of Bach's *Kunst der Fuge*. I should greatly like to have been a Purcell-scholar, but it is too late now, and the best that I could have made of it would have consisted mainly of musical type. One thing I do know, and wish I had contrived to say it, is that no lover of music ought to mention the name of Dryden without passionately reciting the whole of the 109th Psalm.' It would be idle to call his essay 'A Seventeenth-Century Study', but the editors rightly agreed that its exclusion would be a loss to the book.

The 'coming of age' of the Reid Orchestra was celebrated at the beginning of its twenty-second season, October 1937, by a reception given in its honour by the Lord Provost and Magistrates of the city of Edinburgh. A birthday cake with twenty-one small candles amused Tovey almost as much as if it were his own twenty-first birthday, although it was no easy task for his gout-weakened hands to cut it. He was still, in a remarkable way, able to play on the concert platform: 'Praise be,' he wrote to Miss Weisse, in an enthusiastic account of a visit from Rafael Kubelik who was conducting the Czech Orchestra on a tour which included Edinburgh, 'the Pistany Mud is doing my gout so much good that I was able to play almost up to snuff on Sunday (Bach B flat Partita, Beethoven opp. 28 and 111, and a big group of Brahms); he [Kubelik] was most appreciative.'

Miss Weisse was ill at this time and was obliged to remain at her house in Englefield Green until the end of November instead of coming to Edinburgh in October as she usually did. She was greatly disappointed to miss the civic reception to the Orchestra and wrote to me—in the strong, clear handwriting that was so characteristic of her: 'The 20th of October will be, if I am alive, my 85th birthday, and I had had a vision of standing in my red Doctor's robe holding on to my dear Donald's arm for even only one minute, and thanking the Reid Orchestra for the beautiful and noble music they have caused me to hear in these many years.'

After the unfortunate contretemps over the 'cello concerto in 1935, Sir Adrian Boult had assured Tovey that the B.B.C. would certainly do the work 'as soon as we can catch Casals again'. The performance eventually took place on 17 November 1937; Sir Adrian conducted. In a long letter to Miss Weisse, curiously like his boyish ones, Tovey gives an account of a busy week— 'Dearrr Mswicy, Whoosh! What a week! On Wednesday (to continue the alliteration) I went to London, arriving at 5 something, dressing at the Fachiris' and dining with a friend of theirs, in time for the very fine performance at Queen's Hall. I was relieved to find Pablo in wonderful form and such spirits as the state of the world permits. We went to the Fachiris' afterwards till I had to catch the 1.5 a.m. to reach the Usher Hall here for the rehearsal of the enclosed pogrom.' [This was the programme of the third Reid concert at which I—after having conducted it so often for Tovey—was playing the Brahms' B flat Concerto, which was so specially 'his' concerto, and which he could no longer tackle.] 'I wish they had broadcast M.G.'s (and our) playing of the Brahms.[1] . . . Then really a considerable sensation

[1] On this occasion I played almost as I had dreamed of playing. We were all so pleased about the fine broadcast the night before, and Tovey radiated happiness

in St. Mary's Cathedral on Sunday.' [This was a performance by the Reid Choir and Orchestra of Bach's *Missa Brevis*, two of Tovey's own hymns, and Holst's *Hymn of Jesus*, of which, as there was only a leaflet programme, Tovey read the words pontifically from the chancel steps.] 'Snobopolis (bless its three-penny bits) not only crammed the Cathedral to get something for nothing, but was excluded in hundreds for lack of room, the Bishop himself only getting smuggled in by a side door and two of our chief patrons failing to get in at all. Performance really astonishingly good. . . . The Provost and the Bishop much impressed both by the music and the crowd; and determined to make this an annual affair. . . . Tomorrow I have a lecture in Glesgy;[1] and on Sunday, thank goodness, no concert. I'm standing the racket a great deal better than I should have stood it last year.

'No, the proposition of the Gramophone Co. was absolutely inequitable' [this referred to a proposal, to record the 'cello concerto]. '£300 to be guaranteed, or the sale of 100 sets (*by me or my friends*), and on the other hand, *no promise whatever of publication* except as the company chose, and then only under "red label" whatever that may mean.' The rest is unquotable; Tovey was greatly disappointed by the attitude which the Gramophone Company had taken up, but masked this by lapsing into amusing nonsense at the end of the letter.

The broadcast of the 'cello concerto from London was very fine.[2] The performance had a great reception by the public, and

---

and confidence. I always remember the advice which he gave to me when I played the concerto to him some three weeks before the performance: 'forget all about technique now; concentrate upon *declamation*.' But he was unexpectedly firm in vetoing my idea of going to London to hear the 'cello concerto the night before!

[1] This was one of his second set of Cramb Lectures, which he delivered in Glasgow weekly from November 1937 to January 1938, under the title of *The Integrity of Music*.

[2] Suggia wrote from Portugal: 'I heard your concerto through the wireless and it sounded beautiful. I wondered how ever it was possible to master it in such a way and I am convinced that there is only one 'cellist in the world who could have done it'—a lovely tribute from one great player to another. Fritz Busch also wrote from Copenhagen to say how well it had been heard there and what a great impression it had made on him.

critics generally were favourable. A long article entitled *Beauty in Design* appeared in *The Times* two days after the concert criticism, and gave a considered assessment of the work. It remarked on the service which gramophone companies could render to music by recording it: 'for our own part we begin to think of the concerto as a work we could live with. But none of us, except perhaps Señor Casals, can hope to live much with it because it takes up too much space in a concert programme, and there is no other way of living with it except from time to time by poring over the score. It is likely therefore to be the victim of the imperfect conditions in which we all have to take our music.

> *Verily by Beauty it is that we come at Wisdom*
> *yet not by Reason at Beauty.*[1]

'There is no mistaking the beauty at the root of this concerto and by pursuing it we come at more of it, which is wisdom. It is false to imagine, as some have done knowing the composer's reasoning powers, that he has sought through his reason to make a synthetic beauty.'

Tovey had been confident that the 'cello concerto would be recorded this time. 'The point is not my concerto,' said one letter, 'but the opportunity of *An Hour with Casals* on the background of a full orchestra.' When it became obvious that even this was not a sufficient attraction, the brutal fact was forced on him that those who were responsible for the policy of gramophone companies simply did not believe that his music would be of sufficient interest to make the recording a practical proposition. He took this greatly to heart.

Volume 5 of the *Analytical Essays* appeared this month. 'Glorious news!' wrote Tovey to Foss. 'Constant Lambert, not content with being ill-tempered about my compositions (most critics are that) has flown out violently against my programme notes. All I wanted to complete their success was an honestly bad-tempered enemy, especially one who has some following. My next plan of campaign will be to produce some instrumental, not vocal, work

---

[1] Bridges's *A Testament of Beauty.*

of his next year and send him my perfectly polite notes on it. If he doesn't like them, he can write his own (for our programme). Could you procure me a list of his compositions?' But he was also critical of 'the recent extremely generous reception of my collected essays and the erection of me into an infallible oracle to be quoted on all occasions'.

An amusing letter from Tovey to Mrs. Trevelyan, answering an inquiry which she had made, is dated December 1937: 'The only occasion on which I can swear that Bach's E major fugue was actually sung, was in a village school-room in Wales. The Welsh are born in four-part chorus and in full song. I was playing to my cousin Basil Jones' parishioners on a village school-room pianoforte with immovable pedals (fortunately not immovably down), and no nuance but an instructive and inhibitory mezzo-forte. In these circumstances the E major fugue was almost the only thing I could play. I explained that it was exactly like a four-part chorus and I mentioned each voice as it had the subject. I played it three times, and the third time the whole school-room sang it!'

Among guest-artists at the Sunday concerts in the second half of the 1937–8 season were two well-known musicians whose careers had been rudely interrupted by the Nazi régime—Dr. Heinrich Swoboda, the conductor, of Prague, and Karl Klingler from Berlin, the well-known violinist of post-Joachim days. Tovey, who knew both artists well, was not content with the mere friendly gesture of the offer of a concert, but did all he could in other ways to help them. Other refugee artists whom he helped later to take up the broken threads of their career included Frau Doktor Gombrich of Vienna and Dr. Hans Gál. Of the latter he wrote to me: 'As you know, I am in holy terror lest any unbenevolent person should find out what a scandalous state I have got the classroom library into.' [This was an exaggeration.] 'We want to seize the opportunity of getting this distinguished authority's services on an adequate basis; and we have an *excellent* case, such as cannot be made out for anybody else. I regard the matter as urgent, *more on our account* than on international grounds, though these are serious enough. As a matter of fact the Reid Library is a more serious affair than we have ever made of it.' With the addition of Tovey's own music library, gifted to the University by John Tovey in 1942, the Reid Library in Edinburgh is now very fine indeed.

During April and May 1938 Tovey delivered the Alsop Lectures on Music at Liverpool University, a course of four lectures entitled *Musical Art-Forms as Means of Expression*. In May also he lectured in Cambridge for the Cambridge University English Club; 'the subject of the lecture is not announced', it was stated in the *Cambridge Review*, 'but it will deal with some meeting point of Music and Literature.' 'I remember', said Mr. Paul Hirsch, 'that Sir Donald began by saying he hoped nobody would mind if he talked on some other subjects as well, and not directly connected with the official theme! So he talked in a most amusing and fascinating way *de omnibus rebus et quibusdam aliis*, giving occasionally some piano examples.'

On 29 June he gave a lecture in London before the British Academy on *The Mainstream of Music*. 'The room was crowded,' wrote Miss Weisse to me, 'and so was the otherwise very interesting lecture: a quart put into a pint pot, as he sometimes is misguided enough to do.' This was his last public appearance in London; many of his Oxford contemporaries were in the audience on this occasion.

The summer of 1938 was overshadowed for everyone by the gathering war-clouds. It was extremely difficult to get any concrete plans for the next season's University and concert work from Tovey. His despondency was increased by the fact that during several weeks of very wet weather at Hedenham the arthritis in his hands and feet had become very much worse. Even if he had been able to concentrate on composing the violin concerto that was in his thoughts he could not have written anything down without painful effort.

During this summer, and even more during the summer and autumn of 1939, Lady Tovey often wished that Hedenham were more accessible; there were so many busy musicians who would

gladly have paid Tovey a short visit as they passed through
London but who could not spare the time for the tedious journey
to Norfolk. Even Fritz Busch, much as he wanted to see his
friend, found that the cross-country journey from Glyndebourne
was out of the question. Lady Tovey herself was now very lame;
she was patient with her sufferings but impatient with her help-
lessness, and vainly tried all sorts of cures, some of which merely
had the result of making her more ill than she already was. But
all her thoughts were bent on interesting her husband in his
work again, and on getting him well enough for some measure
of musical activity. She was perplexed by conflicting medical
advice, and grieved by the fact that there was so little that even
her devoted effort could do for a man who was so completely
worn out. Their friends were cut to the heart for both of them.

His own despondency did not, however, prevent Tovey from
putting new heart into another great pianist. Although the loss
of the use of his hands was so terrible a thing to him, he never
ceased to appreciate the playing of others. At the Norwich
Festival in 1937 he had heard Myra Hess play the Beethoven
G major Pianoforte Concerto and had written to tell her how
much he had enjoyed the performance. In the following year
Dame Myra was suffering from one of the fits of discouragement
which afflict all artists at one time or another. She asked Tovey
if she might come and play to him and discuss some points in
connexion with the works on the programmes of her forthcoming American tour; 'I shall never forget the inspiration of
those two hours,' she wrote afterwards. But she was deeply
shocked and distressed at the condition of his hands, and had
been thinking what might be done to help him: 'Steinways have
a smaller keyboard and it could be fitted in a concert grand. If
you could bear to banish your giant Bösendorfer temporarily,
the Steinway could take its place and you could also use it for
your concerts. I used the small keyboard and found it tremendously helpful—with my stupid little hands. I only gave it up as
it was too disturbing not to have it always. It was sent by mistake
for one of Harold Samuel's concerts. As you remember his hands

no doubt, you can imagine his description of what happened!'
Tovey was much touched by her thought for him and grateful
for the suggestion. The instrument arrived in the course of the
autumn term, in time to make it possible for him to play the
Schumann Introduction and Allegro at the second Reid concert.

Vaughan Williams's *Sea Symphony* was performed at the
fourth concert this winter. In a postscript to a letter to the composer in November, Tovey wrote: 'About the drum-roll that
supports the chorus on the word "sea" at the very beginning:
what would you think of having the stroke of the big drum on
the first beat instead of on the second? Now that I see you have
the big drum on the second beat I am in two minds about it,
but I had hitherto always thought that a boom on the big drum
would add an oceanic solemnity to the crack of the tympani.'
He evidently had in mind a long-past discussion on this point.
'It must have been in 1909 or 1910,' says Vaughan Williams's
account of it, 'when I first asked Tovey's advice about my *Sea
Symphony*. In my original score, which is still preserved in the
pianoforte score, I started the full orchestra on the first beat of
the bar. I then realized that this would obscure the word "Sea"
sung by the chorus. On the other hand I did not wish to have
nothing for the orchestra and asked Tovey's advice; he suggested
the plan I have carried out—only the tympani and the organ
on the first beat.'

Just before the concert Tovey became ill again; he was
ordered a complete rest for some weeks. 'I am afraid the doctor
takes a rather depressing view,' wrote Lady Tovey to Mrs. Trevelyan, 'but Donald has surprised them all before, let us hope he
will again.'

In the emergency Vaughan Williams agreed to come and
conduct the symphony himself, although it meant that he could
have only one rehearsal on the morning of the concert, and that
with an incomplete choir. (Joint choral and orchestral rehearsals had perforce to take place on Sundays; the concert was
on a Thursday.) He wrote afterwards to Tovey, 'My dear
Donald F., Thursday night was *electrifying*—even if we'd had

six rehearsals together it would have been very good—as it was, it was *miraculous*. Roy Henderson called it the best performance he had ever heard, and he has heard a good many. Both your chorus and orchestra are so *musical*—and I know to whom they owe that.'

Tovey made slow progress towards recovery with many a setback, and he continued to be in very depressed spirits. Miss Weisse still maintained that she did not believe that he had any kind of heart disease, despite the opinion of any specialist; but she was fearful of his high blood-pressure and total nervous exhaustion. Tovey was determined to conduct part of the concert on 9 February when Adolf Busch was to play an unknown Viotti concerto.[1] Once more, contact with his orchestra effected much better results than doctor's treatment. As deputy-conductor I took all rehearsals except the last. I wanted some advice from Tovey about the Schumann C major Symphony—the only Schumann we had never done before—and received after my visit a long (dictated) letter of help: 'I find it surprisingly impossible to do anything to the score of the Schumann C major, except to be very fastidious about the quality of tone, especially in the brass. I have been twice through the score with a quivering pencil, and have found nothing that I hadn't to decide to leave alone. It is not like the other symphonies, which are full of overlapping echoes and of points where you can't tell which of the departments is to lead. It's simply full-swell organ from beginning to end, and hardly moves on two planes of thought at all. . . .

'The slow movement ought to be made to sound very beautiful, but the trills are abominably high, and must be a real *tour-de-force* for smoothness and for lasting to the very last note.

'The finale can hardly go too fast. . . .

'Yours eusebiusly, D. F. T.'

He conducted his part of the final rehearsal seated on a high double-bass stool, and was able to do half of the concert at night

[1] Discovered by Fritz in Italy and copied by him as a birthday present for his brother.

without showing much fatigue. He also conducted half of the following Sunday concert, and was able to play the Mozart D minor Concerto at the seventh Reid concert, when Ian Whyte was guest conductor. This was the last time he played in Edinburgh.

Such was the stimulus of conducting again that Tovey was able to take the whole of the last Reid concert, with this exacting programme:

Kaisermarsch	_Wagner_
Symphony No. 1 in D major	_Dvořák_
Symphonie Fantasia _Pohjola's Daughter_	_Sibelius_
Overture _Cockaigne_	_Elgar_

He also conducted the last two orchestral Sunday concerts; the last, concluding the season on 19 March 1939, was, fittingly, a Beethoven programme. It was his last appearance with his orchestra.

In spite of his remarkable improvement in health since February, Tovey was still a very sick man, and his recovery did not proceed much farther. On 20 April, however, he played the Bach D minor Concerto with the Norwich Chamber Orchestra, though not without difficulty. He also received, and refused, an invitation from the University of California to act as visiting professor from August 1939 to May 1940. An invitation also came from the _Schola Cantorum_ of New York to join its Advisory Committee.

'There is nothing the matter with me', said a typed letter which I received early in June, 'except that I am rather unsteady on my pins at times and that yesterday the ground got up and hit me on the nose, since which I have thought it well to refrain from controversy.' This was alarming, but his letters about the future remained lively, e.g.: 'What we are suffering from is having _too few concerts_. We ought to be able to fill a whole term with a weekly series that expresses something complete as a background for the more capricious incidents.'

He accepted an invitation from the B.B.C. to give a National

Lecture on a musical subject of his own choosing in October. The National Lectures were then given once or twice a year and were among the most important features in the B.B.C. programmes. Tovey chose as his subject Beethoven's *Missa Solemnis*, but the lecture was first postponed and then cancelled because of the war. Letters this summer from Casals at Prades, and Schweitzer in Lambarene, ask about new compositions which both these friends felt sure would follow the 'cello concerto; neither had the slightest idea that Tovey was too ill to think of composing.

In July Tovey's illness became very serious, with such a multiplicity of symptoms that the doctors were both worried and puzzled. When war broke out he was in Westminster Hospital, where he was having new treatment with excellent effect. He even accepted an invitation from Mr. John Christie of Glyndebourne to spend a week-end in Devonshire in September to discuss, with ten other prominent musicians, the formation of a National Council of Music. He had a piano in hospital as part of the treatment. 'Every day he played Bach', said one of the doctors, who was something of a musician himself. 'I listened behind the doors. It was like beautiful and personal singing: almost quite even and regular and somewhat reminiscent of organ-playing.' But the hospital was evacuated, and Sir Donald and Lady Tovey went back to Hedenham. There he slipped back again. The almost illegibly written sentences at the end of a letter to me in October said: 'I'm hoping to get up to Edinburgh sometime about New Year; by which time my handwriting will be presentable. Meanwhile trust your own judgment.'

It had been thought that owing to the war, all the concerts might have to be abandoned. The Scottish Orchestra cancelled its arrangements for the season, but the Reid Orchestra decided, on the vote of all the members who were left, to take the risk of carrying on their concerts—on Saturday afternoons, on account of the blackout. Tovey was pleased when he heard this, and sent a sketch of suggestions at the beginning of November.

He continued, however, to make no progress at all, and

presently ceased even to play; it seemed most unlikely that he would be able to return to Edinburgh at New Year. During this sad autumn the added difficulties of war-time travel made Hedenham more inaccessible than ever. Sir Donald and Lady Tovey were virtually cut off from their friends, and too remote to obtain the skilled medical care of which they were both so desperately in need.

At Lady Tovey's request I went to Hedenham on 27 December. When we talked about the orchestra and music, Sir Donald was so markedly different that the decision was made to return to Scotland in the hope that once more contact with active music-making would do him some good. He returned in February; but this time, alas, the magic did not work, and an attempt to take a rehearsal made it clear that Tovey was too ill for any such exertion. Arrangements were made for him to take a modified Musical Interpretation class in his music room at Royal Terrace, and for some weeks this did effect an improvement— in his spirits at least. Various chamber-music groups (student and professional) rallied round to produce, for this class, works which they thought would interest him, but after a few weeks the effort even of giving a little gentle criticism and encouragement became too much for him.

During the last peaceful months of his life I like to think that his mental ear heard more 'wonderful and beautiful' music than ever existed in physical fact. Indeed I am sure it was so. He died on 10 July 1940, a week before what would have been his sixty-fifth birthday.[1]

---

[1] Lady Tovey died on 20 September 1944 at Hedenham; Miss Weisse died on 10 January of the following year at Guildford.

18

'**D**ONALD was so great a man; that is why he cannot be set down in words,' said one of his oldest friends, Lady Fisher,[1] after his death. It is only through his own writings and his compositions that any comprehensive picture of him can be seen, although legions of anecdotes provide sidelights on his personality. Touching stories abound—such as that about Mrs. Kennedy-Fraser, the collector of Hebridean folksongs: when she lay dying in an Edinburgh nursing-home, Tovey, knowing that she had a wireless at her bedside, arranged that the Reid orchestra should broadcast Bantock's *Hebridean* Symphony for her, as a surprise. She listened happily throughout and died shortly afterwards. Another Edinburgh anecdote concerns a concert of the Scottish Orchestra at which Tovey was playing a Beethoven concerto; the programme-notes contained a story about two English composers, who, on seeing the Albert Hall, likened it to a work of Mendelssohn. In response to the great applause after his playing of the concerto, Tovey came forward and said, '*amende honorable* to Mendelssohn', and played the *Spring Song* enchantingly as an encore. There is also the story told by Lady Cynthia Asquith of how Tovey once played for three hours on end at 'Clouds' (her mother's Wiltshire home), rather to the discomfiture of one of her uncles, who was a prodigious talker. That same evening, however, as the uncle read Browning's *A Toccata of Galuppi's* aloud, he lent special significance to the line, 'I can always leave off talking when I hear a master play'.

There are, of course, endless tales of his phenomenal memory, one of which is attributed alike to Jelly d'Aranyi and to Casals (quite likely the incident occurred more than once). It describes how Tovey arrived for a recital without the piano part of a certain Bach sonata; undismayed, he played his part by heart, with

[1] Cecilia Warre Cornish.

an occasional glance at the string part, but insisted on putting another piece of music up in front of him—*and even turning the pages*—in order to avoid ostentation!

'I shall never forget', said a letter from Lady Betty Balfour to Lady Tovey, 'how once at Whittingehame he gave Arthur the 5th Symphony of Beethoven on the piano, playing by heart. It was quite magnificent and A. J. B. at the end was so moved he could hardly speak.' There were certainly many friends for whom his music had either brought comfort in sorrow or given added pleasure in joy (he must, for instance, have written at least half a dozen wedding marches). Speyer also, in *My Life and Friends*, recalls how, on his ninety-second birthday, 'Donald Tovey, that dear and faithful friend, came with his wife and entertained us royally with his amusing conversation and his very original and lively playing of some Beethoven Sonatas'.

In another vein is Miss Deneke's story of an evening when Tovey joined their music-making and Professor Albert Einstein was playing second violin: 'Donald walked home to Christ Church with Professor Einstein, and the next day gave us a report at considerable length of the latest theories of stars. He was full of what he had just learnt on that evening walk and entirely regardless of his own time or our astronomical ignorance.'

Professor Aitken of Edinburgh University, a distinguished mathematician and an amateur musician who had many hours of discussion with Tovey, gives a description of a mathematical diversion which he sometimes indulged in: 'Tovey was interested in numbers, in prime numbers especially and in factorizations. He seems to have sought occasional relaxation by making palindromes out of squares or cubes—for example 144441, 289982, 343343, and factorizing these into their ultimate factors. And one is assured, from the testimony of two successive professors of mathematics, both friends of his, that he had a genuine perception of the principles involved in non-Euclidean geometry and relativity.'

Another facet of his personality is shown by what he called 'my mild flirtation by post' with Dorothy Sayers. Being at one time an omnivorous reader of detective fiction, he was a great admirer both of her detective novels and of her later, more serious, work. Unhappily his letters to her were lost during the war; his views on Lord Peter Wimsey and his doings were certainly the outcome of intimate knowledge.

It was inevitable that much of Tovey's later life was bound up with the history of the Reid Orchestra. His friends in the south thought it deplorable that he was 'wasted' on Edinburgh. But was he? He was certainly happy in his work there, despite the fact that in the very last volume of *Essays in Analysis* he speaks of 'the heart-breaking task of improving the musical climate of Edinburgh'; and he had wider scope as Reid Professor than he could possibly have had in any other University town, and certainly wider scope than he would have had in London. To many a player the Reid Orchestra was the salvation of his or her musical soul; but for Tovey also it had the saving function of increasing the possibilities of musical expression available to him.

During his twenty-five years tenure of the Reid Chair, Tovey 'put Edinburgh on the map' musically. He built up an orchestra on a part-time basis in the days when a good orchestral player could earn his bread and butter in the theatre or the cinema. Despite its success Tovey was at no time under the illusion that this was other than a temporary and increasingly unsatisfactory basis. His *choice* was an orchestra under these conditions or no orchestra at all; his *aim* was an orchestra on a full-time basis with a pension scheme attached.

The Reid Symphony Orchestra was born during the 1914–18 War, and its founder died at the outset of another and greater war. Once more the orchestra was, despite difficulties of personnel, the sole provider of orchestral music in Edinburgh during the years of war, and its concerts attracted large audiences. It would have been reasonable to imagine that after the war the city would do honour to the memory of the great musician who had spent so large a part of his life in developing its musical resources by establishing the central part of his work on a permanent basis, so that it might be carried on by his successors.

Not so. With the advent of peace, the Scottish Orchestra was revived and Edinburgh once more became a city that was musically divided against itself. There is no doubt that Tovey's intolerance of musical humbug and of false values made enemies for himself and for his work, and that the Reid Orchestra, along with its priceless heritage of tradition and a true sense of style, inherited this enmity. Audiences fell again, and the dearth of orchestral players in the south accelerated the inevitable end of the orchestra after thirty years of existence. Edinburgh has once more decided that nothing but the best from elsewhere will suffice her, and remains incapable of judging whether or not that best is better than what her own native talent, fostered and encouraged, could have provided. As a native of Edinburgh and as a musician, I speak for a minority which regards as a disgrace and a tragedy the ruthless sweeping away of all that Tovey built up.

He would have been the first to concede *autre temps, autre mœurs*. Perhaps it was necessary to destroy in order to rebuild; who can say? He believed, however, that the development of native talent and the visits of distinguished artists from elsewhere were not mutually exclusive, but were the foundations of musical health in any city.

His influence is, and will always be, a living one in the University, where music students may take from the shelves volumes out of his library which contain his vivid marginalia—notes which would almost make another volume or two of Toveyana —and can study his continuo-parts to the B minor Mass, the Magnificat, and other works of Bach. Bantock suggested in 1935 that these should be published; in conjunction with the notes which he wrote for Fritz Busch concerning their use, they would be invaluable for performances of Bach's works. There remain also two Haydn trios which he 'redistributed' but which were never published, although the F sharp minor Trio was already in proof in 1936 and has been played several times in Edinburgh from the corrected proof-sheets.[1]

[1] It has now been published (1951).

There is no doubt that Tovey's death was accelerated by the loss of the use of his hands, but a contributory factor was his despairing feeling that his music was not wanted, and that he was out of touch with the other composers of his day. And yet an article in *Musical Opinion* in November 1939 on modern tendencies expressed the view that a 'much-needed reaction has begun; the bizarre is becoming *démodé*. Walton has written a symphony in a recognisable key. How far will reaction go? Is Tovey wasting his time writing an immense 'cello concerto that ignores other music of the century, or is he leading us back to sanity?' One regrets the loss of the music which he never wrote to the Greek plays, of the opera based on *Twelfth Night* (and on the other libretti which he considered), of the A minor string quartet, the second pianoforte quintet, and the violin concerto, which were all in an amorphous condition during the last years of his life.

'As a lecturer and a writer about music Tovey was certainly without a rival', wrote Trevelyan in assessing his friend's achievements. 'At his happiest moments, when he had leisure to revise, and when he was not trying to say too much at one time, no one could write more lucid, eloquent and witty English prose. But often his writing was almost as much an extemporisation as his talk. He was sometimes obscure and over-lengthy, and would neglect to make the transitions of his thought sufficiently clear and easy for his readers or his audience. Even so, his wonderful command of language, and his fertile imagination made whatever he had to say remarkable. His mind was of a kind that moved slowly and reflectively over his subject, surveying it as a whole, yet at the same time seeing it in all its complexities and details. It is no wonder then if he had not always the time to find a perfect form of exposition, but was apt to wander away into digressions, or else to overlook disconcerting jumps in his arguments. But in spite of such faults, his genius both as a writer and as a lecturer was unique and astonishing.

'His sense of humour was entirely peculiar to himself. At times, when he was in high spirits, his drollery was enchantingly spontaneous and exuberant; but he could also be marvellously and abstrusely witty. He had an illustrative anecdote or a humorous sally lying stored in his mind, awaiting almost every turn the conversation might take. We might sometimes have heard these before, and this he knew well enough; but he could not resist the temptation, nor could we grudge him his repetitions, for his enjoyment of them was infectious. In his happy moods no one could be a more delightful and entertaining companion.

'He was much beloved by all who had the privilege of his friendship; and small wonder; for no one could have a more affectionate and loyal nature. Loyalty and unselfish kindness to others and unswerving faithfulness to his ideals were indeed his most essential characteristics as a man and as an artist. More than anyone I have known, he showed that it was possible to combine the highest intellectual and artistic qualities with a generous and delicate moral sense, and greatness of heart.'

Music for Donald Tovey was ultimately an aspect of truth, and the rich memories of his great personality are for ever associated for me with the lines from Keats's *Ode on a Grecian Urn*, which Holst set so finely:

> Beauty is Truth, Truth Beauty. That is all
> Ye know on earth, and all ye need to know.

APPENDIX

(a) List of Books by Donald Tovey

	Date published
Beethoven's Ninth Symphony	1928
A Companion to the Art of Fugue	1931
Musical Form and Matter (Deneke lecture)	1934
Essays in Musical Analysis, Vols. I & II	1935
,, ,, ,, Vol. III	1936
,, ,, ,, Vol. IV	1936
,, ,, ,, Vol. V	1937
The Main Stream of Music (British Academy lecture)	1938
Essays in Musical Analysis, Vol. VI	1939
A Musician Talks, Vols. I & II	1941
Some English Symphonists	1942
Chamber Music	1944
Musical Articles from the *Encyclopædia Britannica*	1944
Beethoven	1944
Essays and Lectures on Music	1949

(b) List of Compositions by Donald Tovey

(Dates in brackets are those of first performance.)

	Date published
OPERA	
'The Bride of Dionysus' (libretto by Robert Calverley Trevelyan), comp. 1907–18, prod. Edinburgh, 25 April 1932. Pfte. score, Schott	1928
CHORAL WORKS	
3 Anthems for unaccomp. men's chorus. Joseph Williams.	—
'Agnus Dei' for six-part unaccomp. men's chorus. Joseph Williams	—
Motet 'In festo sanctorum Innocentium'	1902

	Date published
25 Rounds, with Appendix of pfte. accompaniments, Op. 5. Joseph Williams	1905
'A Lyke Wake Dirge' (traditional) for 6-part chorus O.U.P.	1931
'The Mad Maid's Song' 3 part. Year Book Press	1920
'On May morning' 4 part. Year Book Press	1921
'The Lord is my Shepherd' 3 part. Vincent	? *c.* 1902

ORCHESTRAL WORK

Symphony, D ma., Op. 32 (1913).

MILITARY BAND MUSIC

National March for the Sultan of Zanzibar.

SOLO INSTRUMENT AND ORCHESTRA

Pfte. Concerto, A ma., Op. 15 (1903). Schott	1906
Cello Concerto, Op. 40 (1935). Full score and pfte. score, O.U.P.	1937
Cadenza to Beethoven's Pfte. Concerto in G, No. 4.	1937
Cadenza to Brahms's Violin Concerto. } O.U.P.	1937
Cadenza to Beethoven's Violin Concerto.	1937

ONE INSTRUMENT AND PIANOFORTE

Divertimento, B flat ma., for oboe (1899)	—
Sonata, F ma., for cello, Op. 4 (1900) } Schott	1910
Sonata, B flat ma., for clar., Op. 16 (1906)	—
Sonata for vn. (1907)	—
'Elegiac Variations' for cello, Op. 25 (1909)	1910

OTHER CHAMBER MUSIC

Trio, B mi., for vn., cello, and pfte., Op. 1 (1900)	1910
Quintet, C ma., for 2 vns., viola, cello, and pfte., Op. 6 (1900)	1912
Trio, C mi. ('style tragique'), for clar., horn, and pfte., Op. 8 (1905)	—
Aria and Variations, B flat ma., for stg. 4tet, Op. 11 (1900)	1913

(Schott)

	Date published
Quartet, E mi., for vn., viola, cello, and pfte. Op. 12 (1900)	1912
Trio, D mi., for vn., English horn, and pfte., Op. 14 (1903)	1913
String Quartet, G ma., Op. 23 (1909)	1914
String Quartet, D ma., Op. 24 (1909)	1914
Trio, D ma., for vn., cello, and pfte. Op. 27 (1910)	1910
Variations on a Theme by Gluck, for flute and stg. 4tet, Op. 28 (1913)	1913
Sonata for 2 cellos (? 1912)	—

(bracketed: Schott.)

SOLO STRING INSTRUMENTS

'Sonata eroica', C ma., for vn., Op. 29. Schott	1913
Sonata, D ma., for cello, Op. 30 (1914). Schott	1913

PIANOFORTE SOLO
'Bagatelles' (1900).
Allegro and Andante (1900).
Variations on an Original Theme (1900).
Passacaglia, B mi. (1908).

PIANOFORTE DUET
'Balliol Dances', Op. 17. Schott.

SONGS
Songs for bass, 2 sets, Op. 2 (1903). Joseph Williams.

ARRANGEMENTS

Trio in A ma. for vn., cello, and pfte. by Joseph Haydn, *redistributed* for the benefit of the vn. and cello by D. F. Tovey. O.U.P.	1939
Trio in F sharp mi. for vn., cello, and pfte. by Joseph Haydn, *redistributed* for the benefit of the vn. and cello by D. F. Tovey. O.U.P.	1951

EDITED WORKS

Beethoven, Sonatas for pfte. and cello, ed. by D. F. Tovey and Percy Such. Augener	1918
Bach, *Das Wohltemperirte Klavier*, ed. by D. F. Tovey and Harold Samuel. Assoc. Board	1924

*Date
published*

Beethoven, Sonatas for pianoforte, ed. by D. F. Tovey and
Harold Craxton. Assoc. Board   1931
Bach, *Die Kunst der Fuge*, edited and completed by D. F.
Tovey. O.U.P.   1931
also *Laudate Pueri*, Sacred Music of the 17th Cent. for high
voices, being the 1st part of *The Northlands Singing Book*.
Selected and edited by D. F. Tovey. Augener   1910
The Kirkhope Choir Magazine, an anthology of pure poly-
phony, edited on new methods by D. F. Tovey. Pater-
son, Edinburgh, Facsimile publication

INDEX